1912–1975

		MACH		
	2·5 2000	3		3·5

BOMBER

PERIOD AND TYPE		
1914 AVRO 504	100	120
1915 BREGUET BM4	600	130
1916 GOTHA G.IV	1,000	185
1917 HANDLEY-PAGE 0/100	2,000	250
1919 VICKERS VIMY	2,476	300
1925 TUPOLEV TB-1	1,650	350
1934 MARTIN B-10	2,260	250
1936 HEINKEL He 111	3,300	200
1937 Savoia-Marchetti SM. 79–1	2,740	330
1938 VICKERS WELLINGTON	4,500	650
1940 JUNKERS Ju88	5,720	450
1941 Mitsubishi G4M "Betty"	2,200	750
1942 BOEING B–17F FORTRESS	6,000	800
1942 AVRO LANCASTER	14,000	850
1943 DE HAVILLAND MOSQUITO	4,000	750
1944 BOEING B-29 SUPERFORTRESS	20,000	1,200
1948 CONVAIR B-36	84,000	3,500
1950 ILYUSHIN IL-28 'BEAGLE'	6,600	600
1951 B-74B		2,000
1955 TU16 "BADGER"		1,800
1957 AVRO VULCAN		2,400
1958 B 52		4,500 with in flight refuelling

THE GUINNESS HISTORY OF
Air Warfare

by David Brown, Christopher Shores, Kenneth Macksey

with specially commissioned paintings and jacket cover by
Michael P. Roffe
and special map and diagrams drawn by Michael Haine

series editor Kenneth Macksey

0 900 424 613   358.400904

GUINNESS SUPERLATIVES LIMITED

2 CECIL COURT, LONDON ROAD, ENFIELD, MIDDLESEX

© 1976 Guinness Superlatives Limited

Published in Great Britain by
Guinness Superlatives Limited,
2 Cecil Court, London Road, Enfield, Middlesex

SBN 900424 61 3

Set in Monophoto Baskerville Series 169
printed and bound in Great Britain by
Jarrold and Sons Limited, Norwich

Facts and Feats Series:

Air Facts and Feats, *2nd ed.*
John W. R. Taylor, Michael
J. H. Taylor and David Mondey

Rail Facts and Feats, *2nd ed.*
John Marshall

Plant Facts and Feats
William G. Duncalf

Yachting Facts and Feats
Peter Johnson

**Structures   Bridges, Towers,
Tunnels, Dams . . .**
John H. Stephens

Car Facts and Feats, *2nd ed.*
Edited by Anthony Harding

Business World
Henry Button and Andrew
Lampert

Music Facts and Feats
Bob and Celia Dearling
with Brian Rust

Animal Facts and Feats,
2nd ed.
Gerald L. Wood

Tank Facts and Feats, *2nd ed.*
Kenneth Macksey

Other titles:

The Guinness Book of Names
Leslie Dunkling

Battle Dress
Frederick Wilkinson

Universal Soldier
edited by Martin Windrow and
Frederick Wilkinson

History of Land Warfare
Kenneth Macksey

History of Sea Warfare
Lt.-Cmdr. Gervis Frere-Cook and
Kenneth Macksey

The Guinness Book of Answers
edited by Norris D. McWhirter

The Guinness Book of Records,
23rd ed.
edited by Norris D. McWhirter

Contents

Acknowledgements

Introduction   vii

Section 1   THE NEW DIMENSION IN WARFARE   1

Section 2   IN SEARCH OF A METHOD   13
            1914–17

Section 3   THE BIRTH OF AIR POWER   44

Section 4   THE INTERREGNUM   60
            1919–39

Section 5   THE HEYDAY OF TACTICAL AIR FORCES 86
            1939–42

Section 6   THE YEARS OF THE HOLOCAUST   141
            1943–5

Section 7   CONFRONTATION:
            COLD AND LIMITED WARS 1945–   199

            APPENDIX
            Trends and Prospects   230

            Select Bibliography   236

            Index   239

Acknowledgements

The authors and publisher wish to thank the many individuals and organisations who gave generous assistance during the preparation of this book – in particular the staff of the Ministry of Defence Library, Whitehall and to Christopher Brown and Peter Hoar.

Thanks are also due to those who gave permission to reproduce material in their copyright. The undermentioned are the major contributors.

Air Ministry, London
Aviation Week/E R Wojtiechowski
Breguet Aviation
Bundesarchiv
Chaz. Bowyer
C.I.C.R./Max Vaterlaus
Crown Copyright
ECA des Armées
ECP des Armées

Keal Photographs Ltd
Imperial War Museum
Indian Air Force
International Defence Review
Japanese Navy
Library of Congress Collections
National Aviation Museum
Photo Safara
Royal Aeronautical Society
Soviet Union Magazine

The Great War
US Air Force
US Army
US National
US National Archives
US Navy
Photo Safara
Hanfried Schliephake
A J Ward
Yasuho Izara

Introduction

It has been of significance to the development of war in the air that the important events in man's conquest of flight have occurred shortly before some major confrontation between nations. **The first man to go aloft in a balloon** did so in 1783, and only eleven years later an observer in a balloon was acting as spotter for the French Army at the Battle of Fleurus (1794), to the alarm and consternation of the opposing Austrian Army which felt naked under the eyes of a man in the sky. A mere eight years after **the first manned flight of a powered aircraft** (1903), machines of this kind were taking part in battle in Libya and in 1914 the First World War produced a titanic conflict that was to hasten the evolution of aircraft and aerial combat beyond all imagination. The demands of war were thus crucial in impelling man's entry into an environment in which he was physically and, to some extent, mentally unsuited. While the early, high-flying balloonists quickly discovered the dangerously inhibiting effects of anoxia above an altitude in excess of 12 000 ft (3700 m) as well as the perils of fire from the hydrogen gas used to lift them, so did the aeronauts in the first heavier-than-air machines come to rely almost entirely upon good design and engineering to support them against the pulls of gravity, the violence of the elements and disorientation. From experience, as speeds increased, they learnt that neither the mind nor the body could cope with the excessive demands of flight and that, in aerial warfare, those demands were uncompromising. Battle compelled man and machines to fly to the limits of their capability. They fought against the enemy, the elements and the limitations of knowledge in a way that had been previously quite inconceivable.

When balloons first flew the first imaginary reaction of the futurists was to adapt them as combat vehicles. Some of the most perspicacious visions of air warfare emanate from the first decade of the 19th century when the means to wage air war were far too primitive for flexible operations. The rapid fading of dreams through lack of technological realism is not therefore surprising, and yet it is astonishing how, even after 1910 when the reality of manned flight in manoeuvrable aircraft was proven, little in the way of strategic or tactical doctrine had been settled by any of the major combatant nations prior to 1914. The likelihood of air reconnaissance, of striking with bombs at fleets, armies and cities, of mid-air combat were all apparent but not converted into policy. The air forces of 1914 flew tentatively into battle and developed the new art empirically and, largely, under the spur of a handful of enthusiastic airmen, who satisfied their individual ambitions by demonstrating the capabilities of the machines in which they loved to fly. Pushing them from behind were the inventors and industrialists who had visions of another kind and improved the machines in response to the enterprise of entrepreneurs. Only random calls for improvement came at first from the leaders in government and from the top sailors and soldiers.

However, isolated successes in the air at once emphasised to the combatants the value of exploiting this new dimension in warfare by extending the age-old advantage conferred by height. This led to a clearer statement of requirements in combat technique as well as in technology. Gradually the first haphazard launching of aircraft into the combat zone was replaced by studied doctrines and careful organisation. By the winter of 1914 nearly all the essential rudiments of future air warfare had been identified. Aircraft were recognised as more than a means of carrying the war to the enemy, albeit in a highly inefficient and ineffectual manner. They were also seen as a factor of immense psychological value. The mere presence of aircraft could destroy or enhance the morale not only of the fighting men but of the civilian populace too. Freedom to fly unchallenged could no longer be allowed to the enemy: control of air space was deemed well worth fighting for.

In 1915 began the serious quest for command of the air, epitomised by ever deeper penetration of an opponent's air space, by reconnaissance and bombing aircraft, and by an intensification of fighting between individual aircraft. In the ensuing years the struggle would be centred upon building aircraft which could fly higher, faster and further than their opponents, and arming them with weapons that could wreak greater destruction upon each other and against targets on the ground. Concomitant with improvements to the aircraft went betterment of communication devices and therefore of centralised control of air forces; simultaneously vast ground facilities sprang into being to support organisations which were ravenous for high capital outlay and the skills of the most highly qualified men, both in the air and on the ground. Those who fought the traditional battles on land and at sea began to find it increasingly difficult to recruit the cream of manpower to fill their ranks; industrial effort was being diverted from the older Services. As a side line to warfare against the enemy, the arbiters of sea and land warfare began to manoeuvre and intrigue for possession of their slice (if not the whole) of the air forces. However, in 1917 it became increasingly clear that the airmen, sensing their power, had ambitions of their own. In 1918 **the creation of the world's first independent air force,** the British Royal Air Force, stimulated a somewhat unwilling recognition of the autonomy of war in the air.

The suggestion that wars could be won from the air by the intervention of aircraft alone absorbed the attention of nations between the world wars. The practical experiences gained by General Hugh Trenchard in command of the British air forces in France when linked with those of the USA's William Mitchell and, later, with a profusion of theory written by Italy's Giulio Douhet, led to a concept of offensive operations being mandatory in the application of air power. From the notion that bombers took precedence over other kinds of aeroplane, such as fighters, evolved an extreme manifestation of contemporary thought that nations could be knocked out by bombers – bombers which, it was claimed, would always get through the defences.

No single air force adopted extremist theories in their entirety, though Britain and Italy tended to run mighty close with their construction of long-range strategic bombers. Germany and Russia put their money into aeroplanes which would lend the best possible support to their armies. Japan did the same and placed even heavier emphasis upon naval aircraft and the techniques of dive-bombing and torpedo dropping. The USA made do with what little money was granted to its air forces prior to 1939 and laid plans, based upon an immense industrial potential, to attempt almost everything when the time came – to support both armies and air forces, to create immense strategic bombing arms and to assist them all with a transport force of immense capacity.

So the Second World War became one in which the limits of technology and production were stretched in order to apply air warfare in all its prospective forms – support of surface forces in combat, delivery of men and supplies in airborne invasions, assaults in depth upon strategic targets and an all-out attempt to destroy civilian morale by an indiscriminate ravaging of cities. Surface warfare without air support became inconceivable even if air forces failed to achieve all that their keenest advocates boasted for them. Combat took place at ever increasing altitude, at longer range and in greater numbers than had been dreamed of, and losses became commensurately higher when each fresh campaign demanded a preliminary struggle for air superiority until one air force or the other was subjugated. And all the time the crucial competition between the scientists and technologists sought advantages in performance which, injected at the right moment, would enable even a few superior aircraft or weapons to eliminate a mass of recently out-moded machines.

Just as the First World War stopped as new visions of air power were beginning to appear, so the Second ended with a highly provocative climax. Jet aircraft with their immense increase in speed and performance at altitude suddenly made most other types obsolete in combat; rocket propulsion opened the way to long-range attacks by unmanned, guided missiles; and the first nuclear warheads made it possible to deliver as one cargo the explosive force that, until then, had demanded an air fleet. The ultimate in strategic air power had been reached. And yet the air battles of the next three decades continued to be similar in method to those of the previous three since nobody resorted to nuclear warfare after 1945. The competition between balancing technologies and techniques remained central to each war, no matter its dimensions, as one side or the other fought for air superiority as the preliminary to winning the surface battle and occupying enemy territory. And the best men with the best brains continued to be absorbed in the process.

Air power has yet to win a war on its own.

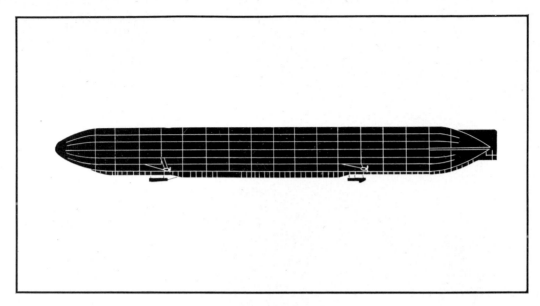

SECTION I

The New Dimension in Warfare

The first free-flight man-lifting aircraft (a hot-air balloon) went aloft on 21 November 1783 from the Bois de Boulogne in Paris, carrying with it François de Rozier. It not only brought man's dream of flight to reality, it marked the culmination of 74 years' endeavour since **the feasibility of going aloft in a hot-air balloon was first demonstrated** with a model by Father Bartolomeu de Gusmão in 1709.

A major step towards lighter-than-air flight was taken in 1766 when the Englishman, Henry Cavendish, isolated 'inflammable air' (or hydrogen, as it came to be named in 1790). But it was not until August 1783 that this gas was used by Jacques Charles to raise an unmanned balloon. That was four months after the Montgolfier brothers' first hot-air balloon had flown and three months before de Rozier went up. The impact upon people's vision of the future was instantaneously immense. At once there appeared a revolution in the published concepts of wars to come: all the pent-up ambitions wrapped in a desire for flight were released to a chorus of imaginative acclaim. In 1783 there was published in Amsterdam a paper envisaging the capture of Gibraltar by 'flying globes'. In 1784 that most far-seeing of Americans, Benjamin Franklin, was forecasting how '. . . ten thousand men descending from the clouds might not in many places do an infinite deal of mischief before a force could be brought together to repel them', showing that Franklin had at once understood the superior mobility offered by airborne forces. Likewise artists grasped the notion of balloon-borne fleets sailing like galleons in the sky, armed with 200 guns apiece and engaged in death grapples as part of an invasion from the sky. Their ideas acquired credibility when a hydrogen balloon **crossed the English Channel for the first**

French observation balloon at the Battle of Fleurus, 26 June 1794.

time in January 1785. Therefore, when France and England once more went to war in 1793, it was tempting for propagandists and alarmists to inspire the dread of airborne invasion at a time when the British fleet prevented any such happening by sea. Yet long before the first imaginative scenario of an airborne invasion of England had appeared in 1798 *(La Descente en Angleterre)*, **the first employment of a balloon at war had taken place** during the Battle of Fleurus, on 26 June 1794, when the French sent up Capitaine Coutelle to make observation of the Austrian dispositions. This ascent led to a classic military response to the air weapon. Among the Austrians there was horror at the thought that no longer could they deploy unobserved – a panic reaction that was typical in the face of a 'secret' weapon before its true value was assessed. As rapidly there ensued the next almost inevitable retrograde step – virtual rejection of balloon companies by Napoleon because their speed of deployment did not comply with his concept of fast moving operations. But in 1810 a Prussian officer, Julius von Voss, saw much further when he wrote, apropos combat by powered dirigible balloons, that they had the task of observing the enemy from afar, but '. . . the enemy, eager to conceal his intentions, did not hesitate to send up his own light craft in order to drive back the enemy balloons; and so in the heavens above skirmishes developed between advanced patrols. . . .' Here was **a first intimation of what actually was to take place a century hence.**

The first aerial bombardment was undertaken by the Austrians against the Venetians in March 1849, when Oberleutnant Franz Uchatius designed and launched several score paper balloons, each carrying a 30 lb (13·5 kg) bomb. The balloons were intended to drift with the wind across the city and release their bombs in response to a time fuse. When at last the wind was favourable and the attack launched it produced one more phenomenon of air warfare among victims and attackers. Though at first alarmed, the citizens of Venice rapidly assumed a disdain for the new method, particularly since no casualties resulted. Equally typical of air enthusiasts, the attackers made exaggerated claims of the damage and casualties they had inflicted and the panic they felt must have ensued. But the experiment was not repeated.

The first design for a powered, steerable balloon was produced in 1784 by a French Lieutenant Jean-Baptiste Meusnier, though it was not until 1852 that another Frenchman, Henri Giffard, travelled in a balloon, for 17 miles (27 km) at 5 mph (8 km/h) propelled by a steam engine of 3 hp driving a three-bladed propeller. From this moment progress with powered airships was quite rapid, though the use of free-flight or tethered balloons in war remained only on a limited scale.

Balloons were used:

- **During the American Civil War** (1861–5) for observation (sometimes towed from a coal-barge) and, **for the first time,** in aiming indirect artillery fire. The balloon corps of the Union side, commanded by Thaddeus Lowe, was disbanded before the end of the war but included many future aviators, including Count Zeppelin.
- **During the Franco-Prussian War** (1870–1) to carry despatches and prominent citizens out of besieged Paris. Sixty-six were launched; a few were fired upon without much effect; many reached safety but were scattered all over the place (eight with the Prussians), some out to sea. One travelled 1400 miles (2240 km) to Narvik in north Norway. Some took carrier pigeons which returned to Paris with microfilm messages. In response, the German firm of Krupp produced primitive anti-balloon guns.
- **During a few colonial campaigns by the British** in South Africa and the Sudan in, respectively 1884, 1885 and during the Boer War when they also used man-lifting kites for observation.

The first successful parachute was used in 1797 by André Garnerin of France and was thereafter developed as much for entertainment as for the lifesaving task it was to assume when aircraft began to fight in earnest.

The first electrically powered dirigible was 'La France', a military project of the French – as indeed were the vast majority of airship projects, due to the difficulty of acquiring funds for expensive schemes of only dubious commercial advantage. 'La France' was intended for reconnaissance but had only a limited range (23 min before the batteries ran flat) and a speed of 10·5 mph (16·5 km/h). Moreover, she was difficult to control. The first petrol-engined airship was that of the German Karl Wölfert, whose 'hot tube' ignition Daimler engine drove this craft in 1888. But in 1897 a similar engine brought a fiery end to Wölfert when the hydrogen ignited at 3300 ft (1000 m) caused by flames from the hot tube. In the first decade of the 20th century the design of airships nevertheless improved along with safer and more reliable means of petrol-engine propulsion. Santos-Dumont and the Lebaudy brothers, in France, and Count Ferdinand Zeppelin, in Germany, showed the way, the latter taking the lead with his 'rigids' which were tailored primarily for military purposes even though they demonstrated a commercial potential.

The first German Army 'Zeppelin', Z_1, was commissioned in 1908 and **the first for their Navy,** L_1, in 1912. Primarily these craft were intended for deep strategic reconnaissance, but as speeds in excess of 40 mph (64 km/h) were achieved, along with the ability to rise above 10 000 ft (3048 m) to keep out of range of guns, other ideas intruded: bombs might be carried. Thus the demand for counter-measures became more urgent as the strike potential of the aircraft was made manifest some time before their engagement in hostilities.

The first sustained flight by a man-carrying heavier than air powered aircraft took place when the Wright brothers' 'Flyer' took off at Kitty Hawk, USA, on 17 December 1903, launching a new era – even though the actual event brought no immediate commercial interest.

The first specification for a military aeroplane was issued by Brigadier-General James Allen of the US Army in 1907, the intention being to obtain an armed machine capable of reconnaissance. A speed of 40 mph (64 km/h) and a duration of 1 hour were demanded for a crew of two.

The first military aeroplane was a Wright delivered to the US Army in August 1909 as a vehicle for trials in the application of aircraft to war.

Four members of the Kill Devil Hills Life Saving Station, admiring the first Wright Flyer during preparation for trials.

The first missile was dropped by Glenn Curtiss in June 1910 with dummy bombs upon the outline of a battleship marked by buoys.

The first firing of a rifle from an aircraft was by Jacob Fickel (USA) in August 1910.

The first take-off from a warship's deck took place in December 1910 by Eugene Ely (USA) who also carried out **the first landing** in January 1911.

The first to land and take-off on water was Glenn Curtiss in January 1911.

The first to drop high-explosive bombs were Myron Crissy and Phillip Parmalee (USA) in 1911 and in that year, too, Capitano Guidoni was **the first to launch a marine torpedo.**

The first to arm an aircraft with a machine-gun (a Lewis) was Charles de Forest Chandler in June 1912, and the first cannon to be fired from an aircraft without disaster was

Captain Chandler with Lewis gun strapped to the rudder bar of a Wright B aircraft, 1912.

the 37 mm COW gun produced by Vickers. It performed successfully in July 1913 but then was allowed to lapse, though this gun was at the root of further cannon development in the 1930s.

The first experiments with catapult launching of aircraft from ships were undertaken by Lieutenant Theodore Ellyson, **the US Navy's first qualified pilot,** in 1912. In that year, too, the British experimented with aircraft **for the detection and attack of submarines.**

Thus the basic essentials of combat aircraft were established in trials over a period of three years, the initial work being done by Americans, with the exception of the Italian contribution to torpedo dropping and the British trial with a cannon and against submarines. To these fighting attributes were added, simultaneously, the elements of a control system by radio.

The first radio signals were sent a distance of 1320 ft (400 m) by Sir William Preece in 1892. Thereafter progress was rapid with Guglielmo Marconi sending a message 1 mile (1·6 km) in 1895 and 3000 miles (4800 km) in 1901. Each new technical development in radio was to impinge upon air power as sets that were smaller and light, more powerful, reliable and versatile were devised.

The most important were:

1904   First use of the heterodyne principle in transmitting and receiving.
        Initiation of work on radio direction finding.
        Use of a vacuum diode valve in a receiver.
1905   The first ground signals received by a British balloon in flight.
1909   The first radio set fitted into the German zeppelin *LZ6*.
1910   The first use of radio between aeroplane and the ground in the USA.
1912   First British aircraft fitted with radio. By 1914 signals were received over a distance of 100 miles (160 km).
1914   First British transmissions between aircraft at a range of 10 miles (16 km).

It thus became possible for aircraft to report and receive information, for their position to be plotted and for instructions to be given to them in flight.

The first official admission that the bombing of England by hostile aircraft was feasible came in 1910 and was followed in 1912 by the statement of Captain Murray Sueter, a naval airman, who told a sub-committee of the Committee of Imperial Defence that '... war in the air, for the supremacy of the air, by armed aeroplanes against each other' was likely. 'This fight for the supremacy of the air in future wars will be of the first and greatest importance, and when it has been won the land and sea forces of the loser will be at such a disadvantage that the war will certainly have to terminate at a much smaller loss in men and money to both sides.' Erroneous though this turned out, the tendency of enthusiasts to exaggerate the effect of the air weapon was established as part and parcel of the evolution of a plausible doctrine.

The first use of aircraft in war was by the Italians in 1911–12 during a war in Tripolitania against the Turks. Capitano Piazza reconnoitred the Turkish lines in a Blériot monoplane on 11 October 1911, an aircraft that was part of an air force comprising nine 50 hp aeroplanes (two French Blériots, three Nieuports, two Farmans and two Austrian Etrich 'Taubes') in addition to a brace of non-rigid airships. Mostly their tasks were reconnaissance, though the

Italian aircraft in Libya, 1911, an Etrich monoplane of German manufacture.

airships dropped $4\frac{1}{2}$ lb (2 kg) Swedish grenades. **The first casualty from enemy action in aeroplane warfare** may well have been the wounding of an observer by rifle fire. It was thus found that rifle fire was dangerous even at 3000 ft (1000 m), despite the difficulty for a man on the ground judging distance in space at that range. The main Turkish response in due course was to obtain aircraft and pilots from Germany for her own use in the Balkans war of 1912.

The dropping of the first hostile bombs by the Italians on Ain Zara caused what was to become an almost inevitable objection to aerial bombardment whenever it occurred in the future. There came an immediate protest from the Turks that a hospital had been hit, though it must be added that a naval bombardment with 152 shells only a few days previously had drawn no such complaint. The upshot was a prolonged press debate on the ethics of air bombing, a debate which continues to this day for both humanitarian and propaganda purposes. In the early instances the chances of error were enormous, for target identification and bomb aiming were extremely haphazard.

The first air operation in direct support of a naval attack (and also the first of any kind by US aircraft) was carried out by Curtiss AB flying boats in a search for mines in Vera Cruz harbour in conjunction with a US naval bombardment during the attack upon Mexico in April 1914. Indeed, reconnaissance was by then fully established as the prime use for aircraft in war, though means to improve the capability to see and record information were essential.

The first aerial photograph had been taken from a balloon by Gaspard Tournachon over Paris in 1858. The technique of reconnaissance by photography did not advance much, however, until aircraft proved feasible. In 1914 great advances were made. In one day, from a height of 5600 ft (1700 m), British Army officers took pictures exposing the entire defences of the Isle of Wight and the Solent, developing the negatives in the air so that they were ready for printing when they landed.

The coming of the First World War found the belligerent nations' air forces in a state of experiment, uncertainty and unreadiness, in contrast to the brash over-confidence of their immense fleets and armies. Although the role of air forces was obscure there was very little to choose between the prowess, strength and technical capability of the contenders, since the international aspects of aeronautics had led to a widespread interchange of ideas and techniques.

The strengths of the main air forces when war broke out in August 1914 were:

	Aircraft	Airships	Remarks
Germany	246	11	
Austria-Hungary	35	1	
Russia	300	11	**These figures are uncertain. There was also an acute shortage of pilots.**
France	160	5	
Great Britain	110	6	
Belgium	25	—	

The performance of the unarmed aircraft was fairly typically represented by the following:

Nation	Type	Speed	Ceiling
Germany	Taube	62 mph	2800 m
France	Farman MF 7	59 mph	4250 m
Britain	BE 2a	70 mph	3300 m

Zeppelin bombardment of Antwerp, 1914. (R G Matthews, 'Great War').

Aircraft such as these were used for various tasks by admirals and generals who had given little thought to what was required of them. In any case there was mistrust of the reports that pilots and observers might bring and an almost total rejection of any suggestion of offensive capability, though many carried darts (called flechettes) for dropping on hostile troops and the pilots had pistols or rifles. The French dropped 50 000 flechettes each day in one period.

The first major participants in air war were the German rigid airships, because they were the best prepared for war and had been allocated specific, if dubious, tasks. **The first attempt to bomb a fortress from the air** was made on 5 August when *Z VI* carried eight heavy artillery shells towards Liège, but, on descending through cloud to 5200 ft (1580 m) in search of the target, was shot full of holes by machine-guns and forced to turn back and crash land. On 21 August Z *VII* and *VIII* tried to make bombing attacks upon French troops in the Vosges Mountains. Z *VII* on coming below 3300 ft (1000 m) found that bombs did nothing to deter the enemy small-arms fire: she was lost, as was Z *VIII*, to the fire of 'friendly' German troops. It was the same at Mlawa in East Prussia on 28 August when Z *V* tried to bomb the railway junction from low level in daylight and was forced to descend by machine-gun fire. A similar fate met a French airship which was shot down by its own ground forces. Any aeroplane was fair game to every rifleman in sight let alone range. British pilots were shot at frequently by both French and English even when far behind their own lines, largely because recognition was not taught but also, one suspects, in a spirit of sport linked to the need to relieve the soldiers' feelings.

The only truly successful deep reconnaissance was made by the Schütte-Lanz airship *(SL 2)* which flew nearly 300 miles (480 km) into Russian territory on 22 August, reported its discoveries to the Austrians at Przemsyl and returned to base at Liegnitz having covered 865 miles (1384 km) in 2½ days (24 hours actual flying). It seems unlikely, however, that her reports were put to much use since the Austrians still permitted the Russian Army to surprise them. For the airmen of August 1914 life was pretty galling as well as hectic, believed by none and shot at by friend and foe as they were.

The first special mountings for mechanised anti-aircraft guns (called balloon guns) were introduced by the German Ehrhardt Company in 1908 by mounting a gun on a pedestal in the back of a lorry. Similar mountings were also made for machine-guns but, for the most part, anti-aircraft fire which dealt quite effectively with the slow low-flying aircraft came from naval guns (1 pdr automatic pom-poms), 3 in (76 mm) and 4 in (101·6 mm) types and field artillery pieces on improvised mountings pointed upwards that fired as rapidly as possible in the general direction of the target. Though it was haphazard, a sufficient volume of fire was bound to hit something in time,

An early German mobile anti-aircraft gun. Note stowage of ammunition and man on the right setting the fuse.

French reconnaissance Blériot sights German columns heading for the Marne, August 1914.

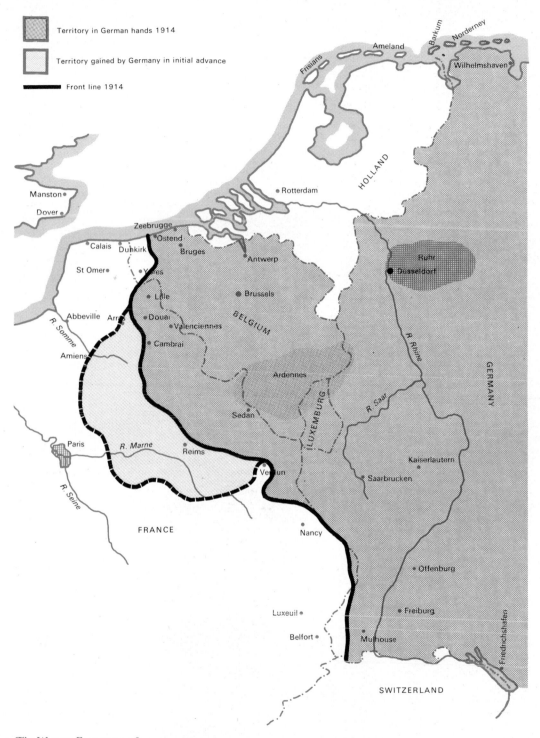

Barkum

Norderney

Ameland

Frisians

Wilhelmshaven

HOLLAND

Manston

Dover

Rotterdam

Zeebrugge

Ostend

Calais   Dunkirk

Bruges

Antwerp

Ruhr

Düsseldorf

St Omer   Ypres

Lille

Brussels

BELGIUM

R. Rhine

Abbeville   Arras

Douai

R. Somme

Valenciennes

GERMANY

Amiens

Cambrai

Ardennes

LUXEMBURG

R. Saar

Sedan

Paris

R. Marne

Reims

Kaiserlautern

R. Seine

Verdun

Saarbrucken

FRANCE

Nancy

Offenburg

Luxeuil

Freiburg

Belfort

Mulhouse

Friedrichshafen

SWITZERLAND

The Western Front 1914–18.

the rate of exchange being something like one aircraft destroyed per thousand shells fired.

The first German pilot to be killed died in a crash on 13 August (the same day on which the first Austrian pilot was wounded) and **the first German forced down** came to earth on 25 August when threatened by three close-flying British pilots in France. More deaths came from crashes before a shot was fired and it was not until 26 August that the Russian Petr Nesterov (who had been **first to loop the loop**) became **the first killed in action** when he rammed an Austrian aircraft flown by Baron von Rosenthal.

What was possibly **the first multi-aircraft mid-air fight** took place on 22 September when a British machine, attempting to drop a bomb upon a German Drachen (kite) balloon (a stable observation balloon developed by the Germans in secret in 1892), was in turn attacked by a German Albatross and the pilot wounded in the leg – the first British pilot to be actually hit. To illustrate the costliness of air support, a German balloon company with two balloons required 232 men and 123 horses with a dozen gas wagons to keep it in action.

The first successful attack by an aeroplane upon a warship took place at Kiaochow Bay near Tsingtao in September 1914, when a Japanese seaplane (a Farman) bombed and sank a small German minelayer by dropping a naval shell, with fins added, on to it. Later, at Tsingtao, Japanese aircraft bombed field positions and put a power station out of action.

The first air to air combat in which a machine-gun scored a kill took place on 5 October, when a German Aviatik was brought down by a Hotchkiss machine-gun fired from French Voisin V89 flown by Sergeant Joseph Frantz. It was a turning point in air warfare since it marked the moment when the vision of Voss in 1810 changed to reality. Already it was realised by the generals that no longer was it permissible for enemy aircraft to have free access to the sky above the land battle. Measures had to be taken to prevent enemy observation; enemy aircraft and balloons had to be destroyed. Yet the threat to the civil populace could not be ignored. Air combat was about to assume a crucial role of its own, transcending the conventional sea and land confrontation.

Paris street scene during an air attack in 1914.

SECTION II
In Search of a Method
1914 – 17

It is a mistake to imagine that doctrines of air power came into being as the result of profound study by acute philosophers of war and much nearer the truth to acknowledge that whatever bore the fruit of action in the air was the outcome of cruel experience in bloody combat. The first air encounters cost the participants very little and made only a marginal contribution to the principal battles. They were the products of partially considered schemes that were tenuously related to policies that were only faintly existent. The pattern of air war which evolved towards the end of 1914 was empirical, forced upon the contenders by the exigencies of a battlefield stalemate. Yet the year of 1915, in particular, was to crystallise the shape of war to come while those to follow merely led to an increasingly thorough refinement of the fundamental concepts that had been identified in the first instance. In the awesome atmosphere of a life and death struggle there was rarely time for mature reflection. One technical improvement would lead to a fresh initiative in the sky and be overtaken by something still more revolutionary before the primary scheme had been fully worked out. Yet a single theme predominated. Command of the air was an irrefutable essential in the business of war.

The first deliberate attempts at carrying destruction by aircraft beyond the immediate zone of the armies was made by the Germans – with the French not far behind. The initial aggressive role of the airships was to bomb fortresses and troops concentrations behind the front. The abortive first attempt by the German zeppelin *L VI* to bomb Liège on 6 August 1914, was followed by a French attempt with an aircraft to bomb the airship hangar at Metz on the 14th. **The first bombs (four) from an aircraft fell on Paris** on 30 August (concurrently with sheaves of **the first air delivered propaganda pamphlets**) and bombs were dropped by a zeppelin on Antwerp on 2 September and Warsaw on 24 September. These raids were aimed at civilian morale with almost as much value placed on the leaflets as the bombs, since the latter contained little more than noise value in high explosive.

What was, perhaps, the first proposal to bomb an enemy headquarters came from a Frenchman, Commandant Barés in September 1914, but was not attempted at the moment.

The first formation specially designated for strategic bombing was the German *Fliegerkorps des Oberstern Heeresleitung* formed in November 1914 for the purpose of bombing London. Under the command of Major Wilhelm Siegert it was given 36 aircraft (mostly small Aviatik B 1s which could carry only a few small bombs) manned by picked crews. The first bombs fell on England at Dover on 24 December, but the preparations by Siegert were mostly concentrated in experimental raids against Dunkirk and the other Channel ports. Without those ports in German hands London lay beyond his range, and there was little chance of their being taken in the immediate future. So, on 23 January 1915, a concentrated raid was aimed at Dunkirk with twelve aircraft, though little damage was caused and one of the bombers was shot down by rifle fire from a British aircraft. There followed a night raid on the 28th/29th but that was all, since shortly after this the Group was transferred to the Eastern front in support of the German offensive in Galicia. It then became **the first fully mobile air unit** based on its own railway trains that could move it from place to place in accordance with demand. Upon the experience obtained by this group the subsequent methods of German strategic bomber forces were built.

Commandant de Göys.

The first French strategic bombing unit (The *1ᵉ Groupe de Bombardement* under Commandant de Göys) came into existence on 13 November 1914 and went into action against Freiburg-im-Breisgau on 4 December. However, neither this raid nor those that followed against industrial, communication, on military or urban targets caused much damage or many casualties. In their novelty and potential, however, they had some value against civilian morale – until their innocuity was comprehended, that is.

The first carefully planned attacks by British Royal Naval Air Service aircraft against zeppelins on the ground were hardly more profitable than the French efforts. The Royal Navy had been given the task of defending England against zeppelin attack and had sent a mixed force of aircraft and armoured cars to Belgium in 1914 which had become engaged in combat with the

Squadron Commander Spenser Grey and Naval aircrew who bombed Friedrichshafen Zeppelin works, November 1914.

advancing German army. The first bombing attack against zeppelins in their hangars at Düsseldorf was made from Antwerp (range 100 miles – 160 km) on 22 September but failed because thick mist obscured the target to all but one aircraft and its three bombs did not explode. A repetition on 8 October brought the destruction in flames of the inflated *ZIX*. On 21 November three Avro 504 biplanes flew from Belfort to Friedrichshafen, a distance of 125 miles (200 km), and bombed the zeppelin works without direct effect, though it made the Germans waste effort on stronger defences which were not to be tested again for a long time. An attempt on 25 December to attack zeppelin hangars near Cuxhaven involved the launching of seaplanes from carriers escorted into the Heligoland Bight by a naval force – **the first offensive strike by shipborne aircraft.** It brought no destruction of value and all the attacking aircraft were lost.

'The hit-and-miss system'; typical early air bombing arrangements.

The main initial attempt by the Germans at strategic bombing involved rigid airships against English cities following a decision taken on 7 January 1915 to attack military targets, an activity which later was varied to permit attacks on London and other cities. Restrictions that forbade the zeppelin commanders from attacking enemy Royalty were made all the more severe since the raids had to be made by night (thus redoubling the problems of navigation and target identification) because of the airship's obvious vulnerability in daylight. **The first raid was** made on 19 January when bombs from two zeppelins were dropped on Yarmouth and other towns on the East Anglian coast. Two people were killed and thirteen wounded; not a shot was fired in retaliation. Thereafter there came a steady, though sporadic, increase in the number and severity of raids. The crucial events and statistics of a campaign which reached its zenith in 1916 are as follows:

First attack on Paris: 21 March 1915   1 Airship   Casualties: 1 killed, 8 wounded.

First attack on London: 31 May 1915   1 Airship   Casualties: 7 killed, 35 wounded.

Flight Sub-Lieutenant R Warneford, V.C. R.NAS.   *The penalty of defeat in aerial combat.*

First airship destroyed by another aircraft *LZ 37* on 6 June 1915 by six 20 lb (9 kg) bombs dropped on it at 11000 ft (3358 m), over Ghent by a Morane-Saulnier monoplane flown by Flight Sub-Lieutenant R Warneford, RNAS.

First airship brought down by defences of England *L 12* on 10 August, 1915 in the sea off Ostend as the result of hits by anti-aircraft guns at Dover.

Most damaging raid, that by Heinrich Mathy a brilliant navigator, in *L 13* on the night of 8/9 September 1915, when he alone caused over £500000 damage to London and the total against England for the whole night's work was £534287. On this night, too, **the first 660 lb (300 kg) bomb was** dropped – the biggest yet. Nevertheless, the chances of a zeppelin hitting so enormous a target as the City of London were remarkably low, particularly since all the raids were in total darkness and could not be in moonlight for fear of detection. Moreover, as the defenders took to extinguishing street and housing lighting (creating the 'black-out'), the problems of navigation and target identification became even more formidable and were multiplied as the defences got stronger (chiefly with AA guns at first), and the airships were compelled to seek greater safety at higher altitudes – often forcing them to fly above cloud level. Attempts to overcome this difficulty by suspending an observation car far below the airship to help plot its course from beneath the cloud base were a failure. Typical of the navigational errors committed were those of *L 12* on 9 August 1915, whose commander thought he had made a landfall in Norfolk when in fact he was over Kent, some 100 miles (160 km) to the southward – at a time when the blackout was far from complete; and on 31 January 1916, when two commanders claimed to have bombed Sheffield three times, Manchester twice, as well as four other northern and midland cities, when nothing of the sort had happened except that the open country had been well spattered by bombs, and Burton-on-Trent had sustained three attacks. But airships continued to have a disproportionate effect on civilian morale despite the irregularity of their attacks. A plethora of ideas to prevent them was considered.

The first effective rocket missiles fired from aircraft were designed in 1915 as anti-airship or balloon weapons. This was a small missile invented by Lieutenant Y Le Prieur of the French Navy and was usually mounted on the outer interplane struts of the aircraft and fired electrically. Unfortunately, the rocket was inaccurate beyond 400 ft (120 m). It was superseded almost immediately when the machine-gun was converted to a more effective role and given more effective ammunition.

The decisive invention in giving fighter aircraft the power to destroy airships (and indeed an advanced capability to fight against all manner of targets) was that of tracer and incendiary ammunition for machine-guns. From about 1910 onwards most nations had been conducting experiments in this field but the attacks by airships in 1915 hastened research, development and production. Britain had an unsatisfactory tracer round ready in 1914 and a serviceable one by July 1916 – the SPK Mk VII T. That month, too, a bullet which was both explosive and incendiary (the invention of Commander F A Brock of the RNAS) was taken into service, as was the Pomeroy bullet in August, an explosive round invented by a Canadian. These bullets were at once mixed in the drum magazines of the Lewis guns with which anti-airship fighters were armed. Their effect was immediately apparent.

The first airship brought down over England was *SL 11* on the night of 2/3 September 1916 by 2nd Lieutenant William Leefe Robinson flying in a BE 2c and using Brock and Pomeroy ammunition which ignited the target at a height of 13 200 ft (4000 m). This was the night of **the biggest airship raid of the war** when fourteen of them crossed the coast and none reached London. By the end of the year five more airships were to be destroyed over England and the airship threat defeated for ever. Further raids would take place (the last on 5 August 1918). They tried to reach safety at altitudes above 21 400 ft (6500 m) and for a while evaded interceptor fighters. However, the problem of finding their targets increased excessively and in due course fighter aircraft were able to climb to the airship's maximum height and shoot them down there. They had caused alarm, despondency and a vast deflection of resources to defence, but the damage they inflicted was in no way commensurate with the effort.

Fate of the German airships built before and during the First World War

No. built	No. destroyed by accident	No. destroyed by enemy action	Remarks
135	52	37	Incl 21 attributed to ground fire

German airship crews lost (killed, wounded and missing or prisoners) as a result of operations against Britain: 270 approximately.

Total German airship crew members lost from various causes throughout the war: 1100 approximately.

Defending British aircraft lost or seriously damaged in combating airships up to the end of 1916: 38.

Defending British pilots killed: 6 (none as result of direct enemy action).

Civilians killed by airship bombing: 501.

Civilians wounded by airship bombing: 1213.

The most important role of aircraft in battle, so far as the total war effort was concerned, remained that of reconnaissance and support of the navies and armies. Allied with these requirements were the demands of navies and armies for aircraft to direct the fire of guns against targets that were out of sight of surface observers.

The first experiments at directing naval gunfire by wireless from an aeroplane began in England in February 1915 and the project was shown to be feasible by trials on 7 April. But already aircraft were directing naval gunfire at Gallipoli in action against Turkish batteries, and a kite balloon towed to the point of action in the ship *Manica* directed its first 'shoot' at Gallipoli on 19 April against a Turkish encampment. Many innovations accompanied the Allied expedition to force the Narrows at Gallipoli in trying to reach Constantinople. For example there was:

● **The first attempt to direct the fire of one ship against another** when *Manica*'s balloon controlled the fire of the battleship *Triumph* against the Turkish battleship *Turgud Reis* on 25 April during the initial British and French landings.

● **The first successful attack against a ship with a torpedo dropped from the air** was made on 12 August when a Short seaplane launched its weapon against a 5000 ton (5050 tonne) Turkish merchant ship from 15 ft (5 m) above the water at a range of 890 ft (270 m). The fact that the ship had already been damaged by a submarine detracted not in the least from the significance of the episode and, a few days later, an unchallengeable sinking was registered.

The first cruiser to be sunk helped by air action was the German *Königsberg* which took refuge in the delta of the River Rufiji in German East Africa in October 1914. Confirmation of her exact location after a prolonged search was made by Sub-Lieutenant H Cutler flying in a 90 hp Curtiss flying boat which had been bought from a South African mining prospector. It took time to assemble suitable forces to attack the cruiser. In January 1915 bombing by Sopwith seaplanes proved impracticable, but in April a Short seaplane took clear photographs of her. Further bombing attacks failed in July. On 6 July monitors were got into position, their fire was directed by wireless aircraft. Finally on the 11th good practice was made and the cruiser was destroyed, the crucial directions to the monitors coming just as the aeroplane was fatally hit by fire from *Königsberg*.

The first land battle in which an air force played a closely integrated part was Neuve Chapelle when the British attacked the Germans between 10 and 12 March 1915. The innovations in **the first battle in which the British tried sophisticated siege techniques** to break the trench warfare deadlock were:

Short 184 being hoisted out from HMS Ark Royal, *Dardanelles, 1915.*

● **A more accurate and simple method of directing artillery fire on to its targets,** known as the 'Clock System' in which a celluloid disc, divided by concentric circles and segments, helped the airborne observer plot the fall of shot in relation to the target which was assumed to be at the centre of the circle. This enhanced the effectiveness of counter-battery work by the British artillery.

● **A more skilled application of photogrammetric techniques** based upon French methods and using the box-type Camera (A) which gave clearer and better annotated information of the enemy defences, and enabled it to be transferred to maps, not only for the artillery, but for use by the assault infantry in finding their way amid the maze of trenches.

● **The systematic medium and long range patrolling of the approaches to the battlefield** to give warning of the movement of German reinforcements.

● **The controlled application of bombing both in time and place** to match the battle plan. The main targets chosen were railway junctions at Courtrai, Menin, Lille, Douai and a headquarters at Fournes. Since only a few bombs, none more than 25 lb (10.5 kg) in weight, were dropped the impact of this first, planned tactical assault was only minimal. Little or no opposition was encountered except from ground fire: more casualties were caused by accidents (including a bomb which exploded when dropped during loading) than by the Germans.

The first of what were to be known as 'Contact Patrols' was flown during the Battle of Neuve Chapelle when two special missions were made in an attempt to discover how far British infantry had advanced. This was necessary once the infantry had moved out of sight and entered the enemy trenches, thus denying their commanders a view of the course of action. The process was formalised during the Battle of Aubers Ridge on 9 May, when the infantry were given strips of white cloth to spread on the ground when they reached their objective, so that aircraft flying at 6000 ft (1800 m) could see them and report their appearance by radio. It was not a success that time because so few objectives were reached, but the system was considered worth while and was further developed.

The first bomb sights were developed simultaneously by each of the combatant nations, starting with devices comprising wires and nails. During 1915, however, the French led the way with the Dorand sight in February and the Lafay in April, while the British Central Flying School produced the CFS sight in June and the Germans their optical Görz. In the USA Sperry developed a Sperry gyro-stabilised sight. The Russians too had a good bomb sight which gave a 60 per cent chance of a hit. Fundamentally these sights helped the bomb aimer measure his speed across the ground and make allowance for drift. The first sights were rudimentary, but at least they improved the chances of obtaining hits from altitudes above tree-top level. Hitting the target was, however, easier than finding and identifying it. The navigation systems of the day, which mostly relied upon good map reading in clear weather conditions, were of doubtful quality. Many targets beyond the immediate front line escaped and even those at close range became increasingly difficult to find as ground camouflage improved. The fixing of an aircraft's position by cross bearing upon radio transmissions was tried by airships but proved of only marginal assistance.

The first attempts at co-ordinated flying by massed aircraft were those practised by the Germans in their January attacks against Dunkirk, described above. Similar techniques were employed by the French 1st Bombardment Group in their subsequent attacks upon South German industry from the area of Nancy-Luneville on those few winter days and in the early spring of 1915 when the weather made long-distance flying feasible. The bombers, Voisin XIII-50s with a speed of 55 mph (90 km/h) and a bomb load of 220 lb (100 kg), did not fly in close formation but took off at intervals behind their leader, making in a swarm for a rendezvous from whence they set course for the objective. These were the last great days of individual aeronauts at war. Close formation flying had not been attempted at first, since the threat from enemy aircraft was negligible, and also because it was felt undesirable to bunch tightly for fear of providing anti-aircraft guns with an easier target.

The first German interceptor force *(Brieftaubenabteilungen Metz)*, was formed in April 1915 to combat the French attacks, could achieve very little with carbines and pistols even when they could locate and get close to the French bombers. Inevitably they fitted machine-guns in rear cockpits since they could not fire forwards through the propeller. In 1915 the French modified their methods by having the bomber swarm fly a little tighter but at varying heights near 6000 ft (1828 m) at which altitude anti-aircraft fire was practically innocuous. Only at the lower levels, where rapid-fire ground weapons could 'hose-pipe' their tracer shots on to the target, was there a deadly threat from gunfire.

Great enthusiasm focused on anti-aircraft guns as the threat of bombing increased. The mere sound of guns had a heartening effect upon those they allegedly defended, though, with the chance of a kill at one aircraft per thousand rounds fired, there was little cause for optimism. The first effective anti-aircraft guns were converted field guns:

Nation	Calibre	Effective vertical range	Rate of fire
Germany	77 mm	4250 m	6-10 rounds per min
	88 mm	3850 m	10 rounds per min
France	75 mm	5000 m	15 rounds per min
Britain	3 in (76 mm)	5500 m	15 rounds per min

Mostly these guns were placed on mobile mountings and fired shells set to explode at a predetermined height. However, accurate fire by individual guns was found to be thoroughly impracticable since the crews could not hope to compute the point of aim even if they knew the target's altitude and speed. It thus came to be directed for groups of guns from a central control post, set to explode their shells in pre-planned barrages in the target's path. A Frenchman called Brocq devised his 'Central Post Instrument' which took information on target height and speed and resolved it into a predicted position of the target so that the correct lay could be given to the gunners along with the fuse setting. This worked quite well providing the operators tracked accurately and the target did not, meanwhile, alter course – and depended upon being able to see the target in daylight or through illumination by searchlights at night. Results were improved but were still much more miss than hit.

Bombing up a Farman bomber. When finally in position the fins protruded above the fuselage, the nose below.

A notable example of the French prowess in bombing was the raid led by Commandant de Göys against a chemical factory at Ludwigshafen on 26 May 1915 as a sort of reprisal in response to **the first poison gas attacks** in battle by the Germans earlier that year. Voisin bombers loaded with 155 mm and 90 mm bombs (artillery shells with fins attached) set off shortly before dawn, found their target, inflicted damage and returned with the loss only of de Göys from engine failure. In August the French could send more than 62 aircraft into a single raid on Germany. But the French, British and Germans were not alone in attempting attacks upon their opponent's hinterland.

Russia's Igor Sikorski had built **the world's first four-engined aircraft,** Le Grand, in 1913 and followed it in 1914 with the even bigger Ilya Mourometz with an endurance of 5 hours (later models 7½ hours). In December 1914 a special self-contained Squadron of Flying Ships was formed and based at Jablonna in Poland. On 15 February 1915 an initial raid by one Ilya was made into East Prussia carrying 600 lb (272 kg) of bombs. Thereafter these gigantic machines were steadily developed and brought into service. Seventy-three were built prior to the Revolution in 1917, and it is claimed that only one was destroyed by enemy action (on 12 September 1916). Armament was increased to seven machine-guns, the Ilya being **the first bomber to install a rear gunner behind the tail.**

Italy had a few tri-motor Caproni 32s with a 7 hours' duration and 600 lb (272 kg) of bombs when she went to war in May 1915 but tended at first to use them against ports and communication centres adjacent to the front rather than against industrial targets. Nevertheless, raids across the mountains into Austria-Hungary were attempted, the first from Pordeone on 20 August 1915.

The turning point in early air warfare came with the realisation that an enemy could no longer be permitted to have unchallenged observation or the freedom to drop bombs

Sikorski Ilya Mourometz bomber.

at will. This point had been reached by the end of September 1914 in unison with a growing belief in the morale value of aircraft despite their doubtful physical contribution. The next critical moment came with the realisation that the most efficient way of shooting down an opponent might be by flying towards the enemy and firing a forward pointing machine-gun aligned to the aeroplane's axis. Aeroplanes specially designed for this purpose had been built before the war: the 'pusher' type Vickers FB with a machine-gun in the nose was a good example and was flying in 1914, having been designed in 1913. As early as 1913, too, experiments had been made in Russia by Lieutenant Poplavko to make a Maxim machine-gun fire bullets through the propeller without striking it. There had also been a device invented by a Swiss, Franz Schneider, and tried by the Germans in 1914. 'Interrupter gears' came under development in France by Raymond Saulnier who at first deferred the idea since it depended upon a reliability in ammunition performance as yet unattained. Saulnier opted for deflector plates attached to the propeller blades and by February 1915 had a crude apparatus ready, one which worked for just as long as the deflectors lasted and so prevented the propeller from being shattered.

The first attack using the Saulnier device took place on 1 April when Roland Garros, flying a Morane Monoplane, crept to within 100 ft (30 m) of an unsuspecting German aeroplane and shot it down in flames. In due course he scored three **confirmed** victories before himself being forced to land with engine failure behind the enemy lines, thus presenting the Germans with the secret of French success.

The first fully effective synchronisation system that enabled a machine-gun to fire through the propeller's arc was designed by the engineers working under the Dutchman Anthony Fokker, whose previous work was aided by a sight of the Saulnier device. The Fokker gear, ready two days after the capture of Garros's aeroplane, activated the firing of the gun at moments of safety after the trigger had been pressed and was not, therefore, an interrupter gear as so frequently described. Its first, unconfirmed, success in battle came on 15 July when Kurt Wintgens claimed a victim that fell in French territory, and so the first confirmed success had to wait until 1 August when Max Immelmann destroyed a British aeroplane over Douai. Nevertheless, the loss of four aircraft by the French *4ᵉ Groupe de Bombardement* on 9 August went wholly to the credit of skilfully handled German Aviatiks whose armament was rearward facing.

The two principal exponents of fighter tactics, as evolved from the introduction of synchronised firing gear, were the Germans Oswald Boelcke and Max Immelmann, particularly the former, who was a supreme instructor. They favoured two main tactical approaches; stalking of two-seater aircraft from below from the 'blind spot' position where the rear gunner was unsighted, or a dive like a hawk from out of the sun, followed by a squirt of machine-gun fire and a continuation of the dive to safety. This second method was further developed by Immelmann with his celebrated 'turn' – a dive followed by a climb, a turn over the vertical and then another dive from the opposite direction; thus a series of attacks aided by the advantage of height could be achieved. Next, Boelcke's suggestion for the establishment of specialised fighter units (instead of the existing organisation of mixed units) was adopted while deliveries began of Fokker E III fighters, which started to

Leutnant Max Immelmann, first German 'ace' with Fokker E I. This particular aircraft is not fitted with a synchronised machine-gun.

appear in quantity towards the end of September 1915; these would occasionally hunt in pairs. The art of aerial gunnery Boelcke also pushed ahead of his contemporaries. No longer would he permit fire to be opened much above 1000 ft (300 m) range: henceforward the problems of allowing for enemy evasion and the usual difficulties of hitting a moving target from a moving platform were to be solved by point-blank fire. From October 1915 onwards the perils of British and French aircraft on the Western Front were sharply increased as the so-called 'Fokker Scourge' began, coincident with the introduction of the special fighter units. However, it is not true, as sometimes is said, that Germany's opponents were 'swept from the skies'. (The Germans themselves were quite unaware of the Fokker's impact.) Simply the work of bombing and reconnaissance was made unhealthy (only sometimes, particularly French strategic bombing, impossible) to accomplish and the Germans were encouraged to foray more often over their enemies' lines.

The first tactical reaction to the Fokker attacks was random attempts at escort to unarmed aircraft. This led to the introduction of **the first close formation flying as a matter of policy** by the French under Capitaine Felix Happe in August 1915 with a V formation. It was found that even the Fokker E IIIs baulked at coming to close combat with a well-disciplined formation of four or more aircraft, since rear-seat gunners could throw up a formidable barrage of self-defensive fire. In point of fact, the Fokker was as vulnerable as any other aeroplane of the day and by no means exceptional **except for its armament and the skill with which it was employed.** Hence competition began to resolve itself into struggles of technology and tactics as both sides endeavoured to develop aircraft which could out-fly their opponents in speed, manoeuvrability and performance at altitude. Predominant were the basic tactics of Boelcke (the *Dikta Boelcke*), but refinements were added as better and – almost as important – more aircraft took the air. It was easily overlooked that, as the quantity of tasks demanded of aircraft by the navies and armies increased, so did the demands of air fighting and formation flying by groups actually reduce the numbers available for basic reconnaissance and artillery direction. That being so the number of aircraft allocated to so-called strategic bombing (of dubious material if not profound moral effect) had to be curtailed while there arose a repetitive cry for more aeroplanes, supporting services and men to run them.

The new aircraft coming into service throughout 1915 and which, in 1916, were to tilt the balance of what had become a battle for air supremacy, may seem only slightly superior, statistically (except in armament), to their precursors of 1914. But their capability to manoeuvre and their reliability were greatly enhanced.

Nation	Type	Date	Speed	Ceiling	Endurance	Armament	Remarks
British	Vickers FB 5	Feb 1915	85 mph	3000 m	4 hr	1 mg	Pusher. Slow climber.
German	Fokker E III	July 1915	87 mph	3800 m	2·75 hr	1 mg	Tractor with sync. gun.
French	Nieuport 11	July 1915	97 mph	5000 m	2·5 hr	1 mg	Tractor with overwing gun. Highly manoeuvrable.
British	DH 2	Feb 1916	93 mph	4750 m	2·75 hr	1 mg	Pusher. Highly manoeuvrable.

Typical of the French aircraft at the front in 1915 was this Farman F-40 'pusher'.

The strict limiting factor to the development of air warfare in 1915 and early 1916 was the volume of production by a brand-new industry that was competing with all the other facets of a burgeoning war industry and the birth pangs of training and maintenance organisations on and behind the airfields. Almost everything had to start from nothing: at best there were to be had as a cadre a few of the pre-war enthusiasts whose knowledge was usually only rudimentary. The bottleneck in aircraft supply was usually that of engines, although the aeroplane industry, which was a craft one, was slow to adopt mass production. British engine production was severely hampered because of a pre-war dependence on German magnetos: they had to buy in France. Fighter production figures speak for themselves.

> Fokker E III   Only 86 were produced by the end of 1915.
> Nieuport 11   Only 210 produced by February 1916
> DH 2   Only one squadron operational by February 1916.

Major developments in air fighting took place as the result of the German attempt to 'bleed the French Army white' at Verdun, beginning on 21 February 1916. A battle of attrition on the surface was reflected by a similar orgy in the sky above. Imbued with the offensive spirit, the French confronted an enemy buoyed up by success as the result of a transitory technical superiority. The Germans committed to the battle:

> 3 zeppelins
> 14 balloons
> 145 reconnaissance aircraft
> 21 Fokker fighters

and employed them in accordance with strategy based on 'barrage' flights. The German aim was to prevent the French penetrating over their own lines; but to do so meant establishing almost permanent patrols which demanded all available aircraft and thus depriving the army of much vital reconnaissance and support in the land battle. **The first German contact patrols were a failure.**

The most extensive air support of an army in 1916 was provided by the French who had developed air photography of the trench battle zone to such an extent that 5000 prints per day were being produced at a forward developing station and could be placed into the hands of the troops within an hour of the picture being taken. Sometimes photos were taken as a battle was going on and the results dropped at intervals to the local commander so that he could have a running photographic commentary on the progress of the battle. But with only a few old Voisins, Caudrons and Farmans, helped by about 36 of the superior Nieuport 11s, the French at first became deprived of this because they were compelled to adopt the defensive. Having once been reinforced they recovered, under the spur of Commandant du Peuty, to their customary offensive, carrying the fight to the Germans and pinning the latter's aircraft to a defensive role. Nothing like this would have been possible for the French, however, but for the arrival of the Nieuport.

Lessons from the French experience were taken to heart by the British. On 19 August 1915, Colonel Hugh Trenchard had been appointed to command the Royal Flying Corps in France. Coming to the work at the critical moment of transition and expansion in aerial warfare, the task of creating a working philosophy of aerial combat in parallel with shifting practice was forced upon him. As a man of strong personality and much staff experience who insisted upon an

Contact Patrol! A Royal Flying Corps BE 2C checks on the progress of the infantry during the Battle of Aubers Ridge on 9 May 1915.

Hugh Trenchard.

offensive spirit in everything, he imposed these convictions on his pilots. In consultation with du Peuty of the French air force, Trenchard preached the attack – meaning, as a matter of principle, that British and French airmen would seek battle over the enemy lines. This put them at an immense disadvantage since, while there was a reasonable chance for the German pilot of a damaged or defective German machine to escape among friends and return to the fray, an Allied airman was more likely to come down among enemies. Moreover, the chances of survival were made even higher for the Germans because they fought mostly with the prevailing wind blowing into their own territory while the reverse naturally applied to their opponents. The gradual changeover to specialised fighter units, which was initiated by the Germans in autumn 1915, was soon copied by the French and British. In January the British laid it down that 'a machine proceeding on a reconnaissance mission must be escorted by at least three other fighting machines. These machines must fly in close formation and a reconnaissance should not be continued if any of the machines become detached.' This rule was taken seriously to heart: for example, on 7 February no less than twelve aircraft were detailed to escort a single BE 2c on reconnaissance of Belgian railways. Teamwork between various types of aircraft was thus being regularised yet, paradoxically, at a time when certain individual pilots were being accorded public adulation.

The French were the first to instigate what became known as aces, pilots who had scored more than five confirmed victories. To begin with the British tended to deprecate

Successful German fighter pilots of 1917. Left to right Kurt Wusthoff, Reinhard, Manfred von Richthofen, Erich Loewenhardt, Lothar von Richthofen.

the system. The first ace was Eugène Gilbert who scored his first victory on 10 January 1915 (by fire from his observer) and eventually (as a pilot) shot down five German aircraft shortly before he was killed (date unknown) in the summer of 1915.

The Germans (who demanded ten victories before pronouncing a pilot as '*Oberkanone*') were first to turn individual pilots' exploits to advantage. Boelke and Immelmann received many decorations and there was a scheme to protect Boelke from being put at risk, although eventually he was killed in collision with one of his own pilots during a dogfight with the British, in October 1916, with his score at 40.

Claims have always been controversial and must be so during intensive combat. The Germans were more accurate because they preferred production of a wreck and this was made all the easier for them since most fights took place on their side of the lines. The French were slightly more liberal and the British the most liberal of all, both they and the French crediting *shared* victories as *whole* victories to the pilots involved.

As the war progressed scores mounted high.

The scores of above 50 victories from all nations are as follows:

Manfred von Richthofen	Germany	80
René Fonk	France	75
Edward Mannock	Britain	73
William Bishop	Canada	72
Ernst Udet	Germany	62
Raymond Collishaw	Canada	62 (incl. 2 in South Russia in 1919)
James McCudden	Britain	57
Georges Guynemer	France	54
A Beauchamp-Proctor	South Africa	54
D M MacLaren	Canada	54
Erich Loewenhardt	Germany	53
William Barker	Britain	52
P Fullard	Britain	52
R F Dallas	Australia	51

Governed by the five-victory convention, the number of aces by nations in the First World War was to come to:

The supreme German award of the First World War, the Pour le Mérité – known as 'The Blue Max'.

Britain and Empire	784	(plus 65 bomber and corps pilots and approximately 50 gunners)
Germany	363	
France	158	plus
The USA	110	(of whom Edward Rickenbacker was top with 26)
Italy	43	(of whom Francesco Baracca was top with 34)
Austria-Hungary	25–30	(of whom Godwin Brumowski was top with 35–40)
Russia	18–19	(of whom A Kazakov was top with 17 at least)
Belgium	7	(of whom Willy Coppens was top with 37)

By 1917 aerial dogfights between opposing scout aircraft over the front were an almost daily occurrence. Here French Spad XIIIs and Albatros D IIIs of the German Luftstreitkräfte meet in combat.

Although the main efforts of Germany, Britain and France were concentrated on the struggle on the Western Front, fighting went on in many other parts of the world – in Africa, China and in Gallipoli as already mentioned; on the Eastern Front, where the Russians fought against the Germans and Austro-Hungarians; in Serbia, where the Serbs resisted the Austro-Hungarians, Bulgarians and the Germans (a war which was to spread throughout the Balkans and then into Rumania in September 1916); and in Italy after the Italians declared war in May 1915. Railways were frequently bombed in the Balkans but with no lasting effect. There was also a considerable sideshow in which the British fought the Turks in Mesopotamia and Palestine. Each of these battle fronts placed demands upon the few available aircraft and their crews at a time when senior airmen, such as the German Thomsen, the British Trenchard and the French du Peuty, were asking for increased resources on the Western battle front to the detriment of the other fronts. So a theatre of war such as Mesopotamia was allocated few aircraft and only obsolete ones at that. Yet in that theatre of war took place:

The first air supply of a beleaguered garrison at Kut-el Amara. The British 6th Division had been surrounded in the town, which lay in a bend of the River Tigris, since 4 December 1915 and, despite attempts at relief, was still besieged in April 1916, by which time rations were practically exhausted. Not until 15 April was the first attempt made to drop food in an effort to satisfy a daily requirement of 5000 lb (2250 kg). Everything was against the project. The few enemy aircraft might interfere, but the effects of weather upon the handful of decrepit aircraft was decisive. In the heat, some aircraft could hardly take off and their ceiling was severely restricted: a machine which

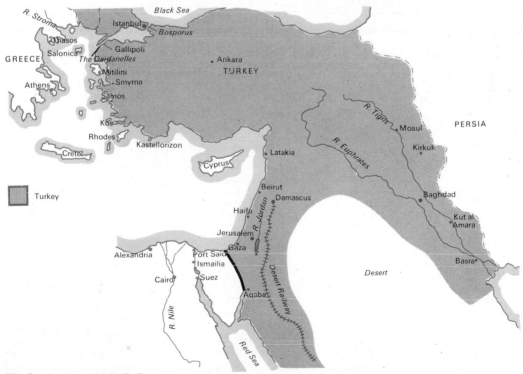

The Dardanelles and Middle East.

Supplies on their way, slung beneath the fuselage, for dropping at Kut-el Amara.

might normally climb to 5000 ft (1500 m) was lucky to reach 4000 ft (1200 m). It was thought that a daily delivery of 3350 lb (1520 kg) might be made, but in the event only 16 800 lb (7636 kg) reached their destination between 15 and 27 April before Kut surrendered. Sometimes aircraft could not take off at all; several times their cargo fell into Turkish hands and occasionally the rudimentary containers (a sack within a sack) burst on impact. There were no parachutes, of course.

Since the first delivery of propaganda material from the air had been made, on 30 August 1914 (see above), demands for this kind of operation had been increasing and acting as a further drain upon resources in aircraft. The early propagandists received little encouragement because there were no official organisations to back them up: hence requests to the air forces to drop paper instead of high explosive were largely rejected – sometimes at pilot level even when official authorisation had been given. The Germans, though first in the field, were soon matched, particularly by the French but also by the British. Deliveries of leaflets and books besides being made through neutral countries, came from drifting balloons, which released their cargo on the action of a time-fuse, or from aircraft. Miniature editions of newspapers and books (notably of *J'accuse* by the French) were printed on a special light-weight paper which had been developed by the autumn of 1915. Partly the material was meant to undermine enemy morale, but some of it to inform the peoples of occupied territory. Except for aircraft delivery it would have been well-nigh impossible; therefore aircraft became essential to a psychological weapon which had a profound effect upon the course of the war. Every combatant nation employed these methods, but the injection of propaganda by air for the most part went on in the West.

The greatest sea battle of the war took place in the North Sea between the fleets of Britain and Germany on 31 May and 1 June 1916. Although five zeppelins were deployed for reconnaissance by the Germans they were of no assistance due to low cloud. The one valid and accurate report submitted by *L 11* on the 1st, as to the location of the British fleet, was underestimated by the German Admiral Scheer. For the British part, a seaplane launched from HMS *Engadine* found the German battle cruisers and reported by radio, but the signal was not received by the British Admiral Beatty. Then the seaplane was forced to land because of a burst petrol pipe. Aircraft therefore paid virtually no part in an encounter in which the commanders of the contending fleets, though conscious of the value of air reconnaissance and in possession of limited facilities, derived nothing of value from that source and blundered from one assumption to another in the formulation of their plans.

Nevertheless, on 27 April three German planes operating in the Gulf of Riga from the converted freighter *Santa Elena* had the distinction of being **the first to hit a battleship with bombs** when they planted three out of 31 dropped upon the Russian *Slava* and caused her to be withdrawn for repairs. This significant event was little remarked upon at the time. On 2 August a Bristol Scout, after taking off from the deck of HMS *Vindex*, intercepted a zeppelin over the sea without, however, making a kill. It thus had the distinction of being **the first aircraft to achieve** this feat though the subsequent need for the pilot to land in the sea may have somewhat damped his enthusiasm.

The major offensive by the British and French Armies on the Somme, beginning on 1 July 1916, had as its prelude a significant struggle for air superiority by the Royal Flying Corps over the German Imperial Air Service. The Germans with 129 aircraft (including 19 fighters) were wholly at a disadvantage prior to the Anglo-French assault (using 386 aircraft, including 138 fighters). Not only had they concentrated every available aircraft at Verdun, where the battle of attrition raged on without pause, but they were suffering from the technical inferiority of the Fokker E III against the French Nieuport 11 (which was also in British service), the newly arrived British DH 2 and another, larger, pusher, the FE 2b. In consequence German balloons were frequently destroyed and their reconnaissance aircraft denied a sight of the British and French preparations while the latter were enabled to do almost as they pleased over the battlefield. The methods of 1915, and those learnt at Verdun, were exploited. While offensive fighter patrols sealed off the battle zone, artillery aircraft were able to give constant help to the guns – particularly in counter-battery shooting – and contact patrols attempted with a modicum of success to trace the progress of the infantry through the trenches. It was now accepted that the contact patrols had to fly low in order to function since there was no guarantee that the infantry would light the flares they carried when they reached an objective. Though low flying sometimes made it possible to recognise different uniforms, it at the same time exposed the aircraft to intense small-arms fire and brought them into the zone of the artillery barrage with an increased chance of being hit by a shell that was intended for quite another sort of target. Meantime the bombing of communication targets and dumps in the German rear went on and with occasional success. Sometimes artillery fire at the front had to be reduced if an ammunition train was hit, because the guns depended upon a steady flow of ammunition from this source and kept low stocks at the pits. Therefore the danger of interruption of train schedules tended to increase dumping at the guns and hence raised the risk of damage during counter-battery work. It cannot be claimed, however, that bombing imposed a

Hermann Thomsen.

profound influence upon land operations. At most the overall effects of air warfare made a limited impact and led to a major reappraisal of policy and organisation by the Germans when their entire war strategy came under review at the end of August. The immediate cancellation of all offensive operations by Field-Marshal Paul von Hindenburg released aircraft for use on the Somme, and the appointment on 8 October of General Ernst von Hoeppner to command a vastly expanded Air Force coincided with a clarification of the air-war scenario. Hoeppner and his Chief of Staff, Colonel Hermann Thomsen (who until then had been Chief of the Air Force in the Field), ratified the previous policy that fighter aircraft were crucial in obtaining command of the air and that in future not only speed but manoeuvrability and rate of climb had to be accentuated. Henceforward German fighters would be concentrated into special *Jagdstaffeln* of fourteen aircraft each (normal operating strength nine), and would tend to fight in larger numbers for command of the air, chiefly where the ground fighting was most critical. The most experienced pilots would go to these special units. They would fly, mostly, in the latest Albatross D series fighters of which the D II came into service in October: its important data were as follows:

Speed 108 mph (173 km/h), Ceiling 18 600 ft (5650 m), Endurance 1½ hr, Armament 2 mg.

Its superiority over those Allied aircraft, described above, needs no emphasis.

A dramatic swing in relative casualties marked the advent of the new German fighters and their organisation into *Jagdstaffeln*. From September to November Boelcke's *Jagdstaffel* 2 destroyed 76 enemy aircraft against the loss of seven, and the total loss of the German Air Force in October was only twelve compared to 27 in September when the Somme battle was at its height.

The greatest changes came about in connection with bombing and support of the armies and navies, however. The German Air Force had failed to support the army as well as it might during the Verdun and early Somme battles, and recognised that its opponents were ahead both in radio co-operation on artillery missions and in contact patrols to help the infantry. At the same time they knew that Allied bombing of communications had been of little effect and that their own airship offensive against England was defeated. Therefore Hoeppner and Thomsen made three important changes aimed:

Ernst von Hoeppner.

● To give priority to artillery co-operation aircraft and in particular to improve radio communication to and from the ground which was already so successfully practised by their enemies.

● To raise the standard of contact patrols which had been a virtual failure until then.

● To run down the airship offensive and substitute heavy multi-engine bombers for attacks upon strategic targets.

      The principal German air strength would be concentrated in the West since Germany was entering a period in which she hoped to rebuild her forces at the same time as the Anglo-French exhausted themselves in forthcoming offensives to recapture lost territory. At sea, too, the emphasis was to be in the West where aircraft were taking an increasing part in the mercantile war that went on both above and beneath the surface. While the zeppelins of the Imperial German Navy withdrew to the sidelines, that service's seaplanes became increasingly active in the seaward approaches to

England and in their efforts to counter Anglo-French air attacks upon port and airfield installations in Belgium.

The change in sea warfare came about as the result of Germany's failure to deplete the British Fleet so seriously that control of the sea passed even temporarily into German hands. Hence Germany decided, towards the end of 1916, to intensify U-boat attacks upon British merchant shipping which had been going on since January 1915. Many U-boats set out on their voyages from the ports of Zeebrugge and Ostend on the Belgian coasts. The British and French based their defence upon Dunkirk and the other Channel ports on both sides of the narrow seas. A battle between surface craft, including light cruisers and destroyers besides fast torpedo boats and submarines, thus opened in 1915 and lasted until the end of the war and included:

● **Attacks upon submarines** both in port and on the sea, the first bombing of Zeebrugge and Ostend being made on 11 February 1916 by flying boats. Soon these were to become a regular but never monotonous feature of the narrow seas' war as the anti-aircraft defences burgeoned and the Germans introduced defending aircraft of their own. Submarine assembly yards at Antwerp also came under air attack. No great damage

Looking aft from the car of a North Sea class airship. Note the Lewis gunner on the lower platform.

was done by these attacks because the bombs were only 25-pounders. Attacks upon U-boats on the surface were rarely successful for the same reason. Seaplanes patrolled against the U-boats, but non-rigid airships were also used with their eight hours' endurance – a type of craft which was produced by the British in three weeks of hectic improvisation.

● **Attacks upon enemy batteries** located on both sides of the lines. Both sides used the conventional artillery control techniques by wireless control from aircraft or telephone from balloons.

● **Attacks upon enemy air bases.** Some of those against German airship hangars in Belgium have been mentioned above and were so effective that the Germans stopped using them after mid-1915. As the rival airfields began to improve and handle more aircraft they naturally attracted retribution by way of bombing, an activity which went on by day and night when the weather was favourable and sometimes when it was not.

● **Attacks upon shipping** either at sea or in port were undertaken by both sides. For example, German seaplanes made repeated attacks against ports on both sides of the Channel and on 1 February 1916 sank a coaster at anchor. And in the Baltic **they were the first to lay mines from the air.** Repeatedly their opponents bombed German destroyers in Zeebrugge and at Bruges in addition to attempts to destroy the lock gates of the canal connecting Bruges with the sea.

● **Interception of raiders,** which was the task, mostly, of land-based aircraft in their endeavours to prevent raids by seaplanes on the ports, but which also included the launching of seaplanes from carriers at sea when conditions were sufficiently smooth to permit take-off. Almost as a matter of course far heavier losses were incurred by accidents than by enemy action. For example, when eleven Sopwith Baby seaplanes were put into the water off Sylt from the carriers *Vindex* and *Engadine* on 3 May 1916, eight failed to take off because of a variety of mishaps, one crashed and one had to land again from engine trouble. The survivor accomplished a sterile mission over enemy waters.

A most important contribution made by the British RNAS to air warfare was the development of heavy bombers and a technique of strategic bombing. Appreciating that the light bombs of 1914, lifted by aircraft of small carrying capacity, were inadequate, Commander Murray Sueter asked in December 1914, for 'a bloody paralyser of an aeroplane', and received, in due course, the Short Bomber and the Handley Page o/100. The single-engined Short would lift nearly 1000 lb (450 kg) of bombs, the twin-engined Handley Page about 1800 lb (820 kg) (see below for more detailed specifications) and both would be ready by the autumn of 1916. In the meantime the French had continued with their strategic bombing of Germany and on 22 June had attacked Karlsruhe, killing 120 people – which was many more than any single airship raid ever killed in England. They were joined at Luxeuil in July by a special Wing, partly manned by Canadians, from the RNAS with a view to making combined raids. A delayed concentration of strength at last led to the first big attack against the important Mauser small-arms factory at Oberndorf on 12 October and resulted in a classic encounter between bombers and defences during a trip of over 200 miles (320 km) in daylight. Sixteen French Breguet IVs and Farmans took off, escorted by twelve of the new Sopwith 1½ Strutters manned by Frenchmen and four two-seater Nieuport 12s. In the next wave came thirteen RNAS single-seat Sopwith 1½ Strutters carrying bombs, and six Breguets, loaned by the French, escorted by seven Sopwith two-seaters in the fighter role. The Sopwith was the most technically interesting aircraft in the raid. Ubiquitous

·and robust, it was more than a match for the Fokkers and could hold its own against the Albatross D II. Once across the German lines the bombers were reported by ground observers and their position plotted. Anti-aircraft fire blossomed in their path and a French Breguet went down. Fokkers and Albatrosses, among other German types, climbed to meet the raiders. Some bombers turned back and only the first French squadron reached the target unmolested by fighters; nine of the French got there in the end but their attack was scattered. Of the British, the Breguets missed their way and bombed the wrong town and only nine Sopwiths put bombs on or in the vicinity of Oberndorf. A running fight took place both on the way to and from the target, the German attacks coming to an end when French Nieuports, manned by Americans of the *Escadrille Lafayette*, met the returning bombers on their way home. The Sopwith fighters did well in helping protect the bombers and claimed three enemy aircraft destroyed (denied by the Germans). To the French it was plain that the slow Breguets were useless in daylight operations so they were relegated to night bombing in all its inaccuracy – the usual reaction when resistance got too hot by day. The British continued to use their Sopwiths until April 1917 and by tight formation flying and close escort reached their objectives without loss in five separate raids. However, nearly always the damage inflicted was minimal.

The first large German twin-engined bombers to come into service were the Gotha G Is, the prototype of which flew in January 1915. Development of the type continued throughout the war along with some other large aircraft built by the Friedrichshafen, AEG and Zeppelin companies. But the Gothas were the most numerous, coming into service in larger numbers and with improved performance towards the end of 1916 as German aircraft production began to multiply. At the same time the British Handley Page 0/400 and the French Caudron R IVs were appearing so that, almost simultaneously, the main combatant powers were acquiring what Russia and Italy had possessed from the outset – the instruments of a long-range bomber force capable of carrying a significant load of bombs. The performance figures for the three aircraft mentioned above bear comparison with each other and their Russian and Italian predecessors on page 22.

Nation	Type	Year	Speed	Ceiling	Bomb load	Armament
Germany	Gotha G IV	1917	80 mph	5500 m	600–1100 lb (250–500 kg)	3 mg
Britain	HP 0/400	1917	97 mph	2800 m	1800 lb (820 kg)	4 mg
France	Caudron R IV	1916	80 mph	3000 m	220 lb (100 kg)	3 mg

At first Germany and Britain, in particular, tended to scatter a few of their large bombers to each of the various fronts rather than concentrate them for a single effort against a particular objective. **The first positive attempt at concentration** came from the Germans when, in the autumn of 1916, the '*England Geschwader*' *(Bombengeschwader 3)* was formed by order of General Ludendorff. With 30 of the latest Gothas it was intended to bomb London as a propaganda terror venture linked to the far more deadly unrestricted submarine attack which was to be launched in 1917 against

British shipping. The attacks were to begin in February 1917, but were delayed because the aircraft were not ready. They would not set forth until May, by which time the war had changed in aspect quite decisively.

The major events which conditioned the future course of the First World War and had their impact upon air warfare after January 1917 were:

- Commencement of unrestricted submarine warfare   1 February
- Start of the Russian Revolution   12 March
- Entry of the USA into the war against Germany   6 April

The first military operations by US Army aircraft took place when the 1st Aero Squadron went into action in support of operations against the Mexicans on 15 March 1916. But already American airmen had joined the French Air Force and they suffered their first casualties near Verdun in June 1916. Nevertheless US air power, as the nation went to war, was virtually of no value, almost wholly dependent upon allies for the supply of aircraft and likely to be many months before a worthwhile number of aircrew and ground staff could be trained.

The principal military winter activities of 1917 in Europe consisted of preparations by the British and French respectively to attack the Germans at Arras and on the Chemin des Dames in April, and by the Germans in building and withdrawing to the shelter of their immensely strong Hindenburg Line – thus partly preempting the Allied plans of attack. The air war was reduced to a relatively low level of activity, chiefly because the weather was some of the worst in living memory but also because both sides were endeavouring to recuperate their strength and restore efficiency after the exhausting battles of 1916. Although aircraft production was rising fast the pilots to fly them, particularly on the Allied side, were mostly short of experience and were only rudimentarily trained. The technical superiority of the German fighters, as demonstrated in October 1916, remained a deadly though somewhat hidden threat because aircraft were so often grounded by bad weather. New Allied fighters were about to come into service but would not be fully proven until May – even those which were in service in March and April. The smaller band of élite German fighter pilots would make up, in no small way, for the numerical disadvantage of the German Air Force as a whole.

The first flights in the air battle to discover the extent and alignment of the Hindenburg Line were made as routine reconnaissance on the few suitable flying days in October and November 1916. From then on every opportunity was taken to photograph the excavations, but had to be made in the teeth of opposition, notably the *Jagdstaffel II* commanded by von Richthofen, located at Douai. Throughout the winter the Germans pressed their technical advantage, adopting the offensive, as in 1915, by tackling Allied aircraft across rather than above their own side of the lines. Yet, faced with these problems, the Allies doggedly declined to abandon offensive flights, as had the Germans in similar circumstances, but continued to attempt deep penetrations of enemy air space. The information they gathered was dearly bought. Salvation could only come from the next generation of planes, while persistent operations were possible only because larger numbers of aircraft and crew were becoming available to replace the heavy losses.

Long before April 1917 – which for the British was to become known as 'Bloody April' – the latest fighters were coming into service:

The Sopwith Triplane.

The Sopwith Pup.

The Albatross D III.

Nation	Type	Date	Speed	Ceiling	Endurance	Armament	Remarks
Germany	Albatross D III	Jan 1917	109 mph	6000 m	2 hr	2 mg	Good climber.
France	Spad VII	Sep 1916	119 mph	5900 m	$2\frac{1}{4}$ hr	1 mg	Very strong.
Britain	Sopwith Pup	Sep 1916	111 mph	5900 m	3 hr	1 mg	Highly manoeuvrable.
	Sopwith Triplane	Nov 1916	113 mph	6850 m	$2\frac{3}{4}$ hr	1 mg	Better than Pup.
	Bristol F 2A	Mar 1917	119 mph	6750 m	3 hr	2 mg	Formidable two-seater.

In view of the obvious superiority of the Anglo-French aircraft over their Albatross adversary the higher German scoring rate in combat has to be explained. During April the British suffered 151 losses against 70 German, and there was a comparable exchange rate on the French fronts, and yet only 114 German machines opposed 385 British fighters over the main Arras front. For a start the Allies had not fully developed the potential of their new fighters, though the Spad, Pup and Triplane held their own. It was tactics which told. The Germans, who used only their most experienced

Jagdstaffel against the British, were intent upon destroying the more vulnerable Allied Corps reconnaissance and support aircraft and would avoid combat with fighters if possible while withholding their own reconnaissance aircraft except for essential tasks. In April Richthofen raised his score from 31 to 52, seven of his victims being BE 2s. The British, despite their losses, were determined to persevere with their offensive policy and had to win their victories against tough opposition while over the enemy side of the lines. Fighter for fighter there was not much in it. In fact 'Bloody April' was to some extent a victory for the Allies, since they maintained their primary aim of assisting the armies and emerged from this gruelling experience in better shape and with improved tactics to fight the battles to come. Bombing raids were pressed against the German Army's rear areas and on at least one important occasion seriously disrupted German counter-attacks by blowing up an ammunition dump. Contact patrols never ceased and in all this, because of their larger resources, the British did better than the French. There was intensive and mounting activity as the weather improved. Combat in the air became less a matter of individual fighting between the hunter and the hunted, but instead a mad whirl of several and then dozens of machines mixed up in what became known as 'dog fights' which could last for nearly an hour with the aircraft ranging from maximum ceiling down to tree-top height.

The claims of air power in connection with operations of war on land were more persistently being pressed by senior airmen. On the day the Arras offensive opened the leader of the French Air Force, Commandant du Peuty, wrote in an official letter, 'Victory in the air must precede victory on land.' He exaggerated but did so, perhaps, because he sought to convince his superiors of the parlous state into which the French Air Force had been allowed to decline. For the oncoming French attack at the Chemin des Dames he could only muster 131 aircraft of all kinds, and most of those were obsolete since production of the latest types had been delayed by industrial troubles. Yet the air-mindedness of the French General Staff was such that they changed the hour of the offensive's start in order to assemble the troops in darkness, since by day they were sure to be seen by German reconnaissance aircraft which operated quite freely on the French front.

The loss of the leading Allied fighter ace, Captain Albert Ball, occurred on 7 May. He had claimed fifteen victories between 23 April and 6 May and thus raised his score to 47, but his loss on the 7th after he had entered a cloud during combat remains a mystery. Lothar von Richthofen was credited with him, but this is contradicted because his claim was for a triplane whereas Ball was flying a biplane SE 5. It is much more likely that Ball became disorientated – quite a common occurrence – and went out of control in zero visibility. Georges Guynemer of France thus became the leading Allied ace at the front.

The implementation of air power in all its aspects demanded even more careful planning and co-ordination. Both sides created extensive early-warning systems to enable ground observers to telephone information of the approach of enemy aircraft so that fighter aircraft could be deployed to attack them at a tactical advantage and balloons and reconnaissance aircraft given time to take evasive action. Elaborate measures to protect bomber formations in daylight were made. On 23 April, for example, a photographic reconnaissance by nine Sopwith 1½ Strutters and a simultaneous bombing attack by nine other aircraft was supported by twelve Sopwith Pups and three Spads, while on 11 May the British made their **first deliberate**

attempt to co-ordinate low-level attacks by aircraft with an infantry assault. Up to then random attacks had been made by contact patrols but on this occasion FE 2bs and Nieuports flew to a timed schedule to attack German infantry beyond the zone of the artillery barrage and then, after the artillery ceased fire, against German infantry opposing the British infantry from shell-holes. **The first attack by a complete Staffel of German aircraft in support of an infantry attack** took place in Flanders on 10 July and was so successful that the Air Command at once began to form special ground attack units *(Schlachtstaffeln)* for direct action at the front against all manner of enemy army installation.

The interdependence of one type of air activity upon another was also clearly demonstrated during the cataclysmic spring of 1917. When the April offensives raged on land and Allied air losses rose, the British were compelled to stop their air attacks, based on Luxeuil, against southern Germany and withdraw the bombers to Flanders. At the same time they transferred Sopwith Triplane fighters from the Channel zone, where the anti-submarine campaign was intensifying, in order to restore the balance against the German Albatrosses near Arras. Yet, when the Germans began seriously to raid England with a few Gotha bombers on 25 May, the British reaction on 13 June was to withdraw two crack fighter squadrons (one equipped with the latest SE 5 machines) from France to England. The speed with which these transfers were made indicated the high mobility of striking power which could be achieved providing adequate ground installations could be maintained in the operational zones.

The first daylight attack by an aeroplane on London was made on 28 November 1916, when a German LVG C II came in high, took twenty photographs, dropped six 22 lb (10 kg) bombs between Brompton Road and Victoria Station and then suffered engine trouble which forced it to land in French territory on the way home. Ten people were injured and £1585 of damage caused. The raid came as a complete surprise. None of the seventeen aircraft which belatedly rose in pursuit got a sight of the raider.

The first bombing attack on England by the Gotha G IVs of Bombengeschwader 3 took place on 25 May 1917. Twenty-three, led by Hauptman Ernst Brandenburg, set out for London and 21 got as far as Gravesend where cloud formations turned them back. Bombs fell on Folkestone as the Gothas made for home. There were no interceptions by the defence, which put 74 aircraft (mostly the totally inadequate BE 2C) into the air. One Gotha was lost out at sea (possibly to an RNAS fighter) and one crashed when landing.

The first Gotha raid on London took place on 13 June. Of the twenty which took off, fourteen reached their objective and, in broad daylight quite undisturbed by the defence, dropped 72 bombs into a square mile of the City. The dead amounted to 162, the wounded to 432 to which were added the observer in a Bristol Fighter killed by cross-fire from the loose, unescorted Gotha formation. More raids would follow and will be mentioned in the next section, as will the resulting reappraisal of future air policy and large-scale reorganisation sparked off by the alarm and fury evoked by the startled Londoners. **For the first time there had been a demonstration of the visions of the past,** the possibility that air power, attacking the heart of a nation, could bring about a major decision. The repercussions from what, for the time being, was a greatly exaggerated menace, were to be enormous.

Another turning point in the evolution of air warfare was thus reached in the spring of 1917, a turning point which coincided with advances in aviation technology which would throw fresh demands upon the air crews, those who controlled them and those whose job it was to make their work easier to perform. By the end of June 1917 most of the techniques that were to be associated with the support of forces on land and sea had been demonstrated – if only in rudimentary form. In essence:

● **The close integration of air attack with surface forces** in addition to reconnaissance and observation had been shown as feasible.

● **The tactics of aerial combat** had been resolved, based upon the single-seater fighter with its forward-firing guns. Even twin-seater aircraft such as the Bristol F 2A had been shown as effective only when flown to make use of the front gun, taking the rear gunner along as a bonus, purely for tail protection.

● **The altitudes at which combat took place** had gone up to about 15 000 ft (4500 m), compared with about 2100 ft (700 m) in 1914. This meant that the airmen were fighting in an atmosphere at which anoxia seriously inhibited their efficiency. The task of swinging or even reloading a machine-gun became more difficult and pilot error more likely above 13 000 ft (4000 m). Yet only a few sets of oxygen equipment had yet been made available (chiefly in the German high-climbing airships and the Gotha bombers). It was to be found, too, that many airmen preferred to do without these aids, rather in the spirit that it was an admission of personal failure to have recourse to them. Severe cold at higher altitudes was

A Fokker Triplane attacks a British observation balloon as the observers parachute to safety, British air crew, other than balloonists, were not equipped with parachutes.

something which the human frame could not easily resist and as yet thick unheated clothing was the only protection. Frostbite was not uncommon.

● **Aircraft speeds had risen** though not so significantly as manoeuvrability and armament. Single-seat fighters operated at about 110 mph (168 km/h) except when in a dive, and multi-gun bombers rarely went at more than 100 mph (160 km/h), so the discrepancy in speed between the two was still quite small. Thus a tail gunner with a good sight of his assailant had a fair chance of defending his aircraft. But gun-sights remained primitive – ring and bead devices which helped little in assessing range and deflection – thus making it almost essential, for the sake of a kill, to fire point-blank, hose-piping bullets by reference to the tracer's stream.

● **Accurate navigation and bomb dropping** remained in the province of guesswork, both largely depending upon visual observation with a minimum of assistance from instruments. Radio position fixing in its infancy could not be relied upon and the existing bomb sights did not provide sufficient information.

● **Ground fire** also depended upon visual acquisition of the target both by day and night since the sound locators then coming into use gave only a rough estimate of an aeroplane's presence, course, speed and altitude. Hence a hit was a matter of chance and impossible to achieve above 19000 ft (6000 m) – the maximum range of the best gun in service.

In fact the application of effective air attack and defence depended more on high numbers than efficient application. Just as 1000 shells were needed to score a single aerial kill, a great many bombs had to be dropped from as low an altitude as possible to hope for a hit on a target – and even then, with the paucity and small size of bombs in use, significant damage was unlikely. In June 1917, as in August 1914, the military possibilities of the aeroplane remained in the nature of a dubious force in aid of, or in conflict with, morale, and as a valuable provider of information about the enemy.

A British RE 8 on contact patrol seen from the trenches.

SECTION III
The Birth of Air Power

The Battle of Messines began at 0310 on 7 June 1917 with the simultaneous explosion of nineteen deep mines beneath the German fortifications. These mines were the result of many months' work by British sappers, and contained among them 1 000 000 lb (450 000 kg) of HE. Immediately, a massive artillery barrage opened, and the infantry moved forward, and as a feature of this battle occurred **the first use of pre-planned intensive low-flying attack as a factor in the initial assault.**

The improved British fighters – particularly those of the RNAS squadrons – were now beginning to take their toll of the Germans. The Pup-flying 3 Naval Squadron had claimed 80 victories by the end of June, but it was the naval Triplane pilots who really got the measure of the *Jastas*. By this same date Roderic Dallas, an Australian pilot, had claimed 29, Robert Little, another Australian, 26, and Raymond Collishaw had brought his personal score to 27. Among Collishaw's victims was Karl Allmenroder, who fell on 26 June, having made 30 claims in five months at the front.

In the face of this increasing opposition, and in the light of their April experience, the Germans instituted some changes. **The first permanent grouping of German Jagdstaffeln** was ordered on 26 June, von Richthofen forming *Jagdgeschwader* I from *Jastas* 4, 6, 10 and 11. **Intensive activity along the Belgian coast and over the English Channel** was generated in the Dunkirk area by Allied seaplanes, bombing aircraft and fighters. After April 1917, despite the departure of many units to aid the RFC at the front, the RNAS still retained 4 Wing with two fighter squadrons and one flight, 5 Wing for bombing and reconnaissance duties, and 1 Wing which undertook purely naval work, spotting for monitors bombarding the Belgian coast, and undertaking reconnaissances. Facing these units in the Ostend-Zeebrugge area were a substantial force of German seaplanes of several types, and a *Marinefeldjasta* with Albatross scouts. **The first attacks with airborne torpedoes to be carried out in the Western war zone** were made by the German Marine floatplanes from Belgium on 19 April 1917, six of these aircraft, three with torpedoes, attacking shipping off Ramsgate and the Downs without success. **The first sinking of a vessel in British waters by an air-dropped torpedo** occurred on 1 May when two seaplanes sank the S.S. *Gema* by this method of attack. Fighter patrols from Dunkirk were sent aloft to intercept such attacks, and on 12 May Sopwith Pups on such a mission met Albatross fighters of the *Marinefeldjasta*, claiming five of them shot down into the sea.

The RNAS fighter units at Dunkirk were well placed to intercept German bombers, both on their way to and from their targets in England. During June the RNAS was introducing another new fighter, the Sopwith Camel, to service with units at Dunkirk, three squadrons being re-equipped with this aircraft. **The first successful interception of a Gotha, and first successful Camel combat,** took place on 4 July 1917, when five Camels intercepted sixteen Gothas north-west of Ostend, returning from an attack on Harwich and Felixstowe. Flight Lieutenant A M Shook shot down one in flames, and a second was claimed out of control.

A reorganisation of the anti-zeppelin defences set up during 1915–16 was enforced by the arrival of the high-performance Gothas over England by day. At once three special day fighting squadrons were set up on lines similar to those at the front, and equipped with Camels and Pups. At the same time, all anti-aircraft weapons and other defences were brought under the control of the London Air Defence Area (LADA), which stretched from Portsmouth in the west to Harwich in the east. All defending aircraft squadrons were organised within this command as the Home Defence Brigade (later VI Brigade).

When the Gothas began night raids in September 1917 separate aircraft and gun zones were instituted. An outer gun barrage was set up for the defence of London, behind which a 'Balloon Apron' was formed around the perimeter of the city. Tethered kite balloons flew at 8000 ft (2500 m), trailing lines of steel cables between them. Above these aircraft patrolled, flights of four flying at 9000, 10000 and 11000 ft (2800, 3100 and 3400 m) respectively. Large numbers of searchlights were added to these zones to work with the aircraft. Initially ten squadrons were involved south of the Wash, with four more based to the north.

The organisation proved effective and in May 1918 the Northern Air Defence Area (NADA) was formed. By the end of the war LADA would have eleven squadrons available, and NADA five, with a total of 400 first-line aircraft and 350 pilots. This force was backed up by ten training squadrons with 227 aircraft and 165 pilots; 174 landing grounds were in use.

The last daylight raid on London occurred on 7 July, while by the end of August the daylight campaign was halted altogether due to the increasing effectiveness of the British defences – particularly the units at Dunkirk. In a total of eight day raids, the Gothas dropped over twenty tons of bombs, killing 401 people and injuring 878 more.

The severe decline in French military strength that ensued after their abortive offensive on the Chemin des Dames in April and which culminated in mutinies within the Army, threw the load of offensive warfare upon the shoulders of the British in the West while the Germans stood on the defensive. The Third Battle of Ypres, which began in July, coincided with a radical re-equipment by both sides with new types of aircraft. Fighters were predominant and over-shadowed in number and performance by the following:

Nation	Type	Date in Service	Speed	Ceiling	Endurance	Armament	Remarks
Britain	SE 5	April 1917	120 mph	5030 m	$2\frac{1}{2}$ hr	2 mg	Fine ac.
	Camel	June 1917	122 mph	7315 m	$2\frac{1}{2}$ hr	2 mg	Excellent in manoeuvring.
France	Spad XIII	Sep 1917	138 mph	6644 m	2 hr	2 mg	Very sturdy.
Germany	Fokker DR 1 (Triplane)	Aug 1917	115 mph	5791 m	2 hr	2 mg	Highly manoeuvrable.
	Fokker D VII	May 1918	116 mph	6980 m	$1\frac{1}{2}$ hr	2 mg	Excellent at high altitude.

Heavy rain and poor visibility fatally hampered the Ypres (Passchendaele) offensive both on

Georges Guynemer.

the ground and in the air, though during September the rejuvenated British squadrons proved very effective in protecting the Corps units from attack. In the II Brigade area no casualties were suffered by Corps aircraft on the first day of the offensive, and of 72 combats reported by the Brigade, only six involved Corps types. Yet September again proved a bad month for the Allies, with overall losses just topping those of April. **The leading Allied ace was lost on 11 September,** when Georges Guynemer failed to return from a sortie. There were some heavy losses for the Germans too; on the 15th, one of the two pre-production Fokker Triplanes was shot down by a Camel, Kurt Wolff, victor of 33 combats, being killed. **The epic dogfight of the war** occurred on 23 September, when Werner Voss, at the time second only to Richthofen in the German air service with a score of 48, was shot down and killed in the other Triplane. The victor was Lieutenant A P R Rhys-Davis (23 victories), who managed to get into a firing position after Voss had fought a long single-handed battle against a flight of SE 5As, all of which were flown by aces of 56 Squadron.

Further British land attacks were made during October and November as the Third Battle of Ypres drew to its end on 10 November. Ten days later a new blow was struck further south in the Cambrai area. In a bold experiment, without initial bombardment, an attack was spearheaded by the first large-scale concentration of tanks. Aircraft, notably DH 5s and Camels, were used mainly in a ground attack role. Complete surprise was achieved and a deep penetration made, aircraft in part doing the work of artillery. Between 20 and 26 November, mainly at ground targets, RFC fighters fired 52 673 rounds of ammunition.

The first employment by the Germans of aircraft in a massed ground attack role supported the counter-attack launched at Cambrai on 30 November. Every available *Schlachtstaffel* – previously used singly – was thrown in supported by *JG I*. The counter-attack was successful and, harried from the air, the British troops were withdrawn to the line of the Flesquières Ridge by 7 December. But the air attack continued just as often as the weather permitted.

A unique innovation in air warfare was essayed on 21 November 1917, when the zeppelin *L 59* set out from Jamboli in Bulgaria in an attempt to carry vital supplies to the

The first major attempts at strategic bombing by the British were made by units of the Independent Air Force. De Havilland DH 9 day-bombers of this force are seen under attack by Siemens Schuckert D. III interceptors of a Home Defence Kesta.

German forces still operating on a guerrilla basis in East Africa. With 22 crew and nearly fifteen tons of cargo (mostly small arms, ammunition and medical supplies) she made her way via Asia Minor and Crete, under the command of Kapitänleutnant Ludwig Bockholt, until she was near Khartoum on the 23rd, where she received a radio report that the Germans had been defeated in East Africa along with orders to return. Despite great difficulties she completed a journey that lasted 95 hours and covered 4200 miles (6720 km) – **the first intercontinental flight** as well as **the first major effort to supply partisan forces at long range by air.**

Meanwhile, the Germans had resumed their raids on England, but this time at night, when **the first organised night raid on England by aeroplanes** occurred on 3 September 1917. The Gothas left their base one every five minutes, rather than in formation, and were very difficult to intercept, though night-fighter squadrons with Camels and Pups did what little they could. **The first Gotha shot down at night over England** fell to guns on 25 September 1917. **The biggest night raid of the war on England** was made on 28/29 January 1918; thirteen Gothas and a single 5-engined Giant set out, but six Gothas turned back in bad weather. **The first successful night interception of an aircraft over England** occurred that same night when Captain G H Hackwill and Lieutenant C C Banks, in Camels, shot down one Gotha in flames.

The largest force of Giants used against England was six on the night of 6/7 March 1918. To support the bombers, three zeppelin raids were launched at this time. **The last bombs dropped on England by a zeppelin** fell on 1 April 1918. **The last raid by bomber aircraft on England during the First World War** was made on 19/20 March 1918; 38 Gothas, two reconnaissance aircraft and a Giant set out, but only thirteen aircraft reached the target. Six Gothas were shot down, three by fighters.

In twenty night raids, fifteen of them on London, $50\frac{1}{2}$ tons of bombs were dropped; 435 people were killed, 997 injured. Disruption of war production in the London area was caused by demoralisation of the work forces. Yet the strength and effectiveness of the German bomber force was reduced by constant night attacks on their airfields by Handley Page 0/100s of the RNAS Dunkirk Wing, which caused the Germans to vacate the airfield at St Denys Westrem completely. Handley Pages also patrolled at night across the path of bombers and *Bogohl* 3 retaliated by bombing the Dunkirk area vigorously during the autumn of 1917. During this period *Bogohl* 3 lost eight Gothas to fighters, twelve to AA, three were missing, one suffered engine failure, and 36 crashed in Belgium for a variety of reasons. **So the Allied defences were the least effective deterrent.**

The last attempted raid on England occurred on 5 August 1918, when five zeppelins approached the coast, but withdrew when *L 70* was shot down in flames by a DH 4. The last six months of the war were without air raids for the British, but a substantial force of night-fighter squadrons and their supporting organisation were tied down in England, when they would have been of great value at the front.

In early 1918, with Russia finally out of the war, the Germans steadily moved all the forces so released to the West.

The main German effort in the air continued to be focused upon the fighter force, the *Jagdstaffeln* enjoying a priority for supplies second only to the submarine service. During early 1918 the number of *Jastas* was doubled to 80, although improved aircraft were still not forthcoming. The increase in pilots was catered for largely by those released from the Eastern Front.

Rear gunner's view from a Bristol Fighter, showing the problem of dealing with a fighter attack from the rear.

The French, without the same calls on their aircraft production for air defence, naval co-operation and anti U-boat patrol duties as the British, were able to concentrate more on the building up of their bomber force into an effective body. By February 1918 there were six mixed day and night bombardment groups with 27 *escadrilles*. These were now reorganised for day and night operations exclusively.

The British bombing force was virtually non-existent. There had been no attempt to carry out any strategic bombing of the German sources of production since the brief efforts of 3 Naval Wing in 1916. But following the start of the German night raids on England it was decided that this should be rectified, and 41st Wing was formed in October 1917, comprising DH 4s and Handley Pages. This small force was active throughout the winter of 1917/18, attacking German military centres.

The principal single-engined bomber aircraft in service towards the end of the war were:

Nation	Type	In Service	Speed	Ceiling	Endur-ance	Bomb Load	Arma-ment
Germany	Rumpler CIV	Nov 1917	106 mph	6401 m	$3\frac{1}{2}$ hr	220 lb	2 mg
France	Breguet XIV	June 1917	110 mph	5791 m	$2\frac{3}{4}$ hr	560 lb	3 mg
Britain	DH 9	Dec 1917	111 mph	4724 m	5 hr	460 lb	2 mg

The British position in January 1918 was quite healthy, and comprised 27 fighter squadrons, four of fighter reconnaissance, seventeen of bombers and eighteen for Army Co-operation (Corps squadrons).

The Belgians had also modernised and expanded their air force, and by the spring of 1918 it comprised three fighter *escadrilles* equipped respectively with Spad XIIIs, Hanriot HD 1s and Camels, a bombing *escadrille* and three reconnaissance units with a mixed bag of Breguet XIVs, RE 8s, Caudron G IIIs and IVs, and a few surviving Sopwith 1½ Strutters.

The first American-service aircrew also appeared at this time, a number of pilots being fed into British fighter units to gain experience. The *Escadrille Lafayette* was transferred to the US Air Service as the 103rd Aero Squadron, but continued to fly with the French for the time being. **The first American air unit to arrive in France from the States** was the 1st Aero Squadron, which was equipped on arrival with Spad XI reconnaissance aircraft, though it was not ready for action immediately. The 1st Pursuit Group also arrived in March, and was equipped with Nieuport 28 fighters, which had been discarded from service by the French.

The great German Spring Offensive was finally launched on 21 March 1918, aimed at the southern part of the British front. The intention was to force a breach in the front at the juncture between the French and British armies, Amiens being the initial objective. Every available British aircraft was thrown in to strafe and bomb the advancing German, with orders that low flying was essential and all risks were to be taken. Faced by a strong concentration of the best *Jastas*, the British squadrons carried out their duties in the face of very heavy losses. Casualties during periods of ground strafing operations sometimes reached 30 per cent. At night FE 2Ds attacked the German airfields, by day combats were frequent and fierce.

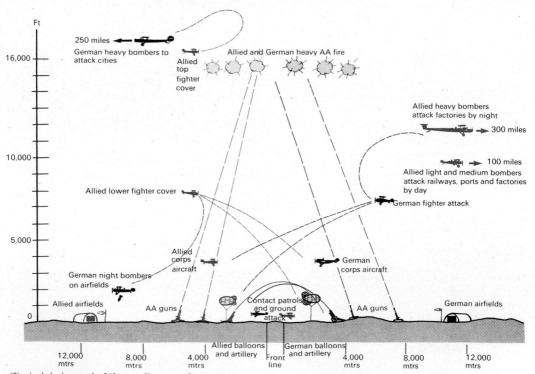

Typical duties on the Western Front 1918.

Damage.

Salvage and repair.

The death of the greatest ace of the war occurred on 21 April near Amiens. Rittmeister Manfred von Richthofen, leader of *JG 1*, had claimed seventeen more victories between 12 March and 20 April to raise his score to 80. Next day he was shot down and killed in his Fokker Triplane. Although claims by infantry in the trenches were made for his demise, his shooting down was credited to Captain A R Brown, a Camel pilot.

Unable to break through the British line, the Germans now attacked the French VI Army on a 35-mile front on the Aisne, north-west of Reims. A large part of the fighter and *Schlacht* force moving down to support this new drive. The modernised French *Aéronautique Militaire*, supported by the newly arrived USAS units and elements of the RAF which moved with the British IX Corps to aid the French, were engaged. The experienced Germans took a heavy toll of the French and American machines. By 30 May the Germans had reached the Marne, and not until 6 June was the advance held.

On 7 June 1918 a new attack was launched against Noyon Montdidier front and RAF bombers from the 9th and 51st Wings of XI Brigade were

thrown in, meeting strong fighter opposition. By 21 June, however, the
immediate danger was past.

This fighting had seen the heaviest losses to both sides to date.
During May German losses rose to 180 aircraft, while, mainly as a result of
the very considerable ground strafing activities, Allied losses topped the 400
mark for the first time. At this time too, the first of the new Fokker D VII
fighters entered service with picked *Jastas*, this proving probably **the best
German fighting aircraft of the war.**

The first aerial victory claimed by an American pilot in a USAS squadron was claimed by
Lieutenant Douglas Campbell on 14 April 1918; this pilot later became **the
first USAS ace of the war.**

The Royal Air Force came into being on 1 April 1918 by the amalgamation of the RFC and RNAS.
Originally it had been intended that the RFC should have a Naval and a
Military Wing, which would co-operate and cross-fertilise, enjoying a unity
of supply and development. In the event the two branches had diverged
considerably, becoming competitors for supplies and resources. Following
the period of the so-called 'Fokker Scourge', reunion had been proposed,
but not proceded with.

The air raids on England, although relatively ineffective, gave further
cause for concern over the lack of co-ordination between the two air arms.
The Gotha raids of June and July 1917 brought matters to a head, and with
a public outcry over air defence as a whole, General Jan Smuts, the notable
South African soldier/statesman, was called in to head an investigation into
the whole matter, commencing with an examination of defence
arrangements and supply. His report advocated unification of the two air
forces, and work to this end began at once. But the decision, let it be
emphasised, was mainly conditioned by political expediency rather than
from military demand.

**The formation by the French of a Division Aérienne, an autonomous unit which could be
moved from front to front as necessary,** took place on 18 April 1918.
This force of nearly 600 aircraft comprised two *Groupements*, one with twelve
escadrilles of Spad fighters and nine of Breguet XIV day bombers, the other
also with twelve Spad *escadrilles,* but with only six Breguet units.

*Breguet XIV bomber of the
French air forces.*

In response to the German bombing attacks on England in early summer 1917, it had been decided to create a combined RFC/RNAS force to bomb Germany, to a large extent as a sop to public opinion. Munitions production and public morale were to be the main targets of the bombers, which were to attack virtually undefended German military centres and arms factories. At first only sufficient aircraft were available to allot a Wing to these duties, but this was subsequently raised to Brigade strength. Between October 1917 and June 1918, 57 raids were made against German towns, with results similar to those in the raids against London.

With the formation of the RAF in April 1918 plans were formulated for an enlarged Independent Force to carry out an extended bombing offensive against German munitions industries. So that a co-ordinated bombing programme might be undertaken without the interruptions which might otherwise be caused by diversion of effort at times on other duties, this force was not to be subordinated to the requirements of the Front.

An Independent Air Force for strategic bombing of the German munitions industry was set up by the RAF on 6 June 1918, under Trenchard. He had been Chief of Air Staff in London during the German land offensive and was, therefore, not a witness of the effects of air attacks on the soldiers' battle during the March Offensive.

A great Allied counter-offensive was launched between Château-Thierry and Soissons on 18 July, French and American forces being supported by the *Division Aérienne*, as well as British troops and aircraft of XI Corps. Allied aircraft losses rose to over 500 during the month. The Independent Air Force also at times suffered heavy losses on its raids into Germany. On 31 July 99 Squadron attacked Mainz, with nine DH 9s of which only one returned to base and one force-landed after damage. The rest all fell to a swarm of fighters from the new home defence *Kampfeinsitzerstaffeln (Kestas)*, formed from second-line fighter pilots. Railways and blast furnaces were the main targets, though out of 550 tons of bombs dropped before the Armistice, 220 were aimed at German airfields. In this period HP 0/400s dropped an average of $25\frac{1}{2}$ tons per month, including **the largest bomb carried** – a 1650-pounder (750 kg).

Tactics were changing. Instead of flying in small formations as in 1917, fighters now generally flew in strengths of at least a dozen aircraft, and frequently in large mixed wings of three to four squadrons. For example, with the RAF, Bristol Fighters, with their additional gunner, flew top cover at 18 000 ft (5400 m), SE 5As at 14 000 ft (4200 m), and Camels at low levels to provide direct support to the ground force and the corps reconnaissance aircraft.

The greatest aircraft losses suffered during a single day were sustained on 8 August 1918, the German Army's 'Black Day'. On this date the combined major British and French offensive, that was to lead to the end of the war, commenced, supported all along the front by concentrated ground attack and bombing sorties. Against the endless targets available, German aircraft were able to shoot down 83 Allied aircraft against a loss of 49. In an effort to keep German aircraft grounded, Allied aircraft frequently raided German airfields, but were successful only against the bombers. Between 5 June and 11 November 1918 not one Allied aircraft was destroyed on its own airfield by opposing aircraft. Typical of the raids on the fighter airfields was that on 16 August when 65 fighter aircraft attacked the German base at La Bassée with bombs and machine-gun fire.

During September, at Marshal Foch's request, the Independent Air

Force co-operated with his forces in their offensive. They came under the command of Colonel William Mitchell, **the first American air commander of a combined Allied force.** Under his direct control were 49 units, half of them French, together with the *Division Aérienne* and nine squadrons of the IAF. This latter force had been reinforced during August by three squadrons of Handley Pages and one of new DH 9A bombers. In September came a Camel squadron to provide escort for the sorely pressed day bombers.

The huge increase in Allied air power, and the concentration by all units on ground support to the troops, resulted in the heavy losses continuing to rise. During September in three days, for example, *JG II* was able to shoot down eighteen US aircraft without loss. **The heaviest Allied losses of the war** were suffered during September, rising to 773 aircraft.

The end of October found the Germans in dire straits, with most of their allies already out of the war, or about to collapse, and with considerable unrest at home. By 9 November they were in general retreat and on 11 November 1918 an Armistice was agreed and fighting ceased. To the end, however, although operations by bombers and reconnaissance aircraft were greatly curtailed by the overwhelming Allied supremacy in the air, the German fighter force was far from defeat. The strength of the German *Luftstreitkräfte* stood at 2390 first-line aircraft on the Western Front and Home Defence. In contrast the French had 4511 aircraft in thirteen fighter groups and twelve independent *escadrilles*, 10 bomber groups, 124 general reconnaissance *escadrilles* and 24 observation units attached to the heavy artillery, while the USAS had increased its component to 1481 aircraft in 45 squadrons, together with 23

Major William Barker V.C., with his Sopwith Camel on the Italian Front 1918.

Hermann Göring, ace of the First World War, wearing parachute harness, standing beside his Fokker D VII.

balloon units. Apart from some squadrons of Camels and US-built DH 4s, it was mainly equipped with French machines.

During the war Allied losses far exceeded those of the Germans, who had claimed 7425 aerial victories (including 614 observation balloons), only 358 of these over the Eastern Front. Their own losses had been of the order of 3000 aircraft, or a little over. Production figures, however, give the main clue to the reason for this discrepancy:

Central Powers	Germany		45704 (20971 during 1918)
	Austria–Hungary		5431
		Total	51135
Allies	France		67982
	Great Britain		55093
	Italy		20000 approx.
	USA		11227
		Total	154302 approx.

While France had the largest air force in continental Europe, the largest overall by far was the RAF. Apart from the squadrons in France, there were 33 more overseas, sixteen on home defence and 37 on marine operations. Over 20000 aircraft were on hand in November 1918, including trainers.

AIR WAR ON OTHER FRONTS

(i) Italy

On the Italian front air activities were mostly desultory, particularly in early 1917. The Italians had reorganised, forming a number of fighter *squadriglie* equipped with licence-built Nieuport 11 and 17 aircraft, and by the spring of 1917 of 62 *squadriglie* available, thirteen were equipped with fighters. The Austrians were also introducing Brandenburg D I and licence-built Albatross D II fighters to service. During the continued fighting in the Isonzo area the great fighter aces of each side had their busiest time as they strove to attack each other's bombing and reconnaissance machines, and to gain aerial superiority over the front. By September Francesco Baracca had nineteen victories, three other pilots in his unit having a dozen or more, while Godwin Brumowski, Julius Arrigi, Frank Linke-Crawford and others were doing well on the other side.

In October 1917, the Austro-Hungarians, strongly reinforced by the Germans both on the ground and in the air, launched the 12th Battle of the Isonzo, which led to huge Italian losses and the disastrous retreat at Caporetto. **The Austro-Hungarian air force was at its zenith for this battle,** but despite this the Italian fighters continued to do well above the battlefield. Other units were hard hit, however, as instanced on 25 October when the Germans shot down five of seven Caproni bombers in a matter of minutes. To avoid a complete collapse in Italy, British and French forces were hurriedly sent in November, bringing with them three French and five British air units. The front was stabilised and operations very similar to those on the Western Front followed, the main difference being the dangerous mountain terrain over which flying took place.

At the close of hostilities the Italians had 68 *squadriglie* available, including a fair-sized Naval Air Arm which had fought a long battle with its opposite numbers in the Austro-Hungarian service over the Adriatic Sea.

Loading the camera on an
Austrian Brandenburg CI
(F Laszlo).

An Italian Caproni Ca 3
(Cross and Cockade).

(ii) Macedonia

The opposing forces around Salonika remained small throughout. The few German scouts enjoyed considerable success early in the year, their handful of Albatross and Halberstadt machines proving superior to anything the Allies had to hand until the introduction by the French of a few Spads.

In spring 1917 an offensive was launched on the Struma Front by the British, but gained little and proved very expensive in casualties, despite a high level of RFC co-operation and perfect flying weather. A number of bombing raids on Turkish and Bulgarian bases was then made, some in co-operation with French units. These met fierce opposition from the small German air component, and by October Lt von Eschwege had pushed his total up to seventeen against these attacks. He then began hunting balloons, shooting down two over the British front. On 21 November he attacked another, but when hit, it blew up and killed him. The observation basket had been filled with explosive, detonated from the ground when he came within range.

Thereafter air superiority moved inexorably to the Allies. In January 1918 modern British scouts reached the area to join the French Spads, and a new fighting squadron was formed in April. In a few months 69 opposing aircraft had been claimed, and opposition was virtually no more. In July 1918 Naval co-operation DH 4s and Camels from the Aegean islands supported an Italian offensive in Albania while on 15 September a major Allied offensive opened all along the front. This was supported by Italian, French and British aviation units, and by the small Serbian and Greek air arms which had been formed with Allied aircraft types. It was everywhere successful, and the British were across the frontier into Bulgaria on 25 September, DH 9s bombing targets as far in the interior as Radomir. Four days later an armistice was agreed, and fighting ceased.

(iii) Egypt, Palestine and Mesopotamia

The use on these fronts of reconnaissance aircraft by the British continued in early 1917, bombing and strafing flights being undertaken as well as general spotting and photographic duties. On the Gaza front hostile aircraft – mainly German flown two-seaters – started to appear at this time; BE 12 and Bristol M 1 C monoplane scouts were then delivered to the RFC to redress the balance, and in June 1917 **the first fighter unit in the Middle East was formed.**

The first air support for a guerrilla force was provided in November 1916 by five BE 2Cs which were detached to co-operate with the forces of the Sherrif of Arabia, who had begun open revolt against the Turks. Remaining until June 1917, the aircraft undertook reconnaissance and strafing attacks in aid of the Arab irregulars.

In March 1918 Arabs under the Emir Feisal, aided and encouraged by Colonel T E Lawrence, were active against the Turks in an area now known as eastern Syria. A flight of Corps aircraft was again sent to aid these forces, but they came increasingly under attack by German aircraft operating in support of the Turks. Consequently in September 1918 a number of Bristol Fighters and a Handley Page bomber were despatched to increase this support, the former aircraft engaging the Germans in a number of air battles which cleared the skies above the Arabs, permitting their activities to continue without interruption.

In Mesopotamia, the general advance which had led to the fall of Baghdad to the British in March 1917, continued. By April the British were in touch by aircraft with Russian forces advancing from Persia in the north. Further operations late in 1917 achieved success, and in February 1918 came the RFC's big chance. The Turks were seen concentrating north of Hit, but the British possessed insufficient troops to attack. Consequently a three day offensive of concentrated air attacks was instituted instead.

In Palestine an airfield which had been set up by the Turks at Amman was heavily attacked during late May and in June, but generally there were only minor efforts by either side until mid September 1918, apart from daily offensive sorties by the RAF. In August two new British units, one with SE 5As and one with DH 9s, became available, and on 19 September General Allenby's great offensive was launched, defeating the Turks utterly. The RAF found the Turkish Eighth Army retreating on the Tulkeram–Nablus road on the first day, and strafed it with great effect.

On 21 September came the first occasion on which a major ground force was virtually annihilated by aircraft alone. The 7th Army was seen trying to escape north-east of Nablus, not yet having been engaged. The road was bordered by steep ravines, and the RAF's attack continued all day, two aircraft appearing every three minutes, with an additional half-dozen each half-hour. Initial attacks blocked the head of the column, and thereafter chaos ensued and multiplied. By the end of the day the 7th Army had to all intents and purposes ceased to exist, and it was only necessary for the advancing British troops to round up the prisoners. With this attack, the campaign in Palestine and Syria was virtually at an end.

NAVAL AVIATION 1917–18

The most vital work carried out by Royal Naval Air Service aircraft during 1917 and 1918 was undoubtedly the protection of merchant shipping against U-boat attack. The operations of anti-submarine (A/S) aircraft – seaplanes, landplanes and airships – were reorganised in December 1916, but their success was limited until the Admiralty introduced the convoy system on a wide scale in mid-1917. Up to then, the A/S aircraft were employed on fruitless patrols of areas of likely U-boat activity, as were the surface vessels. The introduction of convoys resulted in a concentration not only of targets for the U-boats, but also escorts. With their wider field of vision, aircraft were the ideal U-boat spotters and, being faster than the warships, they could investigate or attack possible U-boats before the latter could reach the convoy. Even if the aircraft did not sight the U-boat, it was itself often seen and thus acted as a considerable deterrent. **During 1917, only one ship was sunk while in a convoy with air escort;** A/S aircraft sighted U-boats on 169 occasions and attacked on 106.

The only outright 'Kill' of a submarine by aircraft alone during the First World War took place on 22 September 1917, when a Curtiss H-8 flying boat from Felixstowe sank *UB-32* while on patrol in the southern North Sea. There were no major sorties into the North Sea by the German Fleet in 1917, but the Royal Navy's excursions near the German coast were nearly always shadowed by zeppelins. The existing seaplane carriers could fly off landplane scouts, but the ships were not fast enough to maintain station with the Fleet, and so a light cruiser was fitted with a 20-ft-long platform over the forward gun. The trials were concluded successfully in June 1917 and the ship joined the Fleet to evaluate the 'system' in combat. **The first victory** was scored on 22 August 1917, when Flight Sub-Lieutenant B A Smart took off from HMS *Yarmouth* in a Sopwith Pup and shot down the zeppelin *L 23* off the Danish coast.

The first warship to be converted as an aircraft carrier, HMS *Furious,* joined the Grand Fleet in July 1917. The forward 18-in gun turret had been removed to accommodate a 228-ft flying-off deck, and a hangar was provided to take her three reconnaissance floatplanes and five scouts. The latter were intended to land in the water at the end of a sortie, as no landing facilities were available aboard the ship. *Furious,* however, was a fast ship and aircrew were confident that a Pup could be landed on the forward deck. **The first landing by an aircraft on a ship under way** was made by Squadron Commander E H Dunning on 2 August 1917, who side-slipped the Pup around the bridge superstructure while approaching the deck at a relative speed of less than 20 mph (32 km/h). Five days later Dunning was killed during his third landing attempt and further experiments were forbidden.

The RNAS bomber squadrons based in Flanders played a major role in the naval war in the narrow seas. German U-boats and torpedo-boats were bombed at their bases in Belgium. **Highly effective strategic photographic reconnaissance** was undertaken by naval DH 4 aircraft which, from July, also carried out most of the day bombing along the coast.

The first air anti-submarine school was founded early in 1918 in East Anglia for the familiarisation of aircrew Observers with German U-boat tactics. At this time the RNAS possessed 314 A/S aircraft in home waters, an insufficient number to patrol the coasts and escort convoys. 'Scarecrow' patrols were inaugurated to cover the inshore waters, using inadequately armed training aircraft which were intended to keep the U-boats down by their presence rather than by attacking. Despite the primitive methods, the air A/S forces won the respect of the U-boats, all of which were fitted with 'sky search' periscopes during 1918. Convoy escort was proved to be the most effective form of aircraft employment, for, **during 1918, only two merchant ships were sunk by U-boats attacking convoys with air escort.** Three of the four air-assisted U-boat sinkings occurred around convoys, and a significant feature was that in all three cases the aircraft were from land bases. The higher speed and heavier warload of the large landplane made it vastly superior to either the flying boat or the airship, both of which boasted a better endurance. Probably the best A/S aircraft of the war was the Blackburn Kangaroo twin-engined bomber: less than a dozen aircraft of this type were available between May and November 1918, but they sighted twelve U-boats in the course of 600 hours – in other words 50 hours were flown for every sighting, compared with 196 hours in the case of Curtiss 'Large America' flying boats and 2400 hours in the case of the 'Coastal' airships.

The German High Seas Fleet made few sorties during 1918 and most British fleet activity in the North Sea was connected with the protection of the minefields blockading the German coast. To provide air recon-naissance, large flying boats were towed to the Frisian and Heligoland areas on lighters from which they were launched to carry out extended patrols. One of these lighters was modified to carry a Sopwith Camel, and on 11 August 1918 the scout was flown off and shot down the second zeppelin to fall to seaborne aircraft.

The first air combat between carrier aircraft and aeroplanes occurred on 18 June 1918, when Camels from *Furious* drove off three seaplanes and shot down a fourth from a height of 21 000 ft (6300 m) over the Skaggerack. Anti-zeppelin patrols by shipboard fighters in the North Sea were unsuccessful, but on 19 July, four Camels launched from *Furious* to attack the zeppelin base at Tondern reached the target and dropped two 50 lb (23 kg) bombs each to destroy two hangars and their occupants – *L 54* and *L 60*.

The first true aircraft carrier, equipped to recover landplanes, joined the Grand Fleet in October 1918. HMS *Argus* was armed with Sopwith Cuckoo torpedo-bombers which were to have been used in an attack on the High Seas Fleet in its Wilhelmshaven base, but the war came to an end before the ship and her squadron had completed their work-up.

Fokker's D VIII monoplane, last of his wartime line but withdrawn from service due to wing failures.

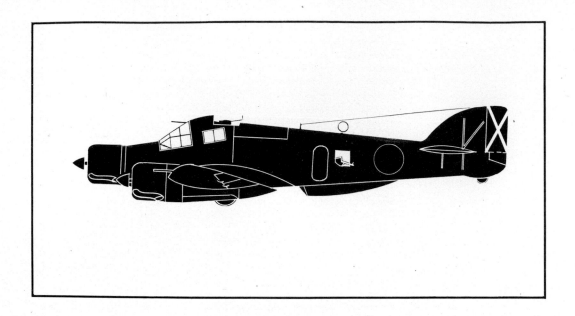

SECTION IV
The Interregnum
1919–39

The Armistice of November 1918 and the collapse of the Central Powers in no way ended the fighting in Europe. The Russian Revolution and its impact upon the shattered Central Powers and the creation of self-governing countries such as Poland, Finland, the Ukraine, Estonia, Latvia and Lithuania gave a stimulus to further violence. For each had designs upon the other and stirred up a cauldron of rivalries and conflict which engulfed Eastern Europe. Inevitably the air warfare that became part of this struggle was a mere extension of the sort of combat that had taken place in 1918, fought by the same pilots in the same types of aeroplanes in pursuit of similar objectives. Indeed, it is a central theme of the two decades that lay between the First and the Second World Wars that, although the foundations of radical change in aerial philosophy, techniques and technology were laid, the final structure had hardly been disclosed prior to September 1939. Apart from rare demonstrations of flashing originality to illuminate the numerous encounters of the period, the underlying tone was of a repetition of air warfare as practised in 1918. There was, in effect, an interregnum concealing the developments to come.

The most widespread outbreaks of air fighting occurred in Russia, although actual Russian participation was on a very small proportional scale. An RAF presence had been established there in May 1918, when British forces were landed at Murmansk on the Arctic coast to forestall any possibility of the Germans establishing a U-boat base (following the Russo-German armistice of 1917), and a flight of DH 4s operated in support of the ground forces in actions leading to the occupation of Archangel in August 1918. Allied forces remained in north Russia to aid the White Russians in their war against the Bolsheviks, and a British-equipped White Russian aviation unit operated with the RAF in this area.

Large-scale air combat took place mostly in southern Russia where an Allied presence was set up following the 1918 Armistice. On the re-opening of the Dardanelles, French, British and American troops were sent to the area, while the RAF provided units to operate alongside the small White Russian air force. Initially a DH 9 squadron was formed to patrol over the Caspian and Black seas, soon joined by a seaplane flight. In April 1919 a composite squadron from Salonika was formed with one flight of DH 9s, one of DH 4As, and one of Camel fighters, and sent to operate in direct support of General Anton Denikin's army, which was launching an offensive up the Don Valley, with Kiev, and then Moscow, as its ultimate objective. The RAF flights were maintained on the vast expanse of the Russian steppe by specially equipped railway trains. Their Camels were particularly effective against the Bolshevik cavalry, carrying out many low-level strafing attacks, as well as escorting RAF and White bomber aircraft.

Combat was fairly frequent. A substantial part of the Bolshevik air force was used on this front, employing aircraft of mainly French origin (taken over from the old Imperial Air Force), together with a few German types; and piloted by a number of German mercenaries. An indication of the level of activity can be gained from the fact that one Bolshevik fighter pilot is believed to have shot down about a dozen White and RAF aircraft during this period, while two RAF Camel pilots each claimed to have shot down at least five opposing machines.

New and quite important air forces were created by the emergent countries, particularly by the long-oppressed Poles who had re-created their nation in October 1918 and were at once threatened by the Bolsheviks. Action flared initially in Odessa, but thereafter for some months the main enemy became the neighbouring

Bristol F2A Fighter of the Polish Air Force, 1919.

Ukraine. During the First World War a Polish Army with its own air element had been set up, trained and equipped in France under General Haller, and early in 1919 this was despatched to Poland, throwing the air balance strongly in the Polish favour. Thus in April 1919 a successful Polish offensive could be launched against the Ukrainians, supported by aerial attacks on cavalry forces and railways.

The first fighter combat over Poland occurred on 19 April 1919 when Lieutenant Stefan Stec in a Fokker D VIII monoplane attacked a Nieuport scout escorting a Brandenburg two-seater, and shot it down. In fact by May 1919, when Haller's army began arriving from France, the Poles already had 40 aircraft deployed on the Ukrainian front, and had achieved a measure of superiority. In September the aircraft of the seven French *escadrilles* which had arrived with Haller in May were handed over to the Poles (including 110 modern Breguet XIV, Spad VII and XIII, and Salmson A2 aircraft) while more Breguets and Spads, 35 Ansaldo fighters and 110 Bristol Fighters were ordered from France, Italy and Great Britain respectively. Most of the 392 aircraft ordered had not arrived by February 1920; Polish strength stood at sixteen squadrons in six groups, plus two squadrons in reserve. By then the Bolshevik Russians were the enemy as the Ukrainians were forced to join the Poles after themselves being invaded by the Red Army.

An intensive air war was assured when, late in April 1920, a Polish offensive was launched to 'liberate' the now-occupied Ukraine, and capture Kiev. Ten Polish squadrons were committed, while facing the Bolsheviks on the static Lithuanian-Belorussian front in the north-east were a further ten squadrons, out of a total Polish strength of about 300 aircraft. The Bolsheviks, too, had about the same number, over half of which were fighters and, emulating the Germans, had concentrated about 30 per cent, including most of their best pilots, on the important front, that in Lithuania-Belorussia.

Technical attrition was the major factor in the battles which developed. By late July 1920 the Poles had only some 30 aircraft serviceable and Russian land forces were approaching Warsaw. At this stage Bristol Fighters began arriving from Britain, and were at once issued to the units. However, by now the Bolshevik air force had few aircraft, due mainly to unserviceability, and no opposition was offered to a series of devastating ground attacks on the Russian cavalry as it advanced to support the main force. From 16 to 18 August the fourteen to sixteen Polish aircraft available flew 190 sorties, firing 27 000 rounds of ammunition and dropping 17 600 lb (8000 kg) of bombs, against Budenny's Cossacks in their drive on Lvov, and contributing to their withdrawal. The Russians began to fall back everywhere, and in October an armistice was signed.

The only role of air forces during the Russo-Polish war was support of ground forces. Between April and October the Bolshevik Air Force flew over 2000 sorties, dropping 14 000 lb (6400 kg) of bombs and engaging in 35 air battles. In the same period the Poles made 3652 sorties, dropped a very much larger quantity of bombs, but lost 34 aircraft to Russian ground fire. During the whole fight for independence, from November 1918 to October 1920, the Poles lost only three aircraft in air combat, claiming in return three Ukrainian and four Russian aircraft, four Ukrainian and four Russian kite balloons. But the Poles also lost 43 aircraft to hostile ground forces, with sixteen more damaged – a significant figure.

The Potez 25A. 2.

AERIAL POLICING

The use of aircraft for the subjugation of dissidents in colonial territories was not an entirely new concept at the close of the First World War. Spanish forces had operated both aircraft and captive balloons against the Riffs in Morocco as early as 1909–13, while the Italians had employed aircraft against the natives in North Africa. Likewise, the use of aircraft against rebel tribes in Mesopotamia during the war had demonstrated to the French and British forces the advantages offered by way of economy in effort and manpower inherent in the armed aircraft engaged in such operations.

The first use of aircraft on such purely colonial activities by the RAF occurred during December 1918, when the Third Afghan War broke out on the North-West Frontier of India. Two squadrons were already available, and four more were sent, equipped with Bristol Fighters, DH 9As and DH 10s. Close reconnaissances were flown, together with bombing raids against the invading Afghans, and on 24 May 1919 a Handley Page V 1500 bomber attacked the capital, Kabul.

As an instrument of policy aerial policing had many facets, of which the suppression of dissidents was but one. While the mobility conferred by aircraft in being able to strike rapidly at distant targets in under-developed countries represented a genuine economy of effort, it was equally apparent that this was not policing in its proper sense, since true policing demands the use of the absolute minimum of force. Dropping bombs on tribesmen or on villages (even after the inhabitants had been warned to leave, as was the practice) were purely punitive measures and only applicable against so-called primitive people, so long as world opinion acquiesced. But the underlying reason for RAF advocacy of this sort of operation could be found in its struggle to consolidate its continued existence as a Service separate from the Navy and the Army. By developing an independent role that aspired to demonstrate air power as a substitute for traditional methods, the RAF was able to expand while attempting to prove it could win wars on its own.

The first territory to pass entirely to air force control became Iraq when the RAF, under Air Vice-Marshal Sir John Salmond, took over as GOC in October 1922. But prior to this the RAF had been kept generally busy by a widespread Arab revolt during 1919–20, as some 200000 Arab nationals attempted to overthrow foreign control of their countries. In Iraq itself during this time 120000 British troops and four squadrons of DH 9As were almost permanently in action, the aircraft firing tens of thousands of rounds of ammunition and dropping nearly 100 tons of bombs for the loss of eleven machines to rifle fire, and damage to 57 more.

Flexible air operations depended upon a mobile ground organisation. With this the RAF was able to switch forces from one end of the Middle East to the other, to be dealing with a revolt in the Sudan in 1920, with a Turkish incursion into northern Iraq in 1921, trouble in Transjordan in 1922 and a host of other operations, including on the North-West Frontier of India. In the process they carried out **the first evacuation of population by air** when, on 5 September 1925, 29 assorted aircraft air-lifted 67 British subjects from the Sulaimaniya district to Kirkuk and then turned to supply-dropping for land forces and flying in troop reinforcements.

While the British were the main exponents of air policing between the wars, they were by no means the only ones. In Spanish Morocco Bristol Fighters, DH 4s, DH 9s and Breguet XIVs were used in a long campaign against the Riffs, led by Abd el Krim, which continued until May 1926. And the French, in French Morocco, having trouble with this same guerrilla leader in 1925, carried on an arduous and costly campaign against him with Breguet XIVs and Potez 25s which did not end until December 1934. In Libya and East Africa, too, the Italians operated against rebellious tribes, developing multi-purpose tri-motor bomber/transport aircraft such as the Caproni 101 and 133, and building under licence the Dutch Fokker C.V as the Meridionali Ro 1

The Meridionali Ro 1.

'general purpose' biplane. And as early as 1919 the United States became involved in activities of a similar nature, when, in February of that year, six Curtiss Jennys of the US Marine Corps were sent with a Marine Brigade to Santo Domingo, where they remained for four years, aiding the government in fighting jungle bandits. A little later that year more marines with Jennys were sent to Port-au-Prince, Haiti, to commence a fifteen-year campaign against rebels, in support of the Haitian authorities. Subsequently the Jennys were augmented and replaced by US-built DH 4s, which also undertook **the first successful casualty air evacuations on a regular basis.**

The first attempt at dive-bombing in action took place at Ocotal in 1927, after Marines were committed to Nicaragua. Here, with the local *Guardia Nacional*, they fought the Moncada and Sandino rebels. They used DH 4s, and later Vought O2U Corsair bomber-reconnaissance biplanes. The Nicaraguan Air Force also took part, dynamite charges being dropped on rebel camps from Laird Swallows.

While the lessons of air policing proved extremely valuable for colonial operations and internal security purposes, experience of work of this nature was of little benefit to air forces which might become involved in full-scale wars. Indeed, the aircraft developed were of little practical application against other than lightly equipped guerrilla-type forces. Their procurement and development, and their maintenance in service, demanded a substantial proportion of funds, which were not then freely available for the development and production of many modern first-line types necessary for national security in times of international crisis.

As can be seen from the following table, the performance of the aircraft employed was not much in advance of those in the First World War.

Nation	Type	Max Speed	Ceiling	Bomb load	Armament
Britain	Westland Wapiti	135 mph	6250 m	500 lb	2 mg
France	Potez 25	137 mph	7200 m	440 lb	3 mg
Italian	Meridionali Ro 1	158 mph	6000 m	500 lb	2 mg
USA	Vought O2U Corsair	170 mph	6250 m	500 lb	3 mg

At the outbreak of the Second World War in 1939 the Potez 25 remained the main colonial type in French service while the British still had large numbers of Wapitis and machines of like performance scattered throughout the Empire.

NEW THEORIES AND NEW AIR FORCES

Although the leading advocate of air power as a war-winning weapon had been the Royal Air Force's Chief of Staff, Trenchard, **the Italian General Giulio Douhet became the internationally recognised apostle of independent air power.** In his book *The Command of the Air* (1921), Douhet expounded a doctrine of attack on the enemy's will to fight by the destruction of his cities and terrorisation of the civilian population. His argument that to achieve this aim the air force must be totally independent of military or naval

Cadenas – ground attack fighter-bomber Heinkel He 51s of the Spanish Nationalist Air Force attack Republican troops, 1938.

Giulio Douhet.

The Handley Page V 1500 which was denied its intended task of bombing Berlin in 1918.

control did not win widespread support immediately: Italy's air force, the *Regia Aeronautica*, was not formed until 1925, and the French *Armée de l'Air* did not become independent until 1934. Of the other major countries with air forces, the United States and Japan maintained separate Army and Navy Air Forces, while the Soviet Union subordinated its entire aviation to the Red Army.

The only country to accept Douhet's theories almost in their entirety was Britain: the RAF became what amounted to an 'all-or-nothing' force, its European order of battle consisting of bombers and defensive fighters, with lip service only being paid to the needs of the Army and Navy. Battlefield support would consist of tactical reconnaissance but no direct intervention since, in the opinion of the Air Force, the war would not be won on the ground, and to allocate too much of its potential to the land war would be a negation of its *raison d'être*.

At the other end of the scale lay the Red Air Forces, dedicated to the support of the ground forces, with each Military District controlling its own individual 'Air Force'. The Long-Range Air Force was controlled by the High Command, but, in spite of its title, was only intended to support the land war by attacks in rear of the enemy on targets which would affect a tactical situation and not to prosecute an independent strategy. The naval air force was tasked with coastal defence and the protection of warships.

The middle ground was occupied by the Germans who, during the 1919–34 period, had digested the lessons of the war to produce in secrecy (the Versailles Treaty prohibiting their possession of an air force) **the most balanced air force in existence.** The bomber force was to be capable of strategic and tactical employment, but the Douhet theory was modified to allow 'terror bombing' only to weaken the enemy's resolve. Wars were to be won by the Army, with effective support given by what was to be the *Luftwaffe* on the battlefield itself.

An unlikely and uneasy collaboration between the Soviet Union and the Weimar Republic began in 1921, enshrined by the Treaty of Rapallo. One immediate outcome was the formation of a joint airline, *Deruluft*, equipped with Junkers all-metal aircraft, but although the Soviet Union began to re-equip its forces with French bombers and British general-purpose aircraft, Germany was the only country to agree to provide technical assistance. Hugo Junkers of Dessau was awarded a 25-year contract to build, equip and run an airframe and aero-engine factory at Fili, near Moscow, that provided an ideal 'shadow' design and construction facility. A secret agreement with the Soviet Union resulted in the creation of a flying training school at Lipetsk in 1924, the students being *Reichswehr* personnel. In exchange, Russian officers of middle rank were sent to the German General Staff School at Berlin, to acquire the arts of administration and command, as taught by former German Flying Service personnel.

Public interest in aviation was fostered in Germany by the formation of the 'Sports Flying Association' *(Luftsportverband)*, unofficially sponsored by the Defence Ministry which wished to develop glider flying as a means of circumventing the Versailles Treaty terms. The Soviet Union soon saw the value of such an organisation and in 1923 the first 'Friends of the Workers' and Peasants' Red Air Forces' were enrolled for engineering and glider flying training. By 1926 the German association had over 30000 members, while there were reputed to be two million 'Friends'.

The Soviet aero-industry expanded remarkably, with the assistance of foreign expertise, and in 1927 Junkers' contract was abruptly terminated, Fili being 'nationalised' as Aircraft Factory No. 22 but continuing to produce Junkers-designed metal monoplanes. From this time, Russian designers had the benefit of the early German work on metal construction and diesel aero-engines, but still depended upon the democracies for the design of petrol engines.

TB-3, developed by the Russians as a strategic bomber, but because of its load-carrying capabilities, utilised as a transport for the Russian airborne forces.

In 1926 the Allies had relaxed the ban on German civil aviation, at the same time placing a restriction on the aviation training of *Reichswehr* personnel. So officers were seconded for air-crew training with the national airline, *Deutsche Lufthansa*, and the aviation industry produced a succession of transports and 'fast mail planes' which were readily adaptable for military purposes. Occasionally the designs were great commercial successes, the best example being the Junkers Ju 52/3m tri-motor transport.

The architects of the re-born German air force were Erhard Milch, Walther Wever and Albert Kesselring. The former had been the chairman of *Lufthansa* since 1926 and had been responsible for the airline's treaty-evading activities; with Hitler's accession to power, he became the Deputy Air Minister under **Hermann Göring,** whose preoccupation with politics considerably reduced his involvement even though he was responsible for major 'decisions and appointments'. Milch and Wever, the latter *de facto* Chief of Air Staff from 1934, built up the service and evolved its policy and doctrine. Kesselring controlled finance and administration and was the first Chief of Staff from 1936 to 1937. Such was their success that, when the *Luftwaffe* was openly formed in March 1935, it possessed 1888 aircraft and 20 000 trained officers and men.

Erhard Milch.

Aircraft performance steadily improved despite limited financial resources. Single-engined biplane fighters had reached speeds of around 155 mph (250 km/h) by the mid-1920s, with static radial or liquid-cooled engines delivering outputs of the order of 450 hp; the fastest light bomber had a similar maximum speed. Engines giving up to 800 hp were available and these would have given increased speed, but the weight penalty involved was excessive. **A major technological advance** was made in 1927 with **the development of a practical supercharger,** a compressor which forced air into the engine carburettor allowing the maximum power to be developed at greater altitudes, at which the less 'dense' air permitted considerably higher air speeds than at sea level. One of the first fighters to appear with a supercharged engine, the British Armstrong Whitworth Siskin IIIA, attained 186 mph (298 km/h) at 15 000 ft (4500 m) but only 156 mph (250 km/h) at sea level.

The first multi-engined monoplane bomber also made its appearance in 1927. This was the Soviet Tupolev TB-1, an all-metal aircraft which owed much to Junkers' technique and which was powered by two licence-built German-designed petrol engines. Normal maximum bomb-load was in the region of 2200 lb

First bomber of the new Luftwaffe, the Dornier Do 22.

(1000 kg) and maximum speed 130 mph (208 km/h) at low level. Load and speed were comparable with those of the biplane bombers being built elsewhere, notably the Italian Caproni and the American Keystone series. Light bombers, with a load of up to 550 lb (250 kg) followed single-seat fighter design and performance closely, the fastest in 1930 being the British Hawker Hart, with a speed of 184 mph (295 km/h) at 5000 ft (1500 m) – only 10 mph (16 km/h) slower than the French parasol monoplane Dewoitine D 27 fighter which entered service in the same year.

Two fighters with speeds exceeding 200 mph (320 km/h) entered service in 1931, the Hawker Fury and the Nakajima A2N (Type 90). The latter was a carrier fighter and was the first completely indigenous fighter design to enter service with the Imperial Japanese Navy, which had depended upon teams of British advisers for the establishment of an aircraft industry until the end of the 1920s. The Japanese lead in shipboard interceptors was to be maintained for a full decade, with the Nakajima and Mitsubishi firms consistently meeting seemingly impossible demands for improved performance and manoeuvrability.

Although the US Navy and Marine Corps fell behind the Japanese in technical development from 1931, they had by that time, in common with most air forces, armed their fighters with light bombs for use as anti-personnel weapons. From 1927, experiments were carried out using large bombs, of up to 500 lb (227 kg) weight, which were released at low level while the aircraft was

The first production dive-bomber; Curtiss OC-2s of the US Marine Corps. in 1930.

The German battleship Ostfriesland, *was reputed to be unsinkable. It was employed in the bombing tests by the US Army Air Corps, who attacked at impractically low altitude to bomb anchored targets which, of course, made no attempt to evade or fight back. It was sunk!*

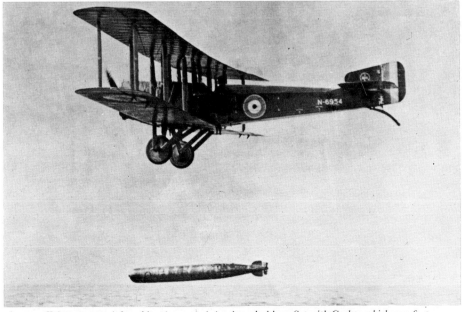

A more efficient way to sink a ship. A torpedo being launched by a Sopwith Cuckoo which was first intended to attack the German High Seas Fleet in 1918.

*William Mitchell, chief
protagonist of air
power in the USA –
and court-martialled for
his temerity.*

diving steeply. In this way, the time of flight, and therefore the cumulative errors in aiming, 'bomb trail' (the forward component imparted to an object released from an aircraft in level or near-level flight), and wind effect were reduced and high standards of accuracy could be attained using a modified fixed gun-sight. 'Conventional' level bombing, from medium altitudes, depended upon a formation of aircraft dropping a sufficient number of bombs to offer a mathematical chance of a hit; accuracy against a small stationary target was poor – against a moving target such as a ship it was lamentable, due mainly to the difficulty in gauging wind and target speeds, allowances for which could be 'fed in' (rather inadequately) to most bomb sights in service in 1930. **The precision attainable with dive-bombing,** and the economy in terms of aircraft size and numbers required made an immediate impression on the US Navy, and from 1929 the series of Boeing and Curtiss fighter-bombers and dive-bombers gave the American carriers a decided advantage over those of Japan and Britain. Germany and Japan were swift to recognise the value of the dive-bomber, the former for close support of the Army and the latter for anti-shipping employment. The RAF, which controlled British naval aviation, never did subscribe to the concept, preferring the more vulnerable low-level attack, using aircraft designed for medium-level bombing.

An important theory widely espoused at this time foretold that:

> 'Tight formations of well-armed fast bombers would always get through to their targets, and would be able to fight off any interception. Dog fights between figher aircraft would no longer be possible, due to the speed and gravitational forces, during manoeuvre, which were a feature of modern high-performance machines.'

In consequence several nations concentrated on bomber development as their main offensive element, treating fighters only as target defence interceptors. The result was a general neglect of the development for offensive and escort purposes of a long-range fighting type of adequate performance, or of a high-performance machine for the direct close support of troops.

Significant advances in heavy bomber design began in 1932. The US Army Air Corps' B-9 was the **first of a succession of famous Boeing bombers to appear,** its main claim to distinction being that it was the first twin-engined bomber to feature a retractable undercarriage, which, with the monoplane lay-out, enabled it to attain 188 mph (300 km/h). **The Russian Tupolev TB-3 was the first four-engined monopolane bomber:** although it was considerably slower than the B-9, it could carry twice the bomb-load twice the distance. Used as a troop carrier, the TB-3 enabled the Red Army to form **the first paratroop assault division in the world,** in 1934. Both the British and the Germans, too, produced successful bombers, but while the former were to lay down specifications for four-engined bombers in 1936 and proceeded with their mass production, the latter abandoned the four-engined bomber in 1937 and with it all pretence to a long-range strategic air force.

By 1936, bomber performances were again approaching those of the best fighters, the fastest being the Russian Tupolev SB-2 twin-engined attack bomber. With a maximum speed of over 260 mph (415 km/h), the SB-2s could leave most Italian or German-built fighters of the day standing. **One of the most outstanding bomber aircraft** was the Italian Savoia Marchetti S 79, a

267 mph (427 km/h) tri-motor aircraft which entered service in 1937, and as an anti-shipping aircraft, armed with torpedoes or bombs it was crewed by men who were fêted as the élite of the *Regia Aeronautica*.

Credit for the first cantilevered wing and retractable undercarriage fighter went to the Soviet Union. The Polikarpov I-16 Type 1 was a small underpowered monoplane with a maximum speed of only 224 mph (358 km/h), though when re-engined with a licence-built 775 hp American engine its speed immediately increased to around 280 mph (450 km/h). However, as an insurance, the Red Air Forces also ordered and received biplane fighters from the same designer, the I-15 series which was considerably slower than the I-16.

Britain and Germany alone dispensed with the first generation of monoplane fighters, preferring to progress from biplanes with metal-framed fabric-covered structures to retractable-undercarriage monoplane fighters with all-metal monocoque fuselages, in which the skin formed part of the load-bearing structure, and enclosed cockpit enclosures. Three of the fighters of this pattern ordered in 1934, the Messerschmitt Bf 109, the Hawker Hurricane (which had stressed-metal wings but a fabric-covered fuselage) and the Supermarine Spitfire, were to be the most successful of the early years of the forthcoming European War.

Initially, Britain possessed a major advantage over Germany, for the experience gained during the successful challenge for the Schneider Trophy, won outright in 1931, had enabled Rolls-Royce to develop a compact 12-cylinder liquid-cooled in-line aero-engine developing 1000 hp and capable of further extensive development without major re-design. **The Rolls-Royce Merlin was produced in greater numbers than any other aircraft powerplant** – over 46000 Spitfires, Hurricanes and North American Mustangs alone were in due course fitted with it. **The Messerschmitt 109D featured a 20 mm cannon,** mounted in the 'Vee' of the engine cylinders – **a position first used by the French;** the shell-firing gun possessed better range and penetration characteristics than the rifle-calibre 0·303 in (7·7 mm) machine-gun preferred by the Royal Air Force, which specified wing-mounted eight-gun batteries in the Hurricanes and Spitfires.

The Thirties saw an end to peace. There was a minor air war in connection with the struggle in the Gran Chaco between Paraguay and Bolivia (1932–5), but **the first major hostilities involving aviation units** occurred in Manchuria, where the expansionist Japanese Kanto Command fought the Chinese after an 'incident' in September 1931. Two Japanese Army squadrons, equipped with Nieuport 29 fighters and Salmson A2 reconnaissance bombers, were available, while the Chinese were supported by a few Potez 25 reconnaissance aircraft. Most of the latter were captured early in the fighting and as the opposition in the air collapsed few were encountered subsequently by the Japanese. In October a squadron of the first **successful Japanese designed and built aircraft for the Army,** the Type 88 reconnaissance bomber, was sent to join in.

The first aerial combat between Chinese and Japanese aircraft occurred over trouble in the International Settlement at Shanghai during January 1932. The Japanese Navy sent first the seaplane carrier *Notoro,* followed by the two aircraft carriers *Kaga* and *Hosho,* to support their forces around Shanghai, the two latter vessels providing a force of 76 fighter and torpedo-bomber aircraft.

First Japanese designed and built aircraft to see action, the Kawasaki Type 88 light bomber, employed during the later stages of the Manchurian campaign of 1933.

During the bombing of Chinese military installations in support of the ground forces, aircraft from *Hosho* met nine Chinese machines on 5 February 1932 and damaged one of them.

The first aircraft shot down by Japanese fighters fell on 22 February when a Boeing 218 demonstration fighter, flown by an American pilot, Robert Short, attacked a torpedo-bomber from *Kaga*, killing the gunner. Three Nakajima A1N fighters then attacked and shot down the Boeing, Short losing his life. Next day a series of attacks on Chinese airfields were begun and on 26 February, over Hanchow airfield, eight Japanese aircraft engaged five Chinese, claiming three shot down. During this period the Navy lost three aircraft to ground fire, but none in combat.

THE ABYSSINIAN WAR, 1935–6

The first attempt to use modern air power with mechanised armies began on 3 October 1935, when Benito Mussolini ordered an Italian invasion of Ethiopia. Against the ill-equipped Ethiopian army, light tanks and infantry with modern weapons were sent in, supported by some 320 aircraft. Most were tri-motor Caproni 101 reconnaissance bomber/transports, joined by a smaller

Italian Caproni Ca 101 bomber-transports over Ethiopia, 1935.

number of the later Ca 111, Ca 133 and Savoia SM 81s. Also used were a number of Ro 1 single-engined reconnaissance bomber biplanes, and eight fighter *squadriglie*, five with two-seat Ro 37 aircraft, the others with Fiat CR 20 single-seaters – a total of nearly 80 aircraft.

The Ethiopians mustered but a handful of obsolete reconnaissance biplanes and civil aircraft. Several were crashed by their foreign mercenary pilots, whilst others were strafed and destroyed on the ground. Lack of opposition in the air led to the Italian fighters being employed almost exclusively for ground strafing and reconnaissance; indeed later in the campaign the designation of these units was changed to that of offensive reconnaissance. The workhorses were the Italian tri-motors, however, which bombed the defenceless Ethiopian troops as they attempted to form up for attack, also dropping mustard gas on them to add fuel to worldwide protests and indignation of the Italian aggression. Apart from their bombing duties, these aircraft also undertook valuable survey work over the unmapped interior, and carried large quantities of supplies and ammunition over the great distances to the troops at the front.

THE SPANISH CIVIL WAR, JULY 1936–MARCH 1939

Within the Spanish air force the majority of aircraft were retained by the Government (or Republican) forces, but most of the experienced officer pilots rallied to the insurgents (who became known as Nationalists). At first the main aircraft types involved were Nieuport-Delage 52 sesquiplane fighters, Breguet XIX and Vickers Vildebeest reconnaissance bombers, plus a variety of miscellaneous types.

The first air combat occurred on 23 July 1936, when a Nationalist Nieuport fighter, flown by Lieutenant Bermudez de Castro, shot down a Government aircraft of the same type over the Pinar region. On the ground the balance of force in Spain favoured the Government, but the experienced and hardy forces stationed in Morocco and composed of Arab volunteers and Spanish legionnaires had rallied to the Nationalists. If they could be transported to the mainland, they could well swing the balance to the Nationalists' favour. But the greater part of the Navy was loyal to the Government, and so a crossing by sea was almost impossible. The Nationalists appealed to the German and Italian dictators. On 27 July a batch of twenty Junkers Ju 52 transports arrived from Germany and next day began **the first major airlift of troops, the first to have a decisive effect on the outcome of a campaign.** Eventually the Ju 52s would ferry across 13 523 troops and 570 000 lb (260 000 kg) of war supplies, joined on 9 August by nine Savoia SM 81 bomber-transports from Italy which maintained patrols against Government naval interference.

Foreign intervention into combat began in earnest when, early in August, six Heinkel He 51 fighters arrived for the Nationalists together with 86 volunteer advisers from Germany. But lack of quick success by the Spanish pilots led the Germans to request and receive permission to fly the aircraft in action. **The first bombing raid by German-flown aircraft** was made on 14 August 1936, when a Ju 52 obtained two direct hits from 1500 ft (450 m) on the Republican battleship *Jaime I,* putting it out of action. On this same date **the first units of Italian Fiat CR 32 fighters and pilots** arrived to begin operations over Spain.

The Republicans turned for help to the Western democracies and Russia. Aid came from France with supplies of fighter and bomber aircraft. Many volunteers of all nationalities flocked to the Republican cause,

Fiat CR 32 fighter of the Italian Aviacione Legionaria.

including numbers of pilots and other aircrew. The main support came from the Soviet Union with tanks, guns, volunteer troops, advisers, and aircraft with crews which began arriving in September and October 1936.

The German Condor Legion was now set up in Spain, comprising a bomber, a reconnaissance, a fighter and a seaplane unit, together with an anti-aircraft element. The Italians formed their own *Aviacione Legionaria* and the indigenous Spanish Nationalist air arm was expanded with German and Italian aircraft types. Initial Nationalist offensives met with success due to the better training of the troops and greater unity of the command, but an advance on Madrid was held by a determined popular defence. Regular bombing of the city followed, and during 1937 the war fermented as the main supporters of the two sides poured equipment into Spain.

A unique opportunity to test theories and new equipment was thus presented. At first Russian Tupolev SB-2 bombers on the Republican side proved very effective, since they were fast and difficult to intercept. **The first fell** to the Spaniard Angel Salas in a CR 32 on 29 October 1936. The Russian Polikarpov I-15 and I-16 fighters also proved much superior to the German He 51, which had to be relegated to the ground attack role at an early stage. But in spring 1937 the introduction by the Germans of early versions of their Messerschmitt Bf 109 fighter swiftly redressed the balance, while their Heinkel He 111 and Dornier Do 17 bombers, with Savoia SM 79s and Fiat BR 20s from Italy, provided a formidable Nationalist day-bomber force which, due to their superior performance, had little to fear from opposing fighters.

The most notorious air action of the war happened during the Northern campaign, when the Basque town of Guernica was bombed to destruction on 26 April 1937 by German He 111s and Ju 52s. Although offering good defensive positions, it fell to the advancing Nationalists almost without a fight two days later. The

Heinkel He 111s of the Condor Legion peel off to attack a Republican target in Spain, 1938.

real reasons for bombing the town were never admitted, but it has been surmised that it was undertaken at German instigation to observe the results of such concentrated attack. The psychological effect on world opinion and morale was significant. Not only was fear of the *Luftwaffe* magnified to exaggeration, but the myth of air power as an instrument of absolute decision deified.

The balance of power between the armies and air forces tipped the Nationalist way in 1938. The Nationalists had 146 aircraft at the front by the end of the year, the Italians 134 and the Germans 106. The situation of the Republican forces was hopeless, and their armies disintegrated in retreat.

This most significant bout of air fighting since 1918 came to an end in March 1939. Since 1936 the Government had received about 2000 aircraft from various sources to add to the 214 with which they started the war. Some 1400 of these came from Russia and, of the total to hand, over 1500 were reported shot down or destroyed on the ground by the opposing air forces. The Nationalist cause received nearly 1200 aircraft, 730 of them from Italy and 400 from Germany. During the fighting the Italians claimed 703 Republican aircraft shot down, the Spanish Nationalists 294, and the Germans 277, plus 108 more by their well-organised anti-aircraft (Flak) defences.

The most successful fighter pilot was Commandant Joaquin Garcia-Morato, Nationalist fighter commander, with 40 victories. **The most successful German pilot** was Leutnant Werner Mölders with fourteen, **the most successful Russian** A K Serov with sixteen, **most successful Italian** Colonel Mario Bonzano with some fifteen, while, so far as can be ascertained, **the most successful Spanish Republican pilot** was Captain Andres Garcia Lacalle with at least eleven. Among the various foreign volunteers an American, Frank Tinker, claimed eight victories flying with the Republicans, and a Belgian, Count Rodolphe de Hemricourt de Grunne, claimed ten flying with the Nationalists.

One of the lessons learned was the fact that modern fighter aircraft could still fight in the traditional manner, and also were necessary to gain air superiority over the battlefield before adequate support could be given to the troops. The use of fighter aircraft for ground attack duties was seen as a very useful development, though this was to some extent overlooked, despite being developed in a small way by the Germans during 1939. However, the lack of real opposition in the air, and of high-performance interceptors in use by the Republican forces, led the Germans and Italians to believe that their fast medium bombers were virtually immune to fighter attack, and did not require heavy armament. It also led them to develop the fighter-bomber into the more specialised dive-bombers and ground assault aircraft, which would only survive in conditions of air superiority. The experience of fighter combat, and the development of new tactics – particularly the classic tactical fighting formation of two pairs, known later as the 'finger four' formation, were later to stand the Germans particularly in very good stead.

SINO-JAPANESE INCIDENT, 1937–39

A full-scale undeclared war between Japan and China began in mid-August. At this time the Japanese Army maintained some 49 first-line units with about 500 aircraft, while the Navy had some 400 more aircraft in 29 units. The Chinese possessed a smaller air force, which had been trained by American and Italian Air Missions, whose countries had supplied large numbers of aircraft.

Initially the Japanese Army committed six squadrons from Manchuria to North China, soon followed by others, while the Navy sent over the carriers *Hosho*, *Ryujo* and *Kaga*, with 264 aircraft. After escorting transport convoys across from Japan, the carrier aircraft went into action over Central China on 10 August, since no land bases on the mainland were immediately available to the Navy.

The first important landmark of the war came on 14 August 1937 when eighteen modern twin-engined Mitsubishi G3M medium bombers flew across the South China Sea to make an unescorted long-range attack on Hanchow. They were intercepted by Hawk fighters which shot several down. In later raids the Chinese claimed eight out of eighteen shot down over Nanking, and a total

Joaquin Garcia-Morato, Spanish Nationalist Fighter leader and top-scoring fighter pilot of the Civil War, with 40 personal victories. He is seen by the tail of his Fiat CR 32, marked with his personal insignia.

of 54 in three raids, while night raids brought further losses. A further débâcle occurred on 17 August when eleven out of twelve biplane torpedo- bombers from *Kaga* were shot down in the Shanghai area.

The first of the new Mitsubishi A5M monoplane fighters arrived on 22 August from *Kaga* thus giving their pilots a crucial advantage against all opposition. Used initially over Shanghai, they swiftly drove the Chinese from the skies. Then, on 9 September, they moved to a landing ground in this area and, equipped with long-range tanks, began escorting G3M bombers on their raids on Chinese cities. The results were dramatic. During their first engagement with defending fighters over Nanking on 18 September, 27 Japanese fighters claimed eleven out of sixteen Chinese interceptors shot down.

An escalation of the intensity and scope of combat was assured when, on 29 August, the Chinese signed a non-aggression pact with the Soviet Union. This brought them immediate assistance in the form of 400 aircraft, mainly I-15 and I-16 fighters, together with two bomber squadrons and four fighter squadrons of Russian volunteers, the former bringing with them SB-2 bombers. But, despite these reinforcements, losses to the sprightly A5Ms remained severe, the Chinese fighter force being virtually annihilated that autumn so freeing the Japanese air forces to do almost as they pleased. **The first combat ever recorded by the Japanese Army Air Force** occurred on 19 September 1937, when Kawasaki Ki 10 biplane fighters engaged six reconnaissance bomber biplanes, claiming four shot down.

The Polikarpov I-15.

The first Japanese fighter pilot to be credited with five victories was Ensign Kiyoto Koga, an A5M flyer, who made three claims on 6 October to raise his score to seven.

Air power contributed strongly to Japanese success against an out-classed opponent. After aiding the ground troops in the capture of Nanking, Navy units concentrated upon operations in South China. Up to October 1937 their land-based bombers made 61 attacks on Chinese cities and in the next year would make 170 more raids on targets in central China, together with some 60 raids on the South.

The greatest success to be claimed by the Chinese occurred over Hanchow on 29 April 1938, when twenty of their fighters attacked an escorted bomber formation, losing eleven of their number for two claims. But 40 Russian-flown fighters then attacked, claiming 34 Japanese aircraft shot down for two more losses. The Japanese Navy fighters counter-claimed 51 intercepting fighters for two losses! Over-estimation of the potential effect of air power has frequently been indulged in by both the aircrew and their supporters.

THE NOMONHAN INCIDENT, MAY–SEPTEMBER 1939

The most intense period of aerial conflict since 1918 – a conflict which, due to European tensions at that time, completely failed to gain the attention of the Western world, began in May 1939, after incursions over the Manchurian border by Mongolian troops were followed by the movement on to Mongolian territory of Manchurian nomads. The bellicose Japanese Army Kanto Command in Manchuria, keen to show its mettle, decided to use its air power at once – to the dismay of the authorities in Tokyo. JAAF strength in Manchuria was well below that of the 1500 aircraft available to the Red Air Force in the Soviet Union's Eastern territories, but it was well equipped, superbly trained, and as a result of the Chinese operations, operationally experienced.

The first big battle in the air occurred on 27 May, when nine I-16s were claimed, seven of them by just two pilots. Next day the Japanese claimed 42 victories against the Russian fighters, the two pilots who had done well the previous day, Captain Shimada and Warrant Officer Shinohara, again coming to the fore by claiming five and six respectively. Shocked by this defeat, the Russians stood back until mid-June, when, along with Mongolian ground forces, they launched an armoured offensive across the Kharkha river. At once the whole of the Japanese air force in Manchuria, the 2nd Joint Air Corps, with 119 serviceable aircraft, was thrown into the battle. Combats between large formations of fighters were common in which an immediate ascendancy was gained by the Japanese whose nimble Ki 27 proved more than a match for the inexperienced Russians in their I-15s and I-16s. On 22 June, in two combats, 49 victories were claimed by the Japanese for the loss of only five aircraft.

Warned by air reconnaissance of the arrival of Russian air reinforcements (and in direct disobedience to the Supreme Headquarters in Tokyo) the Kanto Command directed a series of heavy attacks on Russian air bases on 27 June. In the heavy fighting that ensued 99 Russian aircraft

Nakajima Ki 27 fighters on a Manchurian airfield, 1939.

Warrant Officer H. Shinohara, (standing on right).

were claimed shot down in combat and 111 more destroyed on the ground – all for the loss of five machines. Warrant Officer Hiromichi Shinohara created a new record, claiming eleven victories during the day, **the highest number claimed in a single day by any pilot in the world up to that date.**

During July the fighters were to claim an incredible 560 victories for 31 losses, but despite reinforcements, the Japanese ground forces were driven back. More Japanese aerial successes followed in early August, but the ratio of losses now began to veer as the outnumbered Japanese pilots flagged, and the Russians introduced protective armour for their aircraft with heavier armament and threw in fresh units employing better tactics. Their pilots now avoided dog fights with the Japanese fighters, preferring to dive from above to attack and climb away again, making best use of their aircraft's better maxium speed.

The Japanese planned a counter-offensive for 24 August 1939, but it was pre-empted by a Russo-Mongolian attack with 100 000 men and 400 aircraft committed in support on 20 August. Every possible Japanese aircraft was thrown into an attack on Russian air bases, claiming 61 in the air and 45 on the ground for six losses. Twenty big combats took place in under a fortnight, culminating on 27 August in a fight between formations of fighters over 100 strong. During this particular battle Shinohara was shot down in flames and killed. With 58 victories he was **the highest scoring pilot to appear since the First World War.**

In early September the Russians concentrated their air power in support of their ground forces, while Japanese bombers hammered the advancing enemy at every opportunity. The Japanese were again preparing for a new offensive with a major series of air attacks against Russian air bases on 14 and 15 September. On 16 September 1939, however, a peace formula was agreed and fighting ceased.

The Japanese fighters still appeared to have come out best, even though in some units casualties had exceeded 50 per cent. Fatigue and lack of numbers were considered to be the reasons for these substantial losses. Their achievements blinded the authorities to the lessons of the campaign – the need for heavier armament, greater top speeds, and armour protection for pilots and fuel tanks. The JAAF admitted the loss of 168 aircraft including 96 Ki 27 fighters, with 94 more aircraft damaged; they claimed 1260 Russian aircraft destroyed. The Russians admitted only 207 losses, claiming 660 victories – substantially more aircraft than the Japanese committed to the campaign. Undoubtedly propaganda and some over-claiming distorted most of these figures, and it is unlikely that the true facts will ever entirely emerge.

While the fighting of the Thirties was going on and its lessons being digested or misread (see page 78) **fresh technological discoveries were being made that would revolutionise flight as well as air warfare.**

Great advances took place in radio technology during the 1930s. High-frequency radio-telephone sets were being installed in interceptors of most of the Western air forces and navies, for air-to-air and air-to-ground communication. The expansion of commercial aviation had resulted in the provision of ground radio beacons, to be used in conjunction with airborne direction-finding receivers to give accurate bearings for navigational purposes. A directional beam system, known as the Lorenz Beam, was developed in Germany, primarily as a bad-weather landing aid; with greater transmitted power, it was capable of directing a bomber towards a target along a given track.

By far the most revolutionary invention was that of radar. As early as 1885, a German physicist, Hertz, had discovered that electromagnetic radiations could be reflected by metallic objects in a laboratory, and in 1904 another German patented a primitive radio echo device to prevent collisions at sea. The first serious investigation into radar as an aircraft detection aid began in Britain in 1934, with the secondary object of discovering whether an electromagnetic 'death-ray' could be developed. The latter idea was not feasible, but swift progress was made with the detection of aircraft by using high-power pulsed radio transmissions. The first air warning station opened at Bawdsey in the spring of 1935. Such was its success, a chain of radar stations was built with a minimum of delay, the five stations covering the eastern approaches to London being operational by early 1938, each of the stations having a range of about 70 miles against aircraft at medium level.

Chinese Curtiss Hawk III fighters intercept Mitsubishi G3M long-range medium bombers over Nanking, August 1937.

The British 'Chain Home' radar system was based on a series of plainly visible radar installations.

The first airborne radar, intended to detect other aircraft, was tested in an RAF Handley Page Heyford bomber in 1937. Utilising a substantially higher frequency than the Chain Home sets, the airborne radar was developed for both Air Interception (AI) and Air-to-Surface Vessel (ASV) use, the latter to be used for the detection of ships at sea.

The first steps in the development of jet and rocket propulsion for practical application were also taken in the 1930s. The principle of the rocket was well known, but not until the German Helmuth Walter devised a controllable-thrust unit in 1938 was this a practical proposition for aircraft propulsion, offering thrust which did not vary with atmospheric conditions. The jet engine was intended to produce thrust by compressing indrawn air, heating it in a combustion chamber, and exhausting the heated air at high velocity through a turbine which drove the compressor. In the simplest form of jet engine, the turbine, compressor and connecting spool were the only moving parts, so that not only was it simpler than a reciprocating engine, it was also much lighter and could burn cruder fuel. A Briton, Frank Whittle, filed patents for a jet propulsion system in 1930, but funds were not made available, and thus it was a German aircraft, the Heinkel He 178, which made **the first jet-propelled flight, on 27 August 1939,** the engine having been developed by Hans von Ohain and Max Hahn, both of whom were ignorant of the parallel efforts of Whittle. The German engine was technically superior to Whittle's, which did not fly until May 1941, and it provided the basis for the later full production axial-flow turbojects built by Junkers and BMW.

But so far as the aircraft that would compete in the first two years of the Second World War they were, by and large, the types that were in production on 1 September 1939. The performance table below gives an idea of their relative merits, though it must always be remembered that figures such as these can be misleading since various aircraft perform differently according to the altitudes at which they are engaged and as a result of the pilot's skill in obtaining the best from them.

Bombers in Service with the Combatants—September 1939

Nation	Type	Speed	Ceiling	Range	Max. bomb load	Armament
British	Blenheim I	265 mph	8315 m	1125 miles	1000 lb	2 mg
	Wellington I	250 mph	8791 m	2200 miles	4500 lb	4 mg
French	Breguet 691	301 mph	8500 m	808 miles	882 lb	1 cannon 4 mg
German	Heinkel He 111	248 mph	7000 m	559 miles	3307 lb	5 mg
Italian	Savoia SM-79	270 mph	8500 m	1243 miles	2756 lb	4 mg
Russian	Tupolev SB-2	255 mph	8500 m	746 miles	2205 lb	4 mg
Japanese	Mitsubishi G3M	258 mph	10280 m	2090 miles	1764 lb	1 cannon 2 mg

Fighters in Service with the Combatants—September 1939

Nation	Type	Max. speed	Ceiling	Armament
British	Hurricane I	322 mph	10180 m	8 mg
French	Morane Saulnier 406	304 mph	9144 m	1 cannon 2 mg
German	Messerschmitt Bf 109E	357 mph	10670 m	2 cannon 2 mg
Italian	Fiat CR-42	272 mph	10000 m	2 mg
Russian	Polikarpov I-15	229 mph	9800 m	2 mg
Japanese	A 5M	270 mph	9800 m	2 mg

The Spitfire – ready, but only just, in time for the Second World War.

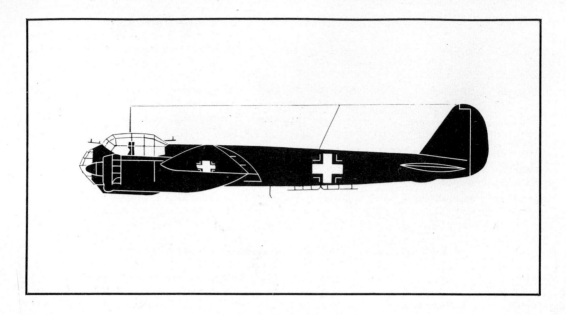

SECTION V
The heyday of tactical air forces
1939–42

THE POLISH CAMPAIGN OF SEPTEMBER 1939 AND THE PHONEY WAR.

Germany's major resort to arms began with the invasion of Poland on 1 September 1939. In support, the *Luftwaffe* initially committed two *Luftflotten* under Kesselring and Loehr with an operational strength of 648 level bombers, 219 dive-bombers, 30 ground-attack aircraft, 210 single- and twin-engined fighters and 474 reconnaissance aircraft, backed up by numbers of transports, liaison and army co-operation aircraft, while other fighter units provided air defence of the main bases.

The Polish Air Force had available 154 bombers, 159 fighters and 84 observation aircraft, plus a variety of Naval, liaison and transport aircraft that were dispersed to well-hidden landing grounds away from the main bases.

The first German air raids of the war were directed against bridges over the Vistula, airfields and targets around Warsaw. Few Polish aircraft were destroyed on the ground, but not many interceptions were made by the Poles either. **The first aerial victory of the war** was claimed by Lieutenant Wladyslaw Gnys, who shot down a Ju 87.

The first fighter *v* fighter battle took place later on 1 September between the Pursuit Brigade and Messerschmitt Bf 110 aircraft over Warsaw. Hpt Schlief claimed one P 11 shot down as **the first German fighter victory.**

The first really effective Luftwaffe attack on a Polish airfield took place on 14 September and destroyed seventeen bombers at Hutnicki. Up to then the Poles had done

*P.Z.L. P.11 of the Polish
Air Force – outclassed by the
Messerschmitts.*

fairly well, though the collapse of their early-warning system on 7 September had fatally reduced the number of fighter interceptions.

Russian forces invaded eastern Poland on 17 September 1939, and the remains of the Polish Air Force were flown to Rumania, where it was interned. Warsaw continued to resist, and on 13 September 183 Luftwaffe bombers began **the first major assault on a fortified city.** A massive raid on 25 September saw 240 Stukas, 30 Ju 52 transports carrying incendiaries and waves of level bombers engulf Warsaw in flame and explosions.

At the conclusion of hostilities the Poles had lost 327 aircraft, about 260 of them to enemy action; some 70 of them shot down in aerial combat, while a great many were lost to the fire of their own ground troops. The *Luftwaffe* had lost 285 aircraft. **The most successful fighter pilot of the campaign** was Hpt Hannes Gentzen, who claimed seven victories in two days flying a Messerschmitt Bf 109D. **The most successful Polish fighter pilot** was 2nd Lieutenant Stanislaw Skalski, whose score was later confirmed at $6\frac{1}{2}$.

A great anticlimax attended the declaration of war by France and Great Britain against Germany on 3 September. From the beginning of September 1939 the RAF sent a substantial force of aircraft to France to support the British Expeditionary Force; this involved ten squadrons of Fairey Battles, four of Hawker Hurricane fighters, three of Bristol Blenheims for long-range reconnaissance, and two of Westland Lysanders for army co-operation in what were part of the Air Component of the BEF and the Advanced Air Striking Force.

During the first three months of the war both British and French reconnaissance aircraft were frequently engaged in fierce battles with German fighters, substantial losses being suffered on occasions. French fighters were also active, claiming their first victories on 8 September, when Curtiss Hawks shot down two of five Bf 109s. By the end of the month they had claimed 27 and ten probables for the loss of four.

The RAF's first raid of the war took place on 4 September, when Blenheim and Wellington bombers raided Wilhelmshaven naval base. Five Blenheims and two Wellingtons were shot down. The Wellington claimed by Fw. Aldred Held was **the first Luftwaffe victory in the West.** Damage to German warships was only slight. Much activity by RAF and *Luftwaffe* units was expended during autumn 1939 against the respective Naval fleets.

The first German attack on a British target took place against warships in the Firth of Forth on 16 October. Two cruisers and a destroyer were damaged, but two Ju 88s were shot down by Spitfires, **the first victories for British-based fighters.**

Fundamental lessons about the vulnerability of unescorted bombers in daylight were learnt during December 1939 in three attacks made on the Heligoland area by formations of RAF Wellingtons. On the second occasion five of twelve were shot down, and on the 18th, when 24 bombers were unable to find German shipping due to cloud, Bf 109s and Bf 110s attacked and shot down twelve, three more force-landing on return. Throughout this period both sides had refrained from making bombing attacks on each other's territory, though British and French bombers had flown many night sorties over Germany, only to drop propaganda leaflets. However, as a result of **the first German bombs falling on British soil** during a raid on the base at Hatston in the Orkneys, on 16 March 1940, Bomber Command Whitleys raided Hornum seaplane base on Sylt next night. The French, however, requested that no further such attacks be made for fear of escalation in an air war they feared from the *Luftwaffe*.

The invasion of Finland by Russia on 30 November 1939 served to expose Russian weakness. Expecting a walkover, the Russians used only second-line troops, supported by some 900 mainly obsolescent aircraft. The Finns possessed 145 operational aircraft of which 114 were serviceable.

The first combat occurred on 1 December 1939, when Lieutenant Eino Luukkanen in a Fokker D XXI, shot down a Tupolev SB-2 bomber. Severe weather reduced operations in the air until January 1940, but on 6 January a complete formation

The principal Finnish fighter during the 1940 'Winter War', the Fokker D XXI.

of seven Ilyushin DB-3 bombers were shot down, Captain Jorma Sarvanto claiming six of these.

Alarmed, the Russians sent in more modern equipment, including 600 more aircraft. In February their forces began a massive offensive, which slowly forced the hard-fighting Finns back. Air reinforcements arrived first from England, and then from France, Italy and the USA. Units of volunteer pilots and other personnel also began to arrive. Growing Russian strength nearly swamped the defenders, however, and their increased force of 196 aircraft could only retain serviceable strength at 112 in the face of some 2000 Russian machines.

With reserves gone and the Russian armies breaking through everywhere, the Finns were forced to accept a humiliating armistice on 13 March 1940. By this time, however, their air force had claimed 200 confirmed and 80 probable victories against Russian aircraft. Their own losses were 67 destroyed (42 in action), with 69 more damaged.

THE NORWEGIAN CAMPAIGN, APRIL–JUNE 1940

An imaginative use of air power characterised the German invasion of Denmark on 9 April 1940. Massed demonstrations by bomber formations and strafing attacks on

Luftwaffe aircraft on an airfield in southern Norway in April 1940. In the foreground are Junkers Ju 52/3 transports, while behind are Junkers Ju 87s.

Skuas dive-bomb the Königsberg.

military airfields suppressed resistance and ensured an almost bloodless occupation by land forces. At the same time fleets of transport aircraft arrived over Oslo in Norway to undertake **the first major airborne invasion,** as naval units entered fjords and harbours in southern Norway. The campaign that ensued was largely one in which troops were deployed by naval power while air forces gave extensive support over land and sea. The negligible Norwegian air force was immediately swept aside, German bombers damaged a few British warships and British bombers tried to do the same to German shipping as well as depriving the *Luftwaffe* of the use of Norwegian airfields. Soon the arrival of Bf 109s and 110s made day bombing too costly. Nevertheless, air activity was intense and seriously inhibited the activities of both navies.

The first dive-bombing attack by fifteen Skuas of the Fleet Air Arm on 10 April in Bergen Fjord against the cruiser *Königsberg* met with complete success. Three 500 lb (225 kg) bombs sank her for the loss of only one Skua, and four days later the troopship *Bahrenfels* was also sunk by Skuas, again for the loss of only one bomber.

Support for British and French land forces sent to central and northern Norway led to some interesting improvisations. The Allied landings were supported by carrier aircraft of the Royal Navy, and carriers remained off the coast in the Trondheim area to give support. Skuas flew many patrols, shooting down *Luftwaffe* bombers, while Swordfish biplanes flew bombing sorties in support of the ground forces. The necessity for carriers to withdraw for refuelling and re-arming at regular intervals made the early presence of land-based air power desirable, in the face of very heavy German air attacks on the Allied forces with Ju 87s, He 111s and Ju 88s. On 24 April the RAF flew Gladiators off the carrier *Glorious* to the surface of frozen Lake Lesjaskog, near Aandalsnes. Spotted at once by the *Luftwaffe*, continued air attacks virtually wiped out the squadron on the lake within 48 hours, although the British fighters managed to shoot down about six raiders. On 28 April evacuation of Namsos and Aandalsnes was ordered, the land operation having failed partly due to the weight of *Luftwaffe* air attack. The evacuation was completed under carrier aircraft cover by 3 May. In the north the land forces were put ashore

Gloster Gladiator of 263 Squadron, RAF, seen here on frozen Lake Lesjaskog, Norway, in April 1940.

around Narvik, but German aircraft were being moved up the country to bases from where they could attack this area. German raids began on 2 June, and thereafter Fleet Air Arm and RAF efforts were mainly concerned with covering a British evacuation. By 7 June the Gladiators had claimed about 30 victories and Hurricanes about a dozen, for very light losses. After the evacuation, fifteen Skuas took off from *Ark Royal* on 13 June in an attempt to repeat their earlier successes, attacking the battlecruiser *Scharnhorst* in Trondheim harbour. But a force of Bf 109s and 110s intercepted them and nine Skuas were lost. Thereafter the Danish and Norwegian coastal area became a regular target for British air attacks as well as coastal minelaying from aircraft. For much of the war beyond effective fighter-escort range, this sector was to see many hard-fought combats. On 9 July 1940, for example, seven Blenheims and two Coastal Command aircraft fell victims to fighters, while on 13 August 1940 eleven of 23 Blenheims failed to return from a raid on Aalborg, all lost to Bf 109s.

THE BATTLE OF FRANCE, MAY–JUNE 1940

In the early hours of 10 May 1940, the German offensive in the West was launched, supported by an immediately serviceable strength of 1016 Bf 109s, 248 Bf 110s, 1120 bombers, 385 dive-bombers, 640 reconnaissance and observation aircraft, transports and 45 gliders.

The main initial operations were directed against Holland and Belgium, troops crossing the Dutch border with Germany, while twelve He 59 seaplanes landed on the Maas River in Rotterdam to debouch shock troops and some 200 Ju 52s dropped paratroops over the same area, 250 more Ju 52s carrying air landing troops followed, landing at Waalhaven and other airfields, after these had been bombed by waves of He 111s and Do 17s. The small Dutch air force, for the loss of 56 aircraft, fought back hard, shooting down at least 25 opposing aircraft, and destroying many of the Ju 52s on the ground, a task in which they were soon joined by RAF aircraft from England. Indeed **the highest number of aircraft ever lost by a single air force in one day's** combat was suffered on 10 May, when 304 *Luftwaffe* machines were destroyed and 51 damaged; 267 air crew were killed.

The most numerous French fighter type in service at the start of the Second World War was the obsolescent Morane 406.

The first successful glider-borne assault was made in Belgium, where nine gliders landed on top of the frontier fortress of Eben-Emael, the troops neutralising the guns and trapping the garrison inside. Ten other gliders landed behind three bridges over the Albert Canal, capturing these and preventing their demolition. Attacks on Belgian airfields destroyed about 30 aircraft on the ground and shot down half a dozen more for only light losses.

The major air battle developed over France, where operations at first were undertaken by the *Luftwaffe* only. An assault on airfields enjoyed less success than hoped for, only 45 French and about fifteen British aircraft being destroyed on the ground. The British and French air forces, covering the planned move forward of the Allied Northern armies into Belgium, were at once in action, British and French fighters claiming some 90 victories during this first day, for the loss of about twenty. With darkness heavy bombers from both forces at once began to attack communications and supply targets across the border into Germany.

Next day, 11 May, the Belgians threw in their few Fairey Battle bombers against the Albert Canal bridges near Maastricht, but to no avail, nearly all the attackers and their fighter escorts being shot down. So great was the threat posed by these bridges that, in the afternoon, French and British bombers, including Blenheims from bases in England, were also thrown in to attack, and the assault resumed with daylight on 12 May, by RAF Battles flown by volunteers, but with total loss and no success. On the 13th more Hurricanes were sent to France to be consumed in the battle.

The most intensive air bombardment of a single target area so far attempted in preparation for an attack by land forces was made along the Meuse River between Sedan and Nouzonville on 13 May 1940. To a timed programme 310 high-level and 200 dive-bombers of the German II and VIII Air Corps rained a steady stream of bombs on the French artillery positions with the aim of neutralising them over the period of the assault crossing of the river. The aim was achieved: few direct hits were obtained on the guns but their fire was practically stopped and the morale of the French soldiers shattered by the noise and concussion. Of anti-aircraft fire, to destroy or deter the German bombers, there was hardly any.

The cause of many losses of and damage to aircraft throughout the war as an essential defence of vital targets, was anti-aircraft guns. By 1939 guns such as the German 88 mm and the British 3·7 in could engage targets up to an altitude of about 32 000 ft (9600 m) (increasing to 40 000 ft (12 000 m) as time passed) with an accuracy that depended almost as much on luck as the range-finders and early manually operated predictor computers could make them. By night they fired a barrage in the path of approaching aircraft to spoil the air crews' aim and determination. At lower altitudes a series of heavy machine-guns and automatic weapons up to about 40 mm were employed to hosepipe shells at their targets: they had a higher rate of success than their heavier sisters since prediction was much more an art than a science. With aimed predicted fire the British 3·7s, for example, destroyed one aircraft per 298 rounds while barrage firing took 2444 each.

Hugh Dowding.

The highest proportionate losses ever suffered by the RAF in a single day were inflicted on 14 May when British and French bombers were committed to an attempt to destroy the bridges built across the Meuse by the Germans and seal the breach at Sedan. Nearly 70 British aircraft (60 per cent of those involved) including 36 Battles, together with more than 40 French machines, were lost to flak and fighters. The same afternoon 86 German He 111s bombed Rotterdam in support of parachute troops, causing great civil destruction, an attack which coincided with the Dutch Government's capitulation. By then the Dutch Air Force had been wiped out and the Belgian *Armée de l'Air* had also undertaken its last sorties, having by now lost 119 aircraft on the ground and 39 in the air.

Due to these heavy losses, Allied air activity was fatally reduced, and the French Prime Minister asked his opposite number in Britain, now Winston Churchill, to despatch ten more fighter squadrons. The latter was persuaded by Air Chief Marshal Dowding, C.-in-C., Fighter Command, to refuse for fear of over-weakening the air defence of the United Kingdom. Despite this, six further Hurricane squadrons were despatched next day. But the German advance continued, unhindered by enemy air attacks yet fully supported by the *Luftwaffe* which bombed opposition ahead of the tank spearheads.

The Franco-British Northern Armies were forced into retreat. Antwerp fell on 18 May, and two days later the Germans reached the English Channel, cutting off the Northern Armies from those in the rest of France. At this stage the RAF Air Component squadrons were withdrawn to southern England. They had claimed over 150 German aircraft shot down, but had lost 75 Hurricanes, 41 Blenheims and half their Lysanders. A further 120 damaged Hurricanes were destroyed on the ground to prevent their capture.

The first all-out attempt by an air force to bring about the capitulation of major ground forces began on 24 May, after the C.-in-C. of the *Luftwaffe*, Hermann Göring, had (for

*The ruins of
Rotterdam.*

prestige and political purposes) persuaded Hitler that the job could be
better accomplished by air power than the victorious tank forces that were
already poised to complete the capture of the last Channel ports and thus
cut off the Northern Allied Armies from escape by sea. By now, however,
the *Luftwaffe* was weakened by battle losses, a degree of unserviceability and
fatigued crews. It still operated from airfields far to the east at a time when
weather conditions declined and this significantly reduced flying hours while
by night it was incapable of delivering a concentrated attack upon the
beaches at Dunkirk, where the armies awaited ships for evacuation. Above
all it met a determined defence by British-based aircraft – mostly Spitfires
and Hurricanes. A pitched air battle broke out over the Channel ports and
their approaches in which both sides operated below full efficiency because
they were at the extremities of their range and lacking well-established
early-warning and control facilities for the co-ordination of their
deployment. By day it became extremely hazardous for ships to work in
Dunkirk and most movement took place at night, but air attacks alone did
not compel men to surrender and so the evacuation continued for just so
long as the armies could hold the perimeter against the German Army.
Some 340000 Allied troops were eventually evacuated – leaving all their
equipment behind, however. In 4000 sorties between 27 May and 2 June,
the *Luftwaffe* lost 189 aircraft, while the British Fighter Command lost 99 in
2739 sorties. So, not only was this an Allied strategic air victory to set
alongside their land defeat, but **the first supreme example of the
inability of air power in isolation to win a land battle.**

Yet the Germans had won total air superiority over France and could do almost as they chose. Prior to the final land offensive opening on 5 June, a series of attacks were launched on airfields and factories. Then the main effort was switched to supporting the army. In response the French *Armée de l'Air*, which had rested while the *Luftwaffe* fought over Dunkirk, enjoyed its best day on the 5th by claiming the destruction of 66 German aircraft for the loss of 24 of their own fighters – but their own bomber losses were also high for no great return in hits obtained and it was a dying effort.

Fighters and bombers from England joined the assault on the advancing German columns, but to no avail. The Allied line collapsed on 7 June. A major attack on Reims and Paris now began, the former city falling on the 11th. Evacuation of the remaining British forces from Cherbourg and St Nazaire under cover of AASF Hurricanes now began. Paris was declared an open city to prevent its destruction, and on 17 June the French sought terms for an armistice. Meanwhile 156000 British troops and 310 guns were successfully evacuated by sea, although the 20000-ton liner *Lancastria* was bombed and sunk in St Nazaire harbour with the loss of 3000 soldiers and sailors. The last British fighters flew out on 18 June, on which day French aviation units began moving to North Africa. And that night the *Luftwaffe* turned part of its attentions on Britain, despatching 100 bombers, seven of which were shot down.

A new contestant entered the ring on 10 June when Italy declared war on the Allies. Initially the *Regia Aeronautica* launched a series of air raids on targets in Tunisia and Corsica. Not until the 13th did Italian aircraft appear over southern France, raids that were repeated on the 15th when there was strenuous combat between Italian fighters and French Dewoitine 520s. Poor weather prevented further raids on France, but attacks on Corsica and North Africa continued until the cessation of hostilities.

The last aircraft shot down during the campaign was a *Luftwaffe* Henschel Hs 126 observation machine, claimed by a French fighter on 24 June, just before the Armistice came into effect, but British bombers with fighter escort continued to attack targets in western France throughout the rest of the month. British losses during May and June 1940 had been 1019, a proportion of them suffered over Norway.

French losses from 10 May to 10 June were later admitted at 306 shot down with 329 destroyed on the ground. So total Allied losses during the campaign, including Dutch and Belgian aircraft, were in excess of 2000. *Luftwaffe* combat losses were, however, the heaviest of any individual air force, totalling 1200 to direct hostile action, together with more than 300 additional operational losses and a substantial proportion of damaged aircraft.

THE BATTLE OF BRITAIN, THE 'BLITZ', AND THE COUNTER-OFFENSIVE, 1940–41

The first check for the Luftwaffe and the first major setback for the dream of reaching a decision in war by the use of air power alone occurred as the result of the Battle of Britain which began in August. Yet this struggle was really only an attempt on the German part to win air supremacy as a preliminary to an invasion of Britain by sea and land forces, though what started as a conventional attempt by the *Luftwaffe* to destroy the RAF and its supporting elements, drifted into an ill-aimed attack upon strategic targets by an air force that was not designed for strategic attacks – in effect as a dying effort to neutralise Britain when it became apparent that she could not be beaten in the air.

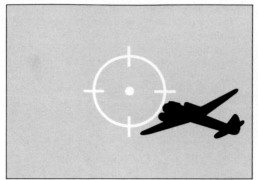

The Reflector Sight. The fighter pilot manoeuvred so as to be flying towards the centre spot of the aiming reticle at an appropriate relative closing speed represented by the outer ring.

A Hurricane on its way down.

The great advantage to the British was the relatively comprehensive chain of radar stations around the eastern and southern coasts of England. Linked directly to an efficient central controlling system, these stations provided a degree of advanced warning of incoming raids far beyond anything previously enjoyed by an air defence organisation.

During a month's probing attacks in July severe fighting took place over the English Channel, some 140 German and 100 British aircraft being lost – the proportion of fighter aircraft included in these figures slightly favouring the *Luftwaffe*. At the same time both sides intensified night bombing attacks on each other's territory.

The first British bomber shot down at night by a German night fighter fell on 20 July 1940, shortly after the formation of the *Luftwaffe's* first night fighter unit, although German night fighters, at this time, did not enjoy the benefit of airborne radar equipment, relying on direction from the ground and chance sightings. **The first victory at night by a fighter carrying airborne radar equipment** was achieved two nights later when an RAF Blenheim shot down a Do 17.

A crucial factor in combat was the inability of German fighters to escort their bombers to the target, since the Bf 109 (the only fully effective German fighter) was limited by range to a penetration of about 125 miles (200 km), escorted operations ended at London. Weather was another important factor and several times prevented operations at a critical moment when the battle had swung the

German way. The German numerical superiority over the British on
1 August was:

	German	British
High-level bombers	1330	not relevant
Dive-bombers	280	none
Single-engine fighters	760	578
Twin-engine fighters	220	58 (night only)

was more apparent than real since the German dive-bombers and twin-
engined fighters, due to heavy losses, were soon withdrawn from the battle,
and the British control system permitted a far more economic employment
of aircraft at the vital points.

The first major assault of the battle was made on radar stations and Manston airfield, Kent, on 12
August. But this attack on one of the most vital parts of the defence system
was never seriously repeated – a most important failure on the part of the
Luftwaffe command, which had underestimated radar's importance. On 13
August a series of raids on airfields and aircraft factories in southern
England began, and two days later, believing all fighters to have been
drawn south for the defence of this area, a force of 113 unescorted bombers
was launched against Tyneside from Norway, expecting no opposition. This
attempt was met by No 12 Group fighters, which inflicted severe losses.
Indeed, **the heaviest losses in one day suffered by the Luftwaffe over
England,** occurred on this 15 August when 73 aircraft failed to return.

The outcome of the battle turned upon the struggle between the Bf 109s and the Spitfires and
Hurricanes. The Hurricanes were outclassed, however, and so, by early
September the raids on fighter sector airfields, and the losses inflicted by the
Bf 109s were beginning to tell on Fighter Command. Supply of replacement
aircraft was satisfactory, due in large part to the new Minister of Aircraft
Production, Lord Beaverbrook, but wastage of pilots was exceeding supply,
and this factor gave the greatest cause for concern.

The first bombs to be dropped on London during the Second World War fell during the night of
24/25 August, dropped in error and against orders by a German bomber
crew. In retaliation **the first air raid on Berlin** was made next night by 29
of 81 Bomber Command aircraft sent out. The psychological effect of the
Berlin raid on Adolf Hitler, together with the *Luftwaffe's* desire to bring all
remaining British fighter reserves to battle, led to the transfer of the main
German effort against London, both by day and night, beginning on 7
September. This proved the salvation of Fighter Command, removing as it
did the weight of attack from the airfields and factories. A series of heavy
battles, with severe *Luftwaffe* losses on 15 September, demonstrated that the
RAF was undefeated. On the 18th, the invasion of England was postponed
indefinitely.

The Battle of Britain was a turning point in the air war for, although not particularly heavy by
standards later in the war, the German losses were at a rate of attrition relative
to the total force available which was unacceptable to the *Luftwaffe* in 1940.
As with the RAF, the loss of trained crews was the most serious aspect.
Consequently, most bombers were transferred to night operations; the last
big daylight battle was fought on 27 September and thereafter only pin-
prick raids were attempted in daylight, a few, with disastrous results for
themselves, by the Italian Air Force.

By the end of October, 1733 German aircraft had been shot down in

BOMBER TRACK DISTANCES

——— German

——— British

- - - - American

Allied bomber bases

Figures at end of routes show distance in miles

0   100   200   300

miles

Murmansk 1,420

Tromso 1,060

Narvik

Trondheim

SWEDEN (Neutral)

Faroe Islands

Scapa Flow

Bergen 300

Oslo

Aberdeen

Stavanger

Skagerrak

Baltic Sea

Newcastle 380

Sylt 360

Kiel

Peenemünde

Danzig

EIRE (Neutral)

Liverpool 340

Hamburg 380

Arnhem

Berlin 580

Rotterdam

Hannover

London 150

Essen 330

Dresden

Antwerp

Cologne 280

Prague

Calais

Schweinfurt 420

Normandy

Amiens

Frankfurt

Nürnberg

Paris

Regensburg 540

Vienna

Munich

Lorient 200

SWITZERLAND (Neutral)

Venice

Bordeaux

Turin 680

Milan

Toulouse

Genoa

Flight distances in western Europe.

four months, and 915 British fighters had been lost during the same period. Through the summer, also, RAF Bomber Command had regularly attacked the Channel ports, where large numbers of invasion barges were being collected. Blenheims also attacked *Luftwaffe* airfields by day, without the benefit of fighter cover due to the operations which Fighter Command was having to undertake over England. These bombers frequently suffered severe losses to German fighters, and by the end of September Bomber Command had lost 165 aircraft by day and night since 1 July. But the British had untapped potential for expansion whereas the *Luftwaffe* was already in decline. In 1940 the latter's losses virtually equalled production while British production exceeded that of Germany.

While British fighter pilots involved in fighting earlier in 1940 had generally been rested and reserved for training jobs during the summer, German pilots had remained in action throughout. As a result the most outstanding were well ahead of their opposite numbers in terms of personal scores by late 1940, but getting tired. When killed on 28 November, Major Helmut Wick had just moved into the lead with 56 victories, closely followed by Major Werner Mölders and Major Adolf Galland, both with over 50. At this time the top-scoring RAF pilots were Flying Officer Eric Lock with 23 and Flight Lieutenant Archie McKellar with 21 victories.

The bomber war now demanded a vast technical outlay and an intricate electronic battle. **The first radio navigation aid employed for bombing purposes** was a beam directed by the Germans over the target along which the bombers flew. A second beam intersected the main one in the target area to indicate when bombing should take place. Known as 'Knickebein'* (bent leg), this device gave the *Luftwaffe* an initial advantage, but was soon discovered by British scientists, who first jammed it, and then introduced more sophisticated counter-measures which deflected the beam a few degrees, causing bombing to take place over open country. **At this time too the Luftwaffe was the first air force to introduce specialist 'pathfinder' units** to lead the main bomber force to the target, and mark it for them. The first such unit, *Kampfgruppe 100*, was equipped with a more complicated radio aid, 'X-Gerät', which was not effectively jammed until early 1941.

Lack of concentration in Luftwaffe attacks was, however, a fundamental cause for their failure to achieve decisive results. Because of bad weather, poor navigation, decoys and general opposition, attacks tended to be spread over wide areas and, when delivered accurately, attenuated by the large percentage of small bombs employed – mostly 110 pounders (50 kg). Parachute sea mines had a far greater blasting effect but could not be dropped accurately. These failures were the inevitable consequences of *Luftwaffe* rejection of strategic air warfare in 1937 – although they were not nearly so fatal to the war's outcome as is sometimes said.

The most damaging night raid of 1940 was made on 14 November when *KGr 100* led 437 bombers to Coventry in bright moonlight, totally devastating the centre of the city. British aircraft production was temporarily cut by 20 per cent making this a tactical victory for the Germans. The British Bomber Command's riposte was puny by comparison. **Its biggest night raid of the war thus far,** on 16 November, put 131 bombers against dock targets on the north German coast.

*Also the name of a German folk-tale character – a magic crow which could fly in the dark.

A Vickers Wellington taxies out for a night raid.

The first effective radar-equipped night fighter, the Bristol Beaufighter, began to enter service at this time, **its first victory** being scored by Flying Officer John Cunningham during the night of 19/20 November.

From small beginnings the British fighters now turned to the offensive in daylight over France, **the first 'Rhubarb' operation** – a low-level nuisance raid over the European coast to attack targets of opportunity – being made by a pair of Spitfires on 20 December, while **the first night intruder operations to intercept German bombers over their own airfields** were flown on the night of 21 December. Despite these developments, **the most damaging night raid on London so far** was made by only 130 bombers on 29 December, the extensive use of incendiary bombs burning out part of the City after high-explosive bombs had cut the water supply to hamper fire fighters.

Another type of RAF offensive operation, the 'Circus' (whereby a small force of bombers was despatched over France with a large fighter escort in order to entice

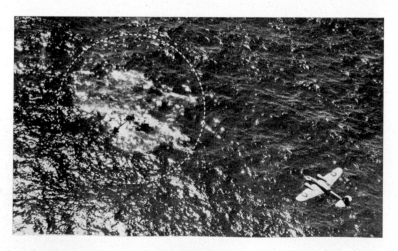

A Bristol Blenheim IV bomber flies over the debris of a vessel sunk by other aircraft of the formation.

THE HEYDAY OF TACTICAL AIR FORCES 1939-42

Luftwaffe fighters to battle) was introduced on 10 January 1941. On that occasion six Blenheims covered by three squadrons each of Spitfires and Hurricanes, raided the Pas de Calais area. Results were meagre, two Bf 109s and one Hurricane being shot down.

The German 'Blitz' entered its final phase on 19 February 1941, raids following every night for the next 81 nights. Between September 1940 and February 1941 the British defences had claimed slightly over 150 bombers brought down, but of these only about 30 had been credited to fighters. The defences began to improve as the weight of German attack increased. During March, 4364 sorties were made by the *Luftwaffe,* but the night fighters were able to claim 22, and the intruders at least two more, while the guns claimed seventeen – the first time their total had fallen below that of the fighters. April saw the heaviest tonnage of bombs dropped on England since the previous November, but during the month the growing number of fighters claimed 48 victories, the guns being credited with 39 more. **The last major raids of the 'Blitz'** (with 550 bombers) took place on the night of 10 and 13 May 1941, though smaller attacks continued throughout the month. Tremendous damage was caused. RAF fighter claims now rose to 96 but since the raids then virtually ceased, the impression was gained that the defences had won. Actually losses were still only a quite bearable 3.5 per cent of sorties flown by the *Luftwaffe,* the true reasons for the departure of the bombers being the forthcoming operations in the East and the Mediterranean. At a cost of about 600 bombers in eight months, the *Luftwaffe* had inflicted much damage, diverted massive resources from other tasks, killed some 40000 people and injured 46000 more.

War in the air now engrossed the combatant nations and affected every activity. The first four-engined heavy bomber for the RAF, the Short Stirling, made its first raid on 10/11 February 1941, when four of them bombed Rotterdam docks. Shortly afterwards the twin-engined Manchester entered action, followed on 10 March by the four-engined Halifax. **The first raid on Germany by four-engined bombers** was made by Halifaxes on 12 March 1941. These were the opening moves in what was to become a main plank in British strategy – the attempt to defeat Germany by air attack by Bomber Command.

A diversion of Bomber Command effort was introduced on 30 March upon the arrival in Brest Harbour of the German battlecruisers *Scharnhorst* and *Gneisenau,* following a successful sortie in the North Atlantic. Many raids were directed against the ships during the next few months, 1161 sorties day and night being made over Brest in eight weeks. **The first major RAF success with torpedo aircraft** was achieved on 6 April when Beauforts of Coastal Command attacked *Gneisenau.* A torpedo from Flying Officer K Campbell's aircraft severely damaged the vessel. Campbell was shot down, receiving the posthumous award of the Victoria Cross. Four nights later Bomber Command aircraft achieved four direct bomb hits on this ship.

Bomber Command launched a new offensive against the Ruhr and Rhineland on 11 June with twenty consecutive raids, but they were to prove disappointingly ineffective. Without adequate navigational aids, many aircraft missed the target area altogether while those that arrived in the right area found accurate bomb aiming very difficult except in conditions of bright moonlight – the same period in which the defences were at their most dangerous.

Loire et Olivier Leo 451 bombers of the French Armee de l'Air and Fairey Battles of the RAF attack pontoon bridges over the River Meuse at Sedan, 14 May 1940.

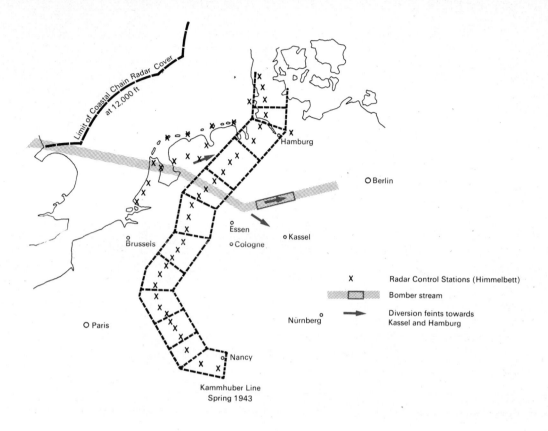

Limit of Coastal Chain Radar Cover at 12,000 ft

Hamburg

Berlin

Essen
Cologne
Kassel

Brussels

Paris

Nancy

Kammhuber Line
Spring 1943

X   Radar Control Stations (Himmelbett)

Bomber stream

Nürnberg

Diversion feints towards
Kassel and Hamburg

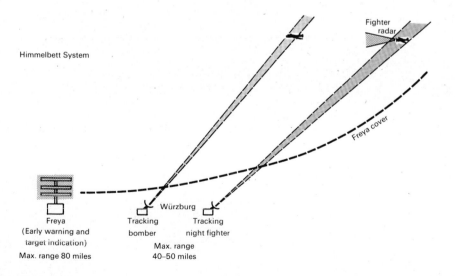

Himmelbett System

Fighter
radar

Freya cover

Würzburg

Freya
(Early warning and
target indication)
Max. range 80 miles

Tracking
bomber

Tracking
night fighter

Max. range
40–50 miles

The Air Defence of Germany.

German defences were improving fast. Still without airborne radar, they were steadily building up a chain of radar 'boxes' right across Western Europe, under the dynamic direction of Generalmajor Josef Kammhuber. Each zone comprised one *Freya* radar set for general surveillance, and two *Wurzburg* sets – one to track an incoming bomber and one to track a defending fighter. Operated in unison, this system could bring the fighter within visual range of the bomber with a good degree of accuracy. Known as the *Himmelbett* (Four Poster Bed) system, the weakness was that each sector could control and direct only one fighter at a time. But since, at this stage, it was normal for Bomber Command to despatch its aircraft singly, and on a broad front, the defence system was perfectly suited.

While the main night-fighter aircraft used was the Bf 110, a second unit had been set up with heavily armed fighter versions of the longer-ranging Do 17 and Ju 88 bombers. These aircraft flew intruder missions over England, attacking the bombers as they returned to land with the crews tired and unwary after their long flights. By the end of July 1941 the German night fighters had claimed approximately 250 victories in their first year of operations, divided equally between intruders and interceptors. Since May 1940 Bomber Command's operational losses to this same date had totalled 543, though quite a number, particularly during the winter, were due to lack of adequate de-icing equipment, heated clothing and inaccurate navigation.

The introduction in March 1941 of a costly anti-shipping campaign by Blenheims and Hudsons of Bomber and Coastal Commands, brought many mast-level attacks off the Dutch and Belgian coasts and in the North Sea generally. Results were overestimated, and a substantial proportion of the 68 Blenheims lost between March and July went down during these operations. More effective was the Bomber Command minelaying campaign which caused considerable dislocation of coastal traffic and forced the Germans to divert effort to the defence of a vital transport system. As the war progressed the intensity of the campaign increased and the resultant effect on German shipping was perhaps **Bomber Command's greatest contribution to the war at sea.**

The fighter operations over Western Europe during the spring of 1941, though kept to a fairly low key, certainly succeeded in bringing the German fighters to battle. Suffering all the disadvantages that had beset the *Luftwaffe* during 1940, Fighter Command now operated at maximum range over hostile territory, with a long over-water flight each way. By 13 June 104 'Rhubarbs' had been flown, but only eleven 'Circuses'. The biggest of the latter had involved 30 bombers and nearly 300 fighters, but the total results had been the shooting down of 16 Bf 109s for a loss of 25 RAF fighters.

The withdrawal of a large part of the Luftwaffe from Western Europe during May and early June for operations in the Balkans, and then against Russia, led the RAF to greatly increase its offensive efforts in an attempt to draw back strength from the East – the only way in which the British, at this juncture, felt they could effectively contribute. Between mid June and the end of July 8000 fighter sorties covering 374 day bomber flights were made. The result was a loss of 123 fighters and fourteen bombers, without a single unit being withdrawn from elsewhere by the *Luftwaffe*. Only 81 aircraft were lost by the two *Jagdgeschwadern* still in the West.

The deepest daylight bomber penetration so far from Britain was made by 53 Blenheims against power stations in Cologne on 12 August, in an effort to put across to the

The splashes of a dozen mines laid by Royal Navy Grumman Avengers mark the closing of another waterway.

Germans that home territory was not safe by day or night and to divert effort from Russia. 1500 Fighter Command sorties and various Bomber Command diversions were flown in support, but twelve of the Blenheims failed to return.

New British types were coming into service, including the first of the fast, unarmed, wooden-construction Mosquitos, initially in the important photographic reconnaissance role. This latter role provided considerable intelligence material and was one in which the RAF excelled, **its high-flying unarmed Spitfires having undertaken this vital task since the very first days of the war.** Both these aircraft survived in daylight because their speed and ceiling took them out of reach of all enemy fighters as well as guns.

The first sorties by bomb-carrying Hurricanes took place against targets in France on 30 October. September had seen **the first appearance of a potent new German fighter,** the Fw 190 and this quickly made its presence felt. 108 British fighters were lost over Europe against 43 *Luftwaffe* machines shot down during September and October, while by the end of the year a further 100 had been lost. For instance, on 8 November during a 'Circus' operation, sixteen British fighters were lost, and only five claims made. Throughout 1941 Fighter Command lost 849 aircraft in 150 828 sorties, 462 fighter pilots failing to return. 800 claims against German aircraft were made, but actual losses inflicted were far lower.

The first of the American Boeing B-17C Fortress I four-engined bombers arrived in RAF service. Operating at 30 000 ft (9000 m) or above in small numbers these soon proved to have insufficient armament for day raids, and small bomb-carrying capabilities. On 8 September 1941 four of them raided targets in Norway, but two were shot down and a third badly damaged. The new heavy British bombers were also occasionally used by day against shorter range targets. On 18 December, 47 Stirlings, Manchesters and Halifaxes raided the warships in Brest Harbour, but five, plus an escorting Hurricane, were shot down.

The best RAF aircraft (including 75 fighter squadrons) were retained in the United Kingdom in case the *Luftwaffe* should return in strength, but the *Luftwaffe* preferred to keep its main strength in two other areas – in Russia and, increasingly, in the Mediterranean (25 per cent of its strength) with just sufficient in the West to contain the growing bomber offensive. The air battles over Malta and the desert had a far more direct influence upon operations than those in the West, and German efforts to block the Suez Canal with air-dropped magnetic mines (beginning in January 1941) had a more disruptive effect than a few bombs on civilian targets when all the latter did was make civilians more angry and determined to fight on. Yet not until spring 1942 was a single squadron of Spitfires sent to the Middle East, even though the Hurricanes and American-built Tomahawks were being out-fought by the numerically inferior Bf 109s, in the series of battles revolving around Malta and the Western Desert.

MEDITERRANEAN AND MIDDLE EAST, JUNE 1940–JUNE 1941

The *Regia Aeronautica* was a relatively large force, with 3296 operational aircraft, of which 1796 were with units. Large commands were situated in Northern Italy, Sicily, and Central Italy; smaller ones in South-East Italy, Sardinia, Albania and Rhodes. A substantial force was based in Libya, half around Tobruk in the east, the rest around Tripoli in the west facing respectively the British and the French. Bombers, fighters, attack and reconnaissance aircraft were backed up by army co-operation and observation aircraft attached direct to ground forces, by coastal seaplane and flying-boat units, and by a medium-sized force of transport aircraft. Additionally, in East Africa, spread between Eritrea, Ethiopia and Somaliland, were a further 338 aircraft, of which 173 were with operational units, though the majority of the latter were obsolescent Ca 133s, SM 81s and CR 32s.

The standard of Italian equipment had fallen below that of other European powers, due mainly to lack of engines of sufficient power, and of good aircraft guns and radios. Medium bombers were of reasonable performance (SM 79, BR 20 and Cant Z1007s), but most fighters were still biplane types (CR 42). Some monoplanes were entering service (Macchi C 200 and Fiat G-50), but their performance generally was below that of the Spitfire. Yet the forces which the Italians would initially meet were no better off and much fewer in number. In Egypt the RAF had but a handful of Gladiator biplane fighters, and Blenheim bombers; on Malta there was a single hastily formed flight of three Gladiators, and the French were fully committed against the *Luftwaffe* in France.

The first Italian strikes on 11 June 1940 were directed against Malta, soon followed by attacks on French bases on Corsica, in Tunisia, and then in southern France itself. In North Africa the RAF took the initiative, striking at Italian airfields around El Adem on the first morning of the war.

A corner-stone of British strategy was reinforcement of the Middle East. Germany on the other hand, looked hardly at all beyond the boundaries of Europe and Italy sought mainly to preserve or expand her colonial territories in North Africa. Hence the air war in the Mediterranean resolved itself into a struggle to support naval and land forces in the accomplishment of those aims and was, therefore, much more tactical than strategic in its application, particularly since few major strategic targets lay within the range of existing aircraft. Before the fall of France a number of Hurricanes were flown out, some to reinforce Malta, but after 24 June fighters could no longer go out by air. A trans-continental route from Takoradi in West Africa, across the Sahara, was planned, **the first aircraft reaching Egypt via this route** on 26 September. Meanwhile, on 3 August a dozen Hurricanes to Malta on the

Used widely by the Regia Aeronautica *in Greece and North Africa was the Fiat G-50 fighter.*

carrier *Argus,* had been flown off. Italian raids on Malta were sporadic, as was initial action over North Africa. On 13 September, however, Marshal Graziani's army crossed the frontier into Egypt in considerable strength, but after taking the airfield complex at Sidi Barrani, the advance ground to a halt in the face of minimal opposition.

A crucial event of the war was the Italian decision to invade Greece on 28 October. While Greek determination on land was enough to throw the invaders back into Albania and 92 Greek aircraft, rapidly reinforced by British bombers and fighters, could match the 283 Italian aircraft initially committed, it was the threat of Allied air bases in Greece to the Rumanian oilfields in Ploesti which gave the Germans most cause for concern. These were vital to the German war effort. Moreover, a British presence in the Balkans posed a further threat to the flank of the operations then being planned against Russia.

British application of air power in the Mediterranean was almost invariably offensive in character. In September Britain's newest fleet carrier, *Illustrious,* arrived and early on 27 November twenty of her Swordfish aircraft attacked the Italian fleet base at Taranto. In **the first decisive strike of the war by carrier aircraft** the battleship *Littorio* was badly damaged, the *Caio Duilio* damaged and beached, and the *Cavour* sunk. By the removal of these capital ships British naval power was made temporarily absolute.

Fragmented British forces in Aden, the Sudan and Kenya were too weak at first to resist strongly. At Aden were some Blenheims, in the Sudan some Vickers Wellesleys, and in Kenya a motley collection of converted Junkers Ju 86 airliners, Fairey Battles and Hawker Hart variants belonging to the South African and Southern Rhodesian Air Forces. Gladiators, Hawker Furies, and the odd Hurricane provided air defence of these areas. Italian air defence proved quite effective, and a substantial toll of the British bombers was taken during 1940 while Italian bombers struck at airfields and convoys in the Red Sea.

The first British offensive of the war was launched in East Africa against areas of the Sudan border occupied by the Italians around Gallabat. Started on 6 November

1940, the offensive came under heavy air attack on rocky ground. On this occasion Italian fighters wrested air superiority from the patrolling Gladiators, inflicting some relatively heavy casualties. As a result of the bombing, the difficult terrain and a stiff Italian defence the British forces were obliged to withdraw.

The first successful British offensive opened on 9 December 1940 in Egypt. Launched as a reconnaissance in force by a relatively small army, it gained immediate success. Air support was furnished by Hurricanes, Gladiators and Blenheims by day, Wellingtons and Bombays by night. An early ascendancy was gained over the *Regia Aeronautica,* which operated under a disadvantage from the start when its forward airfields were overrun. The RAF carried out an aggressive policy of patrolling and airfield attacks, ground strafing being a part of almost every sortie as a matter of policy. While a fair number of Italian aircraft were shot down by Hurricanes a much greater proportion were captured on airfields, either damaged by strafing or unserviceable. On 9 February the campaign ended when the exhausted and overstretched British forces reached El Agheila.

The last fight by Regia Aeronautica in East Africa took place in dispute of a British advance from the Sudan into Eritrea (also supported by newly arrived Hurricane reinforcements), which began on 19 January 1941, joined by an attack from Kenya into Ethiopia on 2 February. *Regia Aeronautica* was steadily worn down by attacks on its bases. 51 CR 42 fighters were flown in, disassembled, in SM 82 transports, while 39 SM 79 bombers also reached the area, but this was the full extent of reinforcements received before the army was reduced to defeat.

The main air battle began to centre over shipping lanes, in the struggle by both sides to sustain their armies on opposite sides of the Mediterranean. Malta had received further reinforcements of Hurricanes, and by the end of 1940 a number of bombers were also based there, attacking convoys from Italy carrying reinforcements to North Africa. In January 1941 *Fliegerkorps* X arrived in Sicily with 132 bombers, 72 dive-bombers and 36 Bf 110s, the initial task being to neutralise Malta and British naval power in the Central Mediterranean and, above all, to prop up the wilting Italians.

The first German assault went in on 10 January when a strong dive-bomber attack was launched on a convoy approaching Malta. The carrier *Illustrious* was severely damaged and next day Ju 87s sank the cruiser *Southampton*. A series of very heavy bombing attacks were now launched on Malta whose defending fighters were able to take a damaging toll but whose bombers were severely restricted and naval surface forces withdrawn. As a result convoys carrying German and Italian troops and armour reached Tripoli safely in February along with Ju 87s, Bf 110s and reconnaissance aircraft. Simultaneously the first Bf 109s took a heavy toll of Hurricanes over Malta, though *Luftwaffe* operations were circumscribed because of supply difficulties in hastily set-up Sicilian bases.

The first British paratroop operation took place at night on 10 February. Eight Whitleys were flown to Malta and while two created a diversion, five carried paratroops to destroy the Tragino aqueduct in Southern Italy, which carried water to Taranto, Brindisi and Bari. The mission was successfully accomplished before the paratroops were captured, but while the demolition caused much alarm in Italy, it had little lasting effect.

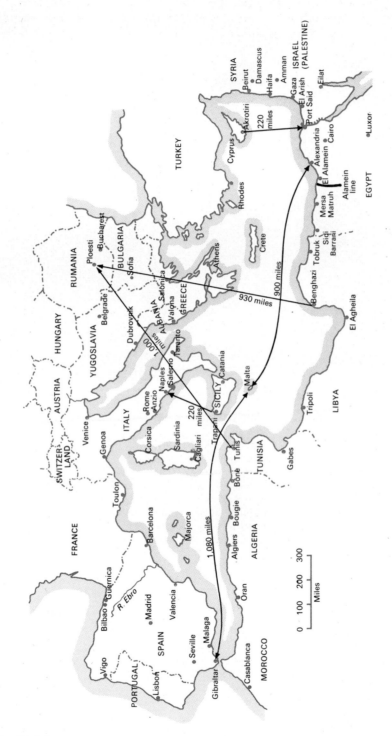

Mediterranean theatre 1940–44.

A German pilot's view of the Desert War in Cyrenaica. Dispersed targets burn.

The German arrival in Rumania and Bulgaria intensified the air war. During late 1940 and early 1941, three fighter squadrons with Gladiators and Hurricanes, and several more bomber units had been transferred from North Africa to Greece, leaving the forces in North Africa critically weakened. The Italians also transferred a number of units of their latest aircraft to Albania, particularly from Sicily. Heavy air fighting broke out over Greece.

At the end of March the Germans, finding the British in the Desert greatly weakened, struck. General Rommel's small but fresh force pushed the British into headlong retreat. Without reserves, the British could only fall back into Egypt, holding on only to Tobruk which was surrounded and invested on 12 April, to become the target for a series of heavy air raids.

The last nations to fall victim in entirety to German Blitzkrieg were Yugoslavia and Greece. On 6 April, following the withdrawal of Yugoslavia from the Axis Anti-Comintern Pact, the Axis launched their armies from bases in Bulgaria and Rumania, supported by some 1200 aircraft of *Luftflotte* 4, plus strengthened elements of the *Regia Aeronautica* totalling some 650 aircraft. Yugoslavia possessed a small but relatively modern air force with 210 fighters, 170 bombers and various reconnaissance types. Over the capital of Belgrade the fighters put up a stiff resistance, but after two days were overwhelmed by sheer numbers. A massive series of bombing attacks aimed with the deliberate intention of stunning morale, shattered the city with great loss of life, but bad weather then reduced aerial activity. The lightning German advance overran many of the Yugoslavian airfields early in the campaign,

Squadron-Leader M T Pattle. and on 17 April the nation surrendered.

A short but intensive air battle also distinguished the Allied débâcle in Greece, its climax coming in a pitched battle over Athens on 20 April when Squadron Leader M T St J Pattle, **probably the highest-scoring RAF fighter pilot of the war,** was shot down and killed. His final total is believed to have exceeded 50 victories. By the end of April surviving British forces had been evacuated under constant air attack to Crete or Egypt. The RAF had lost 151 aircraft since 6 April, but only 72 of these had been shot down, the remainder burnt on the ground when disabled to prevent their capture. *Luftwaffe* losses were recorded as 164.

Axis involvement in the Balkans gave the British opportunities elsewhere. During April *Ark Royal* had made two more deliveries of Hurricanes to Malta and on the 16th a complete Axis supply convoy was sunk off the Tunisian coast. A month later a full Allied convoy loaded with tanks and Hurricanes reached Egypt safely. And during May an Axis attempt to foster a rebellious Iraq was thwarted by air power working in conjunction with land forces, the *Luftwaffe* failing in its effort to strengthen the Iraqi dissidents and Vichy French regulars.

The first wholly airborne invasion to succeed led to the conquest of Crete by the Germans. After the conquest of Greece much of *Luftflotte* 4 had been withdrawn to prepare for the attack on Russia, but 430 bombers, 180 fighters, 500 Ju 52s and 100 gliders had been left behind to deal with the island. Heavy air raids were contested by a handful of RAF fighters until 19 May, when the survivors withdrew. Next day waves of paratroops and troop-carrying gliders were launched, supported by air attack, and the transports returned later in the day, after the capture of airfields on the island, to land still more troops.

The British were ready, and while only seven Ju 52s were shot down in the first attack, the paratroops were very severely handled on the ground. In two days at least 170 Ju 52s were destroyed as they landed, or were unloading. For the whole campaign 4500 'crack' airborne troops were killed. At the same time the Royal Navy flotillas forced the first wave of small craft

Junker Ju 52 transports over Crete, May 1941.

carrying reinforcements and heavy equipment by sea to turn back. The *Luftwaffe* then came to the rescue. Initially Ju 87s sank the destroyer *Greyhound*, while bomb-carrying Bf 109s inflicted serious damage on the battleship *Warspite*. Cruisers and destroyers persisted, but then dive-bombers sank the cruiser *Gloucester*, and Bf 109s sent down the cruiser *Fiji*. Next day, as two more destroyers, *Kelly* and *Kashmir*, were also sunk by Ju 87s, the land battle on the island began to swing the German way and an evacuation soon became inevitable. Quite as inevitably, warships and transports, unprotected by fighter aircraft, suffered heavily from air attack. Yet the high paratroop losses in Crete undermined Hitler's faith in them and they were never again used on that scale in that way by Germans.

A new carrier, *Formidable*, had arrived during March playing a significant part with her Albacore aircraft in torpedoing an Italian cruiser and thus enabling the Italian Fleet to be brought to action at the Battle of Matapan (27/28 March). On 26 May, however, she was discovered by accident by a force of Ju 87s from Libya and badly damaged, thus depriving the Mediterranean Fleet of its air component when it was most needed.

The first large-scale air battle between British and French forces began when the British resolved to secure their rear by occupying Syria on 8 June. The French had just flown in substantial air-force reinforcements following the earlier British bombing attacks that were connected with *Luftwaffe* involvement in the supply of Iraqi dissidents. On several occasions French D 520 fighters got the better of British formations, and both sides suffered relatively heavy casualties in the air. When a column from Iraq moved on Palmyra, in central Syria, it came under sustained French air attack and was brought to a halt for several days. Only when RAF reinforcements arrived and destroyed many French aircraft on the ground could the land forces bring the fighting to a satisfactory conclusion. During the campaign the French employed a total of 289 aircraft, 200 of them modern types. Of these, 179 were lost, 127 of them modern.

By the beginning of June virtually all German forces in Sicily, Greece and Yugoslavia had been withdrawn for the Russian invasion, leaving only those forces employed in North Africa. Substantial numbers of aircraft were now being delivered to Takoradi for the British, to make the flight across to the war zone, and amongst those were quantities of fighters and bombers purchased from the United States. So, while the *Luftwaffe* was about to be overstretched still further, its opponents were gathering in strength around the perimeter of Hitler's Reich.

OPERATION 'BARBAROSSA'; THE INVASION OF RUSSIA, JUNE–DECEMBER 1941.

The German invasion of Russia began in the early hours of 22 June 1941. It was a true gamble, based on the adage of quality over quantity. Designed to succeed at one swift blow, which it might have done, it fell just short of achieving its aim, had the Balkan and Mediterranean operations of April and May not been necessary. Some 60 per cent of the *Luftwaffe's* strength was deployed along the frontier with the Soviet Union, 1400 of the 1945 operational (1280 serviceable) aircraft being gathered in four *Luftflotten* (1-North, 2-Centre (with 50 per cent of the striking force), 4-South, and 5-Norway). All told there were 650 fighters, 831 bombers, 324 dive-bombers, 140 reconnaissance aircraft, to which were added 200 transports plus coastal and reconnaissance machines.

The Germans were supported in the south by a substantial Rumanian

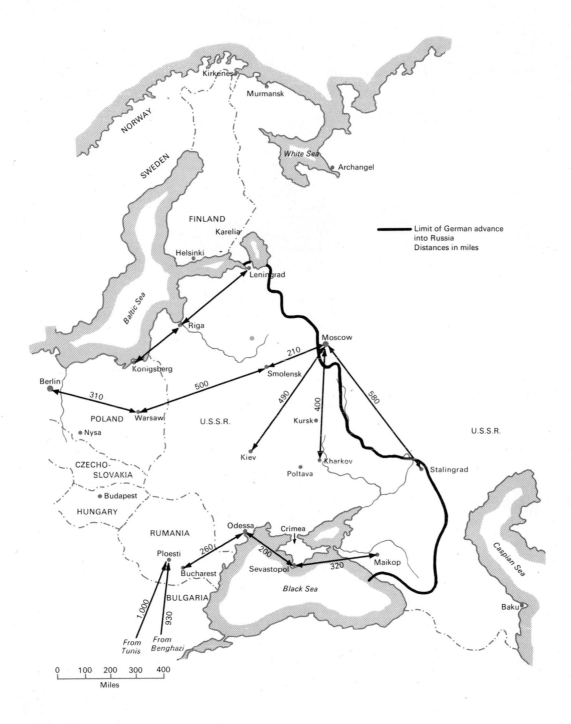

NORWAY

Kirkenes

Murmansk

SWEDEN

White Sea

Archangel

FINLAND

Karelia

Helsinki

Baltic Sea

Leningrad

Limit of German advance
into Russia
Distances in miles

Riga

Moscow

210

Konigsberg

Smolensk

Berlin

310

500

POLAND   Warsaw

U.S.S.R.

490

400

580

Nysa

Kursk

U.S.S.R.

CZECHO-
SLOVAKIA

Kiev

Kharkov

Stalingrad

Budapest

Poltava

HUNGARY

RUMANIA

Odessa

Crimea

Ploesti

260

200

Caspian Sea

Bucharest

Sevastopol

320

Maikop

BULGARIA

Black Sea

1,000

930

Baku

From
Tunis

From
Benghazi

0   100   200   300   400

Miles

Eastern Front 1941–43.

Typical scene on a Russian forward airfield after the Luftwaffe attacks in June 1941. In the foreground is a Yak 4 bomber, while in the immediate background are a Polikarpov I-16 fighter (left) and a Tupolev SB-2 bomber.

army, accompanied by about 230 aircraft of various types, a Hungarian Corps and supporting aircraft (which entered the war a few days after the fighting started) and a token Slovakian air force. Soon after the commencement of hostilities the Finns entered the war (299 aircraft), and an Italian expeditionary force with an air legion was sent to the Southern Front. Later, Croat elements from Yugoslavia and volunteer units from Spain would also arrive.

This total force in no way measured up in size to the Red Air Force, which had some 12 000–15 000 operational aircraft, about 7000 of which were concentrated in Western Europe in 23 Air Divisions. Like the French in 1940, the Russians were in the midst of a vast programme of re-equipment. Not expecting a German attack until 1942, they were also based undispersed and far too near the frontier for safety.

It was in experience that the Luftwaffe really enjoyed a major advantage, as well as in quality of equipment and the elements of surprise.

The first strike was made at 0315 by 637 bombers and 231 fighters against 31 airfields; great success was achieved and only two aircraft lost. Many sorties were flown and by the end of the day 1489 Soviet aircraft had been claimed on the ground and 322 shot down. Panzer columns advanced deep into Russian territory. **The first counter-strike** was made the same day by nine Russian bombers against targets in East Prussia; five were shot down. The usual techniques were employed by the Germans. Stukas and Zerstörer aircraft operated in direct support of the armoured spearheads, acting as airborne artillery, while medium bombers attacked supply and concentration areas, railheads, convoys and other targets further behind the front.

The first tank-air liaison officers were introduced at this time, an Air Force officer in a tank with radio among the leading troops to direct close-support attacks on the Russian tanks and artillery.

In the first week of the campaign 4990 Russian aircraft were destroyed for the loss of 179 German machines. **The biggest battles of the war to date** took place as the German spearheads approached Minsk on 30 June. Large formations of unescorted Russian bombers were thrown in, one German unit alone (*JG 51*) claiming 114 of these. Further north, while defending bridges captured over the River Düna, *JG 54* claimed 65 attacking bombers shot down. On 6 July 73 bombers attacked a German bridgehead at Ostrov and again 65 of them were shot down.

The first air raid on Moscow was launched, after the capture of the Smolensk air bases, during the night of 22 July in an effort to demoralise the population. 127 bombers dropped 104 tons of bombs on this occasion. Next night 115 bombers returned, and 100 more went back on the 24th. Thereafter Moscow was raided regularly by night and day by smaller (30–40) forces but only as a harassment.

During the summer and autumn months of 1941 combat by the German fighters was almost continuous, and Russian aircraft were shot down in numbers previously unheard of. **The first Jagdgeschwader to reach 1000 victories during the Second World War** was *JG 51*, which reached this total during 30 June. On this date Major Mölders, commander of this unit, became **the first pilot to exceed von Richthofen's First World War score of 80,** raising his own total since September 1939 to 82. **The first pilot to claim 100 victories was also Mölders, on 15 July 1941.** (Not including his fourteen victories in Spain.) **The first unit to reach 2000 victories** was again *JG 51*, on 8 September, and two days later its total claims since over Russia from 22 June stood at 1357, with 298 more destroyed on the ground.

Messerschmitt Bf 109F fighter on the Russian Front, 1942.

The first British attempt to give direct aid to Russia took the form of an attack on 30 July 1941 when Albacores, Swordfish and Fulmars from the carriers *Victorious* and *Furious* went for Kirkenes and Petsamo. Little shipping was present in the harbours and damage inflicted was slight. Sixteen British aircraft were shot down, many by German dive-bombers returning from a raid. Concrete British aid came in September when two squadrons of Hurricane fighters were delivered by the carrier *Argus* to Archangel, entering action on 11 September. After initially demonstrating the aircraft in action, the British pilots spent several weeks training Russian pilots to operate Hurricanes, and then handed the fighters over to them. A steady stream of aircraft delivered under Lease Lend followed from both Britain and the United States. Initial deliveries comprised Hurricanes and Tomahawks, soon-followed by P-39 Airacobras.

The first Russian air raid on Berlin was made by a small force of bombers during the night of 7 August. Shortly afterwards the Soviet second city of Leningrad was besieged. The defenders were supported by the gunfire of the Baltic Fleet in Kronstadt harbour, and in an effort to silence these a series of heavy dive-bombing attacks were launched. **The first sinking of a battleship by dive-bombers** was achieved by Leutnant Hans-Ulrich Rudel on 23 September; his 2200 lb (1000 kg) bomb hit the *Marat* (23600 tons) amidships, the ship breaking in two and sinking. Another battleship and a cruiser were damaged. Rudel later became **the most highly decorated airman in the Luftwaffe,** flying over 2000 sorties, and claiming large numbers of Russian tanks destroyed.

Despite tremendous German successes in Russia and tracts of territory occupied, the Russians continued to resist as the weather and utter weariness brought the Germans advance to a halt short of Moscow. The Germans were now beginning to feel the losses that were not being replaced due to dire material and manufacturing shortages at home. In the *Luftwaffe* 1603 aircraft were lost in fourteen weeks' fighting by late September, with over 1000 more damaged, a rate of attrition which had written off a high proportion of the strength with which the campaign began.

The failure of the Germans to prepare for a long war and any sort of strategic bombing now had fatal consequences. The Russians had moved their whole war industry to the east of the Ural mountains – beyond the range of German air attack. Moreover the *Luftwaffe* possessed no long-range strategic bombers and were beginning to suffer from fuel shortage since synthetic plants were delayed in production. As the hard Russian winter found the Germans quite unprepared for its rigours, which grounded aircraft and reduced serviceability to 30 per cent, the Red Army launched a counter-offensive which at first made some ground, supported by new MiG-3, Yak-1 and LaGG-3 fighters, Il-2 ground-attack aircraft (*Shturmoviks*) and Pe-2 bombers, which all supplemented the older types in growing numbers and were more effective in extreme weather conditions.

Pressure on the Germans mounted throughout 1942 as the bomber offensive grew (see page 123), The Russian winter counter-offensive took its toll and the American involvement (see page 126) began to add power to the British punch in the Western and Mediterranean theatres of war. In Russia the *Luftwaffe* retained air superiority, but elsewhere sheer numbers and a gradual atrophy of its technical advantage began to reduce its influence.

The first major airlift in history to support an army was instituted to keep supplied 100 000 German troops trapped near Lake Ilmen in February. Until a counter-attack broke through on 19 May, 32 427 supply and 659 reinforcement sorties had been flown; 64 844 tons of supplies and 30 500 troops taken in, while 25 400 casualties were evacuated. Extensive use of cargo gliders was made. The total cost to the *Luftwaffe* was 265 aircraft. But this operation had ironic consequences; it gave the High Command an inflated notion of the *Luftwaffe's* ability to sustain such activities on a large scale.

Most Luftwaffe operations continued to be in direct support of ground operations as their summer offensive got under way. By far the most effective Russian aircraft at this time was the Ilyushin Il-2, a very heavily armed and armoured single-engined attack aircraft, known by the generic term '*Shturmovik*'. These proved difficult to shoot down and, at this stage, were unique in the service of any of the Allied air forces.

Due to the inherently tactical nature of the air war in the East, most activity took place at a very much lower altitude than in Western Europe. Because airfields were close to the front, sorties were generally quite short, and consequently many more could be made in a given period. Conditions in fact were very similar to those pertaining to the Western Front in 1917-18.

Albert Kesselring (right) and Erwin Rommel (centre) in the desert. Kesselring had command of all German troops in the Mediterranean and employed the Luftwaffe with great skill. He eventually became C.-in-C. South with command over all three services.

In the West and the Mediterranean air activity of a routine nature was frequently illuminated by dramatic encounters when entire air fleets were drawn into action – usually in connection with major ground offensives or a big naval operation – often at longer range. The recurrent desert battles in the approaches to the Suez Canal absorbed much effort and the thrust and counter-thrust by both sides in endeavouring to supply or prevent supply by sea and air of the forces in

North Africa provoked one long, drawn-out engagement. Malta as often as not stood at the centre of operations. For example, late in March 1942 a small convoy reached Malta, and while all ships were eventually sunk, two which went down in shallow water had their cargoes salvaged, allowing the beleagured island to fight on. But on occasions only five serviceable aircraft were available.

On 20 April a major delivery of 47 Spitfires was made to the island by the aircraft carrier USS *Wasp*. Within two days only seventeen of the new aircraft remained serviceable, as successful attacks on the airfields were made by the *Luftwaffe*. At the same time air reconnaissance noted signs of preparations which the Germans and Italians were making to launch an airborne invasion of the island. Early in May *Wasp* returned with the carrier HMS *Eagle*, and 64 more Spitfires were flown off. This time the Spitfires were not caught on the ground, and in three days *Luftwaffe* bomber losses reached a higher figure than they had done during the whole of a five-week period up to the end of April. Moreover, it was to be shown in mid-June, when another convoy was being run to Malta from Gibraltar, that carrier aircraft, however inferior in performance they were to the best of the *Luftwaffe*, could hold off air attacks sufficiently well to avert serious ships' losses. Only after the carrier force had been withdrawn in the Sicilian Narrows did the sinking of merchantmen pile up.

HMS Eagle *flies off Spitfires for the RAF Squadrons on Malta, July 1942.*

The biggest convoy to set out for Malta to date sailed from Gibraltar on 11 August, escorted by three aircraft carriers, with one more carrying further Spitfires for the island. On the first day the carrier *Eagle* was sunk by a submarine, while on the 12th the carrier *Indomitable* was damaged by bombs. Despite this, the carrier fighters had their greatest success so far in holding off the attacking bombers and torpedo-bombers, and not until after the carriers had turned back as darkness fell did the convoy suffer substantial further losses.

The biggest British operation in Western Europe during 1942 was launched on 19 August, as 6000 British and Canadian troops were landed at Dieppe. While USAAF B-17s and RAF light bombers struck elsewhere as a diversion, a maximum Fighter Command effort was made, with 2339 RAF and 123 USAAF fighter sorties over the area dawn to dusk. Aware that such an operation was impending

Leutnant Hans-Ulrich Rudel of Stukageschwader 2 dives in his Junkers Ju 87B Stuka to sink the Russian battleship Marat *in Kronstadt harbour, 23 September 1941.*

and wishing to discourage any larger scale attempt, the Germans made a maximum effort. British aircraft losses totalled 106, plus eight more American Spitfires, while the Germans lost 48, with 24 more damaged.

Preceded by an air offensive, the British launched their victorious offensive at El Alamein on the night of 23 October. Air attacks in all sectors of the front slowed down Axis attempts to regroup and supply their forces. Following the Allied breakthrough early in November came **the first great Anglo-American amphibious landings of the war** when their forces came ashore at Casablanca, Algiers and Oran in North-West Africa. Hence the greatest fleets of Allied aircraft carriers and other warships yet assembled supported the assault. Initial Vichy French resistance led to some air fighting for the

An Axis supply train comes under attack from RAF Bristol Beaufighters on the Libyan coastal railway.

carrier air groups, but this was swiftly terminated. From Gibraltar squadrons of British and American fighters soon flew in to take over the air defence of Algeria, while USAAF P-38s, B-26s, and B-17s, RAF Beaufighters and Bisleys, came direct from England. Feldmarschall Albert Kesselring, the senior German officer in the Mediterranean, despatched German fighter aircraft and dive-bombers to Tunisia. But the uninvited arrival of Italian fighters prompted the local French forces to swing irrevocably to the Allied side.

On 14 December the Allies found themselves held up, under heavy air attack from Ju 87s, Bf 109s and MC 202s because they were beyond the range of really effective air cover by Anglo-American units and lacked a good early-warning system.

A British parachute landing to secure the port and airfield at Bône, carried out moments before a similar German operation could be launched, improved the situation slightly. Malta was relieved and the initiative of the air war had passed to the Allies as the African front contracted into Tunisia. In an effort to supply

the much-increased Axis forces in Africa, large numbers of German and
Italian transport aircraft were moved to Sicily to fly to Tripoli and Tunis,
but these came under frequent attack from Malta-based fighters, and losses
were often heavy. At the same time **the first regular attacks by escorted
formations of USAAF heavy bombers** were being met by the German
fighters in northern Tunisia and it was here that the German tactics devised
for combating these formidable opponents were initially improvised.

AIRCRAFT AGAINST SUBMARINES

At the outbreak of the Second World War the RAF had 196 aircraft based in the United Kingdom for
maritime reconnaissance duties. **None of the squadrons was tasked for A/S warfare, nor were the
aircrew trained for other than naval co-operation tasks,** the belief being that no specialised
aircraft or training was required to find and attack submarines, in spite of the lessons of 1917–18. The
French *Aeronavale*, equipped for A/S warfare with a wide variety of flying-boat types, shared similar
opinions. Of the RAF's A/S aircraft, only the 12 Lockheed Hudsons and 18 Short Sunderland flying boats
were capable of operations more than 300 miles from their bases.

The first aircraft-assisted kill occurred on 30 January 1940, when a Sunderland escorting a convoy
off Ushant shared in the destruction of *U-55* with surface escorts. Before
Allied aircraft could achieve any further successes against U-boats at sea,
the *Seeluftstreitkräfte*, the German Navy's air arm, forced **the first
surrender of a submarine to an aircraft,** the boat in question being
Seal, damaged by a mine in the Kattegat and unable to dive.

Italy's declaration of war in June 1940 placed a considerable strain on
the twelve RAF flying boats divided between Gibraltar and Malta, these
aircraft being required more for Fleet reconnaissance than A/S duties.
Nevertheless, **the first submarine to be sunk by air attack alone** was
the Italian *Argonauta*, despatched by a Sunderland from Egypt on 28 June
1940. The mere presence of aircraft had a harassing effect on the U-boats,
which were frequently driven down out of sight of the convoys or forced to
return to base, damaged by the inadequate weapons of the Coastal
Command aircraft. By midsummer 1941, the combined effects of increased
numbers of surface escorts and aircraft had forced the U-boats into the mid-
Atlantic, beyond the range of aircraft.

Air-to-Surface Vessel (ASV) radar was fitted to Coastal Command Hudsons as early as February
1940, but it was not until the autumn of that year that its fitting to A/S
aircraft became general. With a 10-mile (16 km) range against a surfaced
U-boat, ASV was an invaluable night and bad weather detection aid, but
the lack of a suitable means of illuminating the target at night – the U-boats'
favoured time for attack – prevented the maximum advantage from being
gained from the device.

The first ASV-assisted kill was made on 30 November 1941 by a Whitley which sank *U-206*,
approaching through cloud as the U-boat was heading across the Bay of
Biscay on the surface. British and Allied forces had sunk 100 submarines by
the end of November 1941, but at the beginning of December the German
Navy alone had 90 U-boats operational.

A major A/S victory was scored by the Royal Navy during the second half of December 1941. Convoy
HG 76 left Gibraltar for the UK on 14 December with a powerful escort
which included **the first escort carrier** (CVE), HMS *Audacity*. The
convoy was opposed by a dozen U-boats, assisted by long-range maritime

Nakajima Ki 43 fighters of the Japanese Army Air Force strafe a British airfield in Northern Malaya as Brewster Buffaloes attempt to get into the air, December 1941.

reconnaissance Focke Wulf Fw 200Cs, but the battle which lasted from 17 to 21 December saw the destruction of four U-boats, one shared by the carrier's Grumman Martlet fighters, and two Fw 200s. Only two of the 32 merchant ships were sunk, but one destroyer and the carrier herself were sunk. After the loss of *Audacity* air cover was provided by Consolidated Liberators operating from Northern Ireland, over 900 miles (1440 km) from the convoy. Meanwhile, at Gibraltar, Royal Navy Swordfish, survivors of the sunken *Ark Royal*, were flying nightly patrols against U-boats trying to pass through the Straits into the Mediterranean. Twelve ASV-assisted attacks were made during the month, five inflicting severe damage and a sixth sinking **U-451, the first U-boat to be sunk at night by aircraft.**

The U-boats were given a new lease of life by the entry into the war of the United States. Their appearance off the US East Coast in mid-January 1942 marked the beginning of a seven-month-long slaughter of merchant shipping. The American A/S forces were even less prepared for war than those of France and Britain had been. The US Navy had only 60 long-range flying boats and a single squadron of Hudsons to cover a 1400-mile (2240 km) coastline. As a proper convoy system was not inaugurated until the late spring of 1942, the efforts of the aircraft were largely devoted to fruitless patrols, by USN and, from March, USAAF aircraft.

The first kill by an American aircraft occurred off Newfoundland in March 1942, while escorting a British convoy, and it was not until July that a U-boat was sunk off the US coast, by an Army aircraft on patrol. By the end of July, no fewer than 423 ships had been sunk between Nova Scotia and Trinidad; aircraft had played a part in the sinking of six out of the eleven U-boats destroyed in the area. From August, the increasing scale of air and surface escort for American convoys drove the U-boats back to the mid and eastern Atlantic areas, where they suffered heavy losses to the now-efficient British air A/S forces. Between August 1942 and January 1943, the latter sank eleven U-boats in the vicinity of convoys and five while on patrol over the U-boats' transit routes; five more were sunk by aircraft in the Mediterranean, and American and Canadian aircraft destroyed another nine in the western and south Atlantic areas. The sudden increase in the rate of sinkings was due almost entirely to the introduction of a new explosive filling (Torpex) and a shallow-firing depth-charge pistol which detonated the charges around the diving targets, instead of far below.

The most effective aircraft for convoy duties was the Liberator, in service with one Coastal Command squadron and with the USAAF; with only six aircraft available, No. 120 Squadron RAF's escort missions had made four of the eleven kills during the period.

THE STRATEGIC BOMBING OFFENSIVE

RAF Bomber Command's offensive continued to grow. By 1 September 1941 200 Wellingtons, 120 Hampdens, 60 Whitleys and 40 of the new heavy bombers were available, though raids by more than 150 aircraft were rarely made. **The first examples of a new radio navigational aid,** 'Gee', became available during the autumn, as did the first really large bombs of 4000 lb (1818 kg). At the same time the bombers were relieved of the danger of enemy intruder attacks as they returned to base when, during October for political reasons, Hitler ordered that all night fighters were to operate over Europe, where their accomplishments could be seen and improve the morale of the populace.

Although German oil refineries and synthetic fuel plants had priority for attack up to 8 July, only 8 per cent of the effort had been devoted to those targets, whereas nearly 30 per cent of the bombs had been intended for ports, naval bases and shipyards, to break up the invasion forces gathered in 1940 and thereafter to make a contribution to the defence of Allied trade. Assisted by Coastal Command aircraft, Bomber Command had attacked the French Atlantic coast U-boat bases, but had inflicted damage on only one U-boat. Due to the lack of suitable aids for navigation over long distances **it was estimated that only three night-flying crews in every ten were releasing their bombs within five miles of the intended target.** In other words, against an 80 mile^2 (128 km^2) city area, only 30 per cent hits could be expected, the remainder of the bomb-load being dropped on the wrong target, in open country, or on the excellent decoy targets supplied by the Germans.

The German active defences were also becoming formidable. Many of the *Flak* and searchlight batteries were radar-controlled, and **the combination of the Kammhuber Line and the newly introduced night-fighter radar** resulted in heavier losses for Bomber Command, which between August and November 1941 lost 516 out of 10179 aircraft despatched on night raids while the less numerous day bombers lost 73 from 912 sorties over occupied territory.

The bombing of Germany was virtually suspended in November 1941, in order to enable Bomber Command to expand and re-equip with the new types of heavy night bomber. In consequence, the proportion of effort devoted to naval bases and railway facilities in France and Belgium was greatly increased, with 40 per cent of the bombs targeted for the battlecruisers *Scharnhorst* and *Gneisenau* at Brest.

Bomber Command's greatest contribution on the occasion of the battlecruisers' escape in mid-February 1942 was made by the minelaying Hampdens. Having survived naval and air attacks undamaged, both ships were badly damaged by air-laid magnetic mines.

The appointment of Air Marshal A T Harris as C.-in-C. Bomber Command had the most profound effect on the strategic air offensive. Harris, who took up office in February 1942, was a disciple of Trenchard – whose statement that the moral effect of strategic bombing was twenty times as great as the material effect was based on the slender evidence of the results of the 1918 operations of the Independent Air Force but had become an article of faith in Air Force teaching. With the concurrence of various Ministry experts, Harris propounded his theories on the supreme effectiveness of 'Area Bombing', directed at the built-up areas of towns and having as its objective the disruption of the lives of the German working population, with a consequent loss of industrial output. The presence of industry in towns would result in damage to factories and plants, but this would merely be a by-blow, since the whole town would be the target. The proposal was all the more acceptable because of the low standard of navigational accuracy at the time, and the British War Cabinet accepted the plan on 13 February 1942.

Arthur Harris.

Thus began one of the most expensive campaigns of the war. Between 13 February 1942 and 6 March 1944, Bomber Command was to drop 194000 long tons of bombs aimed at German cities – 84 per cent of the total dropped during the period. By the end of the campaign, 23000 acres (9200 ha) in 42 German cities lay devastated and over half a million casualties had been inflicted, at a cost of 4285 bombers.

The first major milestone in the Area Bombing campaign was the bombing of Cologne on 30 May/1 June 1942. Over 1000 bombers were despatched, the numbers being swelled by the inclusion of training units and Coastal Command aircraft.

Co-ordination of this force was provided by the adoption of a new technique, that of sending the bombers out in a stream to a time-table along a pre-determined route, instead of permitting crews to select their own lines of approach and times of attack. The target was marked by aircraft equipped with the 'Gee' radio navigation equipment, the fires started by the first bombers to arrive providing aiming marks for the remainder. The German night-fighter defence system was not prepared for the saturation of just one sector of the radar 'fence', but 41 of the bombers were shot down.

Two more huge raids were carried out in June 1942, against Essen and Bremen, but both targets were obscured by cloud and the raids were unsuccessful. Other, smaller raids brought the total of sorties for June to 4801, but at a cost of 212 bombers destroyed or damaged beyond repair – 4.4 per cent of the total despatched.

A stream of Avro Lancasters form up over England in preparation for a night raid on Germany.

The United States Army Air Force flew its first strategic bombing mission in Europe on 17 August 1942. The target for the 12 B-17E Fortresses was a rail marshalling yard near Rouen: 16½ tons of bombs were dropped, of which more than half fell on the yards and workshop. Nine squadrons of RAF Spitfires provided escort and support, and no B-17s were lost to the few German fighters which attempted to intercept. Prior to the arrival of the Eighth US Army Air Force (under Ira Eaker) in Britain, considerable pressure had been put on the USAAF to employ its B-17s and B-24s on night raids, the RAF believing that no bomber force could operate over Germany by day in large numbers. Greatly to the credit of the Americans, they pursued their own policy and from the beginning of the Eighth AF's operations the four-engined bombers were used for daylight formation precision attacks on strategic targets – individual factories, oil refineries, shipyards, rail installations and 'military' objectives. USAAF bombing philosophy proposed that the enemy's *means* to wage war should be destroyed by direct attack, rather than by the indirect effect of area attacks of reducing his *will* to wage war, as propounded by the RAF.

Yet the RAF did undertake daylight precision attacks with heavy bombers during 1942, **the most successful being that delivered on Augsburg** by twelve of the new Lancasters, on 17 April. Heavy damage was inflicted on the MAN factory which was building a large proportion of the engines for U-boats, but seven of the bombers were shot down. Such losses deterred Bomber Command from developing the low-level daylight precision technique, but on the basis of the April 1942 night-bomber loss rate, an area attack on Augsburg by 350 aircraft would have cost twelve bombers destroyed and 39 damaged, with no guarantee that the MAN plant's output would be reduced.

THE FAR EAST, 1940-2

The first appearance of the Japanese Mitsubishi A6M 'Zero' was startling. Continued Chinese fighter resistance over Chungking led to the despatch of a test batch of these Navy fighters to take part in the continuing Chinese war at the end of August 1940. They first engaged interceptors on 13 September, having flown 575 miles (920 km) to the target and, without loss, claimed all 27 I-15s and I-16s shot down. After further successful sorties in early October, they moved to Indo-China, gaining equal success from here over Kunming, where the Chinese government had set up its new seat. Sorties were also flown over Chengtu, where on 14 March 1941 twelve A6Ms claimed 24 of 30 Chinese aircraft shot down. **These operations by the A6Ms were the furthest-ranging fighter operations so far undertaken anywhere in the world.**

The Japanese had learned many more true lessons during the four years over China than had been learned in Spain. Yet the début of the 'Zero' fighter was completely overlooked by the Western world. Indeed the superior equipment, training and experience of the Japanese air forces was at this time appreciated fully only by the Russians. This experience was to stand the Japanese in very good stead during the early years of the Pacific War, particularly their nagivational skill to attack targets accurately at very long range, and to provide effective fighter escort for their bombers.

Against the lightly armed and armoured Chinese aircraft, however, they had not yet learned the real value of heavy armament, armour protection, and high top speed.

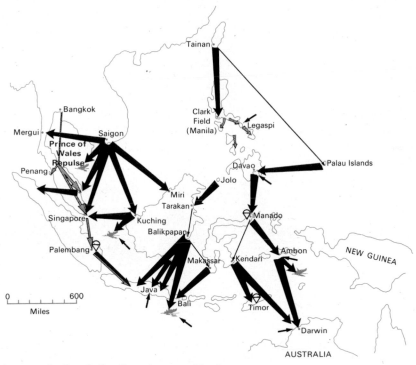

The Japanese advance to the East Indies, December 1941–March 1942.

THE WAR IN THE FAR EAST, 1941-2

The military principles of concentration, mobility and surprise were the key to the immediate success of Japanese aggression. The Allies – Britain and the Dominions, the United States and the Netherlands East Indies (NEI) – were at a disadvantage through their dispersal and lack of a common defensive policy, to say nothing of their qualitative material shortcomings in the matter of aircraft equipment.

The boldest and best known of the Japanese air attacks on the first day of the Pacific War was the carrier strike by Admiral Nagumo, without declaration of war, against Pearl Harbor, on Sunday 7 December 1941. In the space of less than two hours, 167 torpedo- and dive-bombers sank four of the US Pacific Fleet's battleships, damaged three others and inflicted loss and damage on many smaller units. At the same time, 105 other bombers, assisted by many of the 78 Mitsubishi 'Zero' fighters, destroyed or damaged beyond immediate repair 310 of the 400 US Army Air Force, Navy and Marine Corps aircraft on Oahu Island. Twenty-nine Japanese aircraft failed to return to the carriers, victims of anti-aircraft gunfire and of the few USAAF fighters which had taken off to intercept the second wave of raiders.

    The Pearl Harbor attack succeeded in its main strategic objective, that of preventing the US Pacific Fleet from going to the assistance of US forces in the Philippines, but failed in one important aspect. Neither of the two operational American carriers was present and so a major threat to the Japanese remained at large.

Mitsubishi A6M 'Zeros' and Aichi D3A 'Vals' on the deck of Soryu, *about to take off for the attack on Pearl Harbor, 7 December 1941.*

The opening shots of the Pacific War were fired on the day before the carrier attack. A British Catalina flying boat shadowing a Japanese convoy off Cambodia was shot down by a (JAAF) Ki 27 formation escorting the convoy – **the first aerial combat victory** of the war. Part of the convoy arrived off the north-east coast of Malaya in the early hours of 8 December (7 December in Hawaii) and the ships were attacked before dawn by Royal Australian Air Force Hudsons. At much the same time, JNAF medium bombers flying from Indo-China made a token attack on the city of Singapore, inflicting civilian casualties but little military damage. At first light, the JAAF bombers based in Thailand carried out intensive raids on the airfields in northern Malaya and by nightfall only 50 out of 110 RAF and RAAF aircraft in the area remained servicable.

The third major success of this first day of war was achieved by JNAF units based on Formosa. Intended to attack at dawn on 8 December, fog delayed take-off until noon, but although the USAAF command in the Philippines was expecting raids, the fighter defences failed to prevent the 108 medium bombers from attacking the Clark Field complex with great accuracy. Out of 90-odd USAAF aircraft destroyed, 75 were modern Boeing B-17 Fortress bombers and Curtiss P-40 fighters – half the effective strength in the Philippines.

These initial victories gave the Japanese air forces a moral ascendancy which was to continue unchecked for six months. The Allies, surprised by the quality of the opposition in spite of continued warnings from China, never regained their balance after the first day's defeats: no coherent strategy could be formulated as long as the available forces had to be used to restore an increasingly unfavourable situation.

American air and naval power in the Philippines was broken on 10 December, when JNAF medium bombers destroyed the Cavite Navy Yard, Manila, and damaged cruisers of the US Asiatic Fleet. Total superiority at sea in the South China Sea was also assured on this day, when 84 land-based torpedo-bombers and level bombers caught H.M. ships *Prince of Wales* and *Repulse* without fighter cover off the east coast of Malaya and sank them in 90 minutes – **the first capital ships to be lost in the open sea to air attack alone.**

Allied bomber operations were limited by the early losses and by the Japanese aerial superiority. Daylight raids by unescorted RAF Blenheims were abandoned after 9 December, but not before Squadron Leader A S K Scarf had won **the first Victoria Cross in the theatre** for a single-handed attack on Singora. The Dutch Navy Dornier Do 24K flying boats based in Java carried out long-range night raids on the Davao area of Mindanao, but a major reverse was suffered on 23 December, when five failed to return. In the Philippines, the remaining B-17Ds flew less than a dozen effective sorties before 17 December, when they were withdrawn to a secure base in Australia; thereafter a few 'shuttle' missions were flown via Mindanao against the shipping at Davao and Lingayen Gulf, Luzon. Dutch Army Martin 166 bombers based in Borneo sank **the only Japanese ship to be lost to air attack during the month,** but they were unable to prevent the occupation of the Sarawak airfields and the arrival of JNAF fighters and bombers from Saigon.

The Japanese Third Air Army in Malaya made a major contribution to the swift advance of the troops on the ground, providing close support and attacking lines of communication; by 30 December, medium bombers had moved forward to bases from which they could attack Singapore Island, where the 160 remaining RAF and RAAF aircraft were all gathered on four airfields.

In spite of its isolation, Singapore received a large number of replacement aircraft. Sixty-four bombers arrived from Britain, Egypt and Australia, six Catalinas came from Gibraltar and Java, and, on 13 January, 51 Hurricane fighters arrived by sea. The Hurricanes did not turn the tide against the vast numerical superiority of the Japanese, and by the end of January, when all but a token defensive force were withdrawn to Sumatra, only 25 remained combat-worthy.

The British anti-shipping bomber force had been broken on 26 January. Attempting to deliver a daylight attack on a Japanese beach-head at Endau, thirteen out of 24 biplane Vildebeeste and Albacore torpedo-bombers were shot down and most of the remainder damaged by fighters.

The last defensive mission from Singapore was flown on 9 February 1942. On the following day, the surviving Hurricanes were flown out to Sumatra, leaving the island without further air cover until its fall, on 15 February.

The Japanese southward drive through the Philippines and northern East Indies was also moving fast. **The first airborne assault of the Pacific War** was mounted on 11 January 1942, when 28 medium bombers of the 21st Air Flotilla dropped 334 naval paratroops in an attempt to capture Manado airfield, Celebes. The first JNAF bomber raid was mounted from the newly acquired airfield four days later.

Java, the ultimate objective, was bombed for the first time on 3 February, the JNAF concentrating, as usual, on eliminating the air opposition. In addition to the NEI Army aircraft which had survived deployment to Singapore in December, the USAAF was basing B-17s and P-40s on Java, and on 27 and 28 January the only Allied Fleet carrier in the Indian Ocean, H.M.S. *Indomitable*, had flown off 48 Hurricanes to Batavia; 39 more Hurricanes arrived aboard a transport on 4 February, bringing the total of reinforcements of this one type to 138 in three weeks. Of 68 USAAF P-40s despatched from Darwin between 20 January and 19 February, only 36 arrived, thirteen of the lost aircraft being shot down *en route*.

Air raids on Java and bases in Sumatra cost the Allies over 70 aircraft up to 7 February, with negligible losses for the Japanese. A week later, **the first Japanese Army paratroop assault** contributed a prelude to a seaborne invasion of the Palembang area of Sumatra. RAF bombers struck back effectively and delayed the landings by 24 hours, but only by accepting heavy casualties. By 17 February the RAF had withdrawn into Java, which was now under attack by aircraft from Sumatra, Borneo, Celebes, Ambon and Bali.

The fate of Java was sealed on 19 February, when Allied air and naval forces suffered shattering losses. JNAF and JAAF aircraft made continuous raids on Javanese airfields and harbours, while to the east, the six large carriers which earlier had attacked Pearl Harbor launched 188 aircraft to strike at Darwin, the main sea and air staging post for the reinforcement of Java. Seventeen Allied aircraft were destroyed and eleven ships sunk in the harbour, for the loss of one 'Zero' fighter, while 84 medium bombers from Ambon and Bali added to the carnage.

Japanese carrier and land-based aircraft controlled the sea approaches to Java, preventing the Allied cruiser force from acting against the build-up of invasion shipping and also destroying much of the reinforcement traffic. Less than 50 serviceable combat aircraft were available to contest the Japanese landings on Java on 1 March 1942, against over 500 at the disposal of the invaders. The 44 Allied bomber sorties on this day were unable to turn the tide and three RAF Vildebeestes were shot down. The destruction of all nine of the remaining P-40s eliminated the USAAF's fighter presence on 1 March, and the Dutch Buffaloes flew their last combat mission on 5 March. **The last mission by the Allied air** force in Java was flown by two Hurricanes on 8 March, the day before the island commander surrendered.

Allied air losses in this phase of the war were staggering, the RAF losing all but a handful of the 476 aircraft committed to Malaya, the Dutch nearly all their 200 combat aircraft, and the USAAF some 340 aircraft in the Philippines and Java. JNAF combat losses in all theatres in the same period came to about 250 carrier and land-based aircraft; Army Air Force losses are not clear but amounted to less than 150 aircraft.

Only over Burma were the Japanese defeated during the first month of the War in the East.

Claire Chennault.

Few aircraft were available to the Allies in this theatre, though at Toungoo the three squadrons of the American Volunteer Group were under training. This, **the only mercenary 'air force' raised during the War,** called the 'Flying Tigers', was led by Claire Chennault, an American in the service of Chinese Generalissimo Chiang Kai-shek. They were to defend the 'Burma Road', by which all war supplies reached China, and were initially equipped with 36 Curtiss P-40Bs.

The first determined attacks on Rangoon were costly for the Japanese bombers. Allied fighters, warned by the only radar set in Burma, were ready for the 160 bombers and escorts which attacked on 23 and 25 December 1941, and 27 JAAF aircraft were destroyed for the loss of two P-40s and four RAF Buffaloes, the latter being on the ground. But there were over 5000 dead in the city. The credit for this victory goes to the advanced tactics of the American pilots who gave the Japanese fighter escort no chance to inflict the customary losses and prevented them defending the bombers adequately.

A renewed attempt to gain air superiority resulted in a JAAF offensive against Rangoon between 23 and 29 January 1942, but some 50 aircraft were lost and again the Japanese had to abandon day attacks for a month. Hence RAF attacks against Japanese shipping and the invading Japanese Army proceeded without loss in February. And during **the heaviest raid on Rangoon** on 25 February newly arrived Hawker Hurricanes helped inflict losses of 37 out of 170 attacking JAAF aircraft – a reverse that led to the Japanese remaining clear of the area until the fall of the city to the steadily advancing Army. There was therefore no aerial interference with the evacuation of Rangoon, which fell on 9 March.

However, on 21/22 March, 239 Japanese aircraft attacked British airfields at Magwe in five raids. Radar gave little warning and only seven JAAF aircraft were shot down, for the loss of three Hurricanes in combat and thirteen assorted aircraft on the ground. From then on the Japanese possessed air supremacy as the British withdrew. Yet although defeated by weight of numbers after a three-month campaign, the Allied aircrew had destroyed over 150 JAAF aircraft and had materially assisted the out-generalled Army, thus **permitting the only orderly Allied evacuation in the opening stages of the war with Japan.**

The last unquestionable victory enjoyed by the Japanese carrier fleet occurred over and around Ceylon on 5 and 9 April 1942. Ceylon was the main base for the British Eastern Fleet and the 73 fighters and 34 bombers and maritime search aircraft based there represented the bulk of British air strength remaining in the Eastern theatre. The Fleet included two modern carriers and the old, small *Hermes*. but between them they could muster only 27 fighters and 58 torpedo-bombers to pit against 117 'Zeros' and 260 'Kates' and 'Vals' aboard five Japanese carriers.

Twenty-seven Hurricanes and Fulmars were shot down for the loss of nineteen Japanese aircraft. Nine warships were sunk around the island, including HMS *Hermes*, **the only British carrier to be sunk by air attack.** RAF Blenheims attacked the enemy on 9 April, becoming **the first Allied aircraft to sight the Japanese fast carriers.** But altogether 43 British aircraft were shot down and thirteen destroyed on the ground between 4 and 9 April.

The first major air lift by Allied air transport was begun after the Japanese cut the Burma Road early in April 1942, and was to continue for three years as the only supply route to the Chinese Government or the American forces based in China. It was on this 'Hump' route, 530 miles (848 km) long and across mountains that were 12 000 ft (3600 m) high, that the Douglas DC-3 Dakota proved its versatility, shifting the bulk of the fuel, arms, aircraft spares and personnel.

The airlift from Assam to Kunming was first executed by USAAF and Pan-American Airways C-47 and DC-3 Dakotas which carried 25 000 gal of aviation fuel intended to refuel the 16 B-25 Mitchells which attacked Tokyo on 18 April (see p. 134). As none of the B-25s arrived intact, the fuel was available for the AVG's P-40Bs and P-40Es, all of which were now based in China.

The main task of the AVG, as decreed by Chennault, **was the destruction of Japanese aircraft** and the pilots were paid bonus money for confirmed kills. Over 300 JAAF aircraft were claimed up to 4 July 1942, when the AVG's contract expired, but by that time the P-40s had also given close support to the Chinese Army in western China. The USAAF took over the AVG's role in July and Chennault, recalled to the Service, took command of the China Air Task Force.

The China Air Task Force was perpetually short of fuel, but the four squadrons of P-40s and the single squadron of B-25s were used boldly to attack JAAF airfields and shipping in the harbours of Hong Kong, Canton and Haiphong.

Few military commanders have employed such slender resources with such imagination and to such effect as did Chennault.

The most efficient air freight unit to operate between Assam and Kunming was the China National Aviation Corporation, a civil airline leased by the US Army in September 1942. From October, deliveries increased to over 800 'short tons' (1 short ton = 2000 lb – 910 kg) for the first time. By January 1943 the figure had risen to over 1260 tons and the USAAF Air Transport Command had become the main service operator, using Curtiss C-46 Commando and converted B-24 Liberators as well as Dakotas. By September 1943, ATC had 225 aircraft in Assam, only 82 of which were Dakotas, and this fleet delivered an average of 23 tons per aircraft per month; in the same month the 23 Dakotas of CNAC delivered 49 tons per aircraft. The 6330 tons delivered in this month still fell below the requirements for Chennault alone.

C-46 Commando of Air Transport Command on the 'Hump' route showing the inhospitable country.

The most remote American island base, Wake Island, fell to the Japanese Navy on 23 December 1941. The air garrison of twelve USMC Grumman F4F-3 fighters and a single battery of 3-in AA guns could not be expected to stave off for long the JNAF medium bombers from the Marshall Islands or reinforcements of carrier aircraft. Nevertheless, the Marine pilots destroyed half a dozen bombers and sank **the first Japanese surface warship to be destroyed by American aircraft – a destroyer.**

Japanese fast carriers also assisted in the occupation of Rabaul, on 22 January 1942, this naval air base in New Britain becoming the most important Japanese outpost in the south-west Pacific. The subsequent expansion in the area was intended to ensure its security.

The first offensive action by US Navy carriers occurred on 1 February 1942, when two ships sent 92 bombers to attack airfields and shipping in the Gilbert and Marshall Islands. Two merchant ships were sunk and eight others (50 000 tons) damaged, while fourteen aircraft were destroyed for the loss in action of eleven Douglas Dauntless dive-bombers.

The efficiency of the JNAF's maritime reconnaissance was well demonstrated on 20 February – the day after they had struck devastatingly at Darwin – when the carrier USS *Lexington* was approaching to attack Rabaul. Flying boats located the force 375 miles east of Rabaul and summoned a raid by 18 Mitsubishi 'Betty' bombers. In spite of radar warning and fighter patrols, the bombers got through to near-miss the carrier before all were shot down by F4Fs, **Lieutenant E O'Hare becoming the US Navy's first 'ace' during** the action.

The Japanese invaded Papua early in March in order to establish an outer defence perimeter for Rabaul. Port Moresby was their main objective, but an Australian P-40 Kittyhawk squadron defended Port Moresby single-handed between 19 March and 28 April 1942, preventing the almost daily medium bomber raids from Rabaul from inflicting major damage on the rapidly expanding Allied base.

Rabaul was the target of the first sustained Allied bomber offensive in the Pacific. RAAF bombers made small-scale night raids, while from April 1942 the USAAF sent B-17s and Martin B-26 Marauders to attack by day. The results of the 140 daylight sorties in April and May were not encouraging, but the Japanese were forced to retain a large number of fighters at Rabaul instead of being able to deploy them to gain complete air superiority over Papua.

The first USAAF fighters (P-39s) arrived at Port Moresby towards the end of April. Vastly inferior though they were to the 'Zeros', their presence decided the Japanese to invade Port Moresby from the sea; a naval landing force occupied Tulagi Island in the Solomons, as a preliminary, to establish a reconnaissance seaplane base.

These moves provoked the first carrier-versus-carrier battle. Warned by its Intelligence organisation, which had broken the Japanese naval cypher, the US Navy moved two carriers into the Coral Sea while the Japanese provided a light carrier to cover the invasion convoy and two large carriers as heavy cover. The battle was fought in three separate phases between 4 and 8 May 1942, opening with an attack by *Yorktown* on Tulagi, where several ships were sunk and the air reconnaissance force destroyed. *Yorktown* and *Lexington* then moved west to block the route to Port Moresby from Rabaul and on 7 May *Yorktown*'s aircraft sank the small *Shoho*, **the first Japanese carrier to be sunk.** The climax of the Battle of the Coral Sea occurred next day when the opposing carrier task forces struck simultaneously at one another. The two

The light carrier Shoho, *already on fire from bomb hits, takes a torpedo amidships during the Battle of the Coral Sea.*

American ships launched a total of 69 attack aircraft in two separate and unco-ordinated strikes, whereas the 51 Japanese dive- and torpedo-bombers attacked as a single force, which overwhelmed the ineffective US Navy long-range air defence. *Yorktown* received moderate bomb damage, but *Lexington,* was hit by two torpedoes as well as bombs. Although able to steam and operate her aircraft, the latter was lost later in the day as the result of a petrol explosion and subsequent fires. *Yorktown*'s strike inflicted severe bomb damage on *Shokaku,* but *Zuikaku* escaped without damage.

Japan itself had been attacked on 18 April 1942, sixteen B-25 Mitchell medium bombers taking off from USS *Hornet* to raid Tokyo and three other cities. The surprise attack inflicted little damage, but the moral effect in both Japan and America was considerable. The potential striking capability of the US carriers was therefore a menace which the Japanese Navy wished to eliminate as soon as possible.

The setting for a decisive battle was to be the seas around Midway Island, 1300 miles (2080 km) west-north-west of Pearl Harbor. An invasion force, covered by four large carriers, approached the island at the beginning of June, while two other carriers made diversionary attacks on the Aleutian Islands. The US Navy was again prepared, thanks to the 'code-breakers', and three carriers were despatched to cover Midway. The island itself was reinforced, and on 4 June the US Navy had available 232 carrier aircraft plus 82 USAAF, USMC and USN aircraft on Midway, to oppose 254 Japanese carrier aircraft.

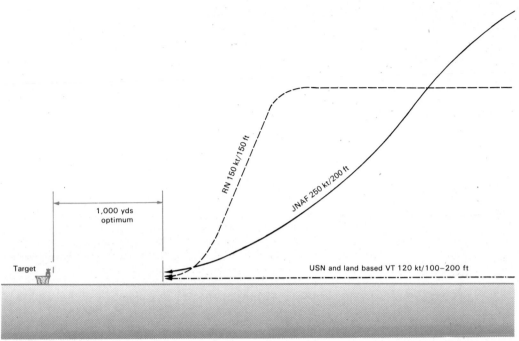

1,000 yds
optimum

RN 150 kt/150 ft

JNAF 250 kt/200 ft

Target

USN and land based VT 120 kt/100–200 ft

Torpedo Attack Profiles 1940–2
The characteristics of torpedo aircraft and of their weapons dictated tactics, the Royal Navy's slow biplanes being obliged to dive to the release point, the US Navy, handicapped by a poor torpedo, attacked at low level and a vulnerable speed while the Japanese, unfettered by aircraft or torpedo restrictions, were able to attack and release at high speed.

The Battle of Midway began on 4 June with a dawn strike on the island, in which the Japanese strike and escort destroyed sixteen out of the island's 28 USMC fighters and inflicted moderate damage on the base. At the same time, the 53 Midway-based B-17s, dive-bombers and torpedo-bombers made piecemeal attacks on the Japanese carrier force, losing seventeen of their number but failing to score hits. Inefficient reconnaissance failed to locate the American carriers before the latter launched their strikes, and in mid-morning dive-bombers from *Enterprise* and *Yorktown* inflicted fatal damage on *Akagi*, *Kaga* and *Soryu*. Douglas TBD Devastator torpedo-bombers from all three US carriers had attacked earlier, but had succeeded only in drawing the 'Zeros' out of the Dauntlesses' way – only six of the 35 Devastators escaped. The undamaged Japanese carrier struck back with dive-bombers and torpedo-bombers, seriously damaging *Yorktown*, but *Hiryu* was then put out of action by American dive-bombers, sinking on the following day. *Yorktown* was finished off by a submarine three days after the carrier battle. With the loss of all four carriers, the Japanese abandoned the Midway operation. **The battle had been decisive, but the result was unexpected.**

Allied air superiority over Papua was achieved in August 1942, following the Allied invasion of Guadalcanal. Realising the threat posed to Rabaul by the occupation of the airfield on the island, the Japanese reacted swiftly to the invasion on 7 August. On that day and the next, 67 JNAF bombers attacked the shipping off the beach-head, but Grumman F4F-4 Wildcats from three carriers and the ships' own AA gunfire destroyed 36 bombers and several escorting

'Zeros'. **The first premeditated suicide attack** was delivered by two Aichi 'Val' dive-bombers, which hit and destroyed a transport off Guadalcanal, but the loss of over 40 aircraft in two days effectively drew the teeth of the Japanese Eleventh Air Fleet.

The first ferry carrier operation by the US Navy in the Pacific saw the delivery of USMC Wildcats and Dauntlesses to Henderson Field, Guadalcanal, from the escort carrier (CVE) *Long Island*, on 20 August. Joined later in August by USAAF P-400 Airacobras, the Marine Corps aircraft supported the Marine troops fighting to drive back the Japanese from the American enclave and fought almost daily air superiority battles against 'Zeros' flying down from Rabaul. In these combats the honours usually went to the JNAF, though the 'Zeros' suffered heavy non-combat losses during the 1300-mile (2080 km) round trip.

The third carrier battle of 1942 was precipitated by a Japanese attempt to reinforce their troops on Guadalcanal. The Japanese carrier covering force, comprising three carriers with 174 aircraft, was opposed by three USN ships with 253 aircraft, but only two ships and 174 aircraft actually took part in the **Battle of the Eastern Solomons,** on 24 August. Like that in the Coral Sea, the carrier battle was a tactical draw, with the Japanese again losing a small carrier (*Ryujo*) and about 90 aircraft, while USS *Enterprise* was damaged and had to return to Pearl Harbor for repairs. **The strategic victory** was won on this occasion by USMC Guadalcanal aircraft and USAAF B-17s from the New Hebrides: on 25 August, Dauntlesses damaged two transports and B-17s sank a destroyer – **the first Japanese ship to be sunk by USAAF level bombers.**

A 'Kate' passes through the screen to attack the US carriers at the Battle of Santa Cruz, 27 October 1943.

The climax of the struggle came on 26 October, when the four Japanese carriers, which were to have supported the expulsion of the Americans from Guadalcanal, were engaged by the US Navy's two serviceable carriers in the Battle of Santa Cruz. On this occasion, the US Navy was seriously out-numbered, being able to oppose only 169 aircraft to the 207 of the Japanese, and the result was a clear tactical defeat, with USS *Hornet* sunk and *Enterprise* damaged and forced to withdraw. Dauntlesses put two enemy carriers out of action, and the Japanese lost over 100 aircraft, so that, although they could remain at sea, they could play no part in the Guadalcanal operation.

The decisive battles for Guadalcanal were fought during the second week in November 1942. The Japanese made a determined attempt to send 11 000 men in an eleven-ship convoy, supporting the movement by bomber raids from Rabaul and battleship bombardments of Henderson Field. Over 40 JNAF aircraft were destroyed on 11 and 12 November, and on the 13th the island's Dauntlesses and Grumman TBF Avengers sank the disabled Japanese battleship *Hiei*, damaged during the previous night's action. On 14 November, the reinforcement convoy came under attack from aircraft from Guadalcanal and *Enterprise*. Two small Japanese carriers operating to the north of the Solomons could do little to protect the convoy, which lost seven ships sunk. A supporting cruiser force also came under attack and one cruiser was sunk and three others damaged by USN and USMC aircraft. That night a battleship action resulted in the sinking of a second Japanese battleship, and on the following day repeated air attacks on the four remaining transports saw the end of the crisis. Fewer than 2000 Japanese soldiers struggled ashore on 15 November, lacking weapons, food and supplies. **American carrier and land-based air power** had swung the balance on Guadalcanal.

The first daylight raid by B-17s staging through Henderson Field took place on 18 November and was escorted by USAAF P-38 Lightnings, making their South-West Pacific début.

On Guadalcanal, Marine and USAAF aircraft gave continuous close support to the ground troops, using improvised petrol fire-bombs – **the fore-runner of napalm** – for the first time on 14 January 1943. JNAF strength at Rabaul had been just under 200 aircraft at the beginning of the year, but losses during January approached 100, with 36 shot down in the last three days of the month as they tried to cover preparations being made for evacuation. Only the arrival of some 50 JAAF fighters and reconnaissance aircraft enabled the 11th Air Fleet to continue in action while the Navy evacuated 13 000 men, between 1 and 7 February 1943.

Guadalcanal was the vital campaign of the Pacific War. The US Navy and Marine Corps, supported later by the Army, had forced upon the Japanese a war of attrition. America could make good her losses, but Japan's less developed industrial capacity and smaller population could not replace the sunken shipping or the crews of the 1000 aircraft lost during the six months of the Guadalcanal campaign. The JNAF alone lost 1960 aircraft in combat between December 1941 and February 1943; with them went the cream of the veteran air crews who had won the early victories.

At the turning point of the war the Allied air forces began to take a firm grasp upon their opponents with an air superiority based upon larger numbers more than technical superiority. The performance of typical aircraft in service was epitomised by the machines in the tables below. Comparison can be made with the table on page 85 to show how relatively slight was

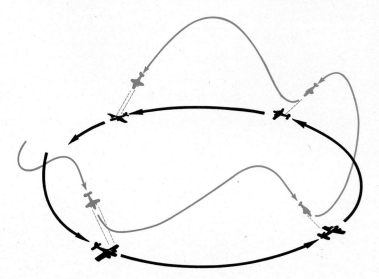

Fighting on the climb-and-dive. The tight-turning qualities of an opponent could be neutralized by a higher-speed aircraft utilising its rate of climb to describe an undulating circular flight-path which intersected the smaller radius at intervals.

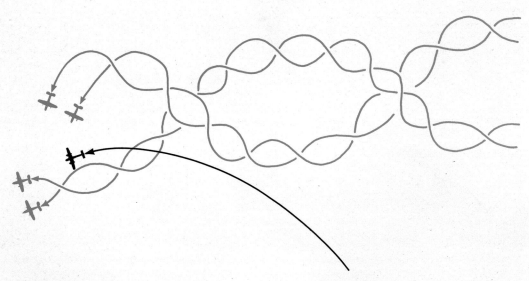

The 'Thatch-Weave', by which a pair of aeroplanes 'scissoring' were able to maintain a continuous watch on one anothers' tails. With pairs duplicating this manoeuvre mutual support against hostile aircraft attempting to interfere could be given at any point.

During the winter of 1943–4 the losses of RAF Bomber Command during night raids over Germany reached a peak. A radar-equipped Messerschmitt Bf 110G night fighter fitted with upwards-firing 'Schräge Musik' guns, puts paid to an Avro Lancaster bomber. Beneath a city burns.

the change since 1939, though tables cannot demonstrate techniques and the virtues of training and morale of the aircrews – and the latter was often the crucial imponderable in deciding battles.

Bombers 1942

Nation	Type	Max. speed	Ceiling	Range	Max. bomb load	Armament
British	Avro Lancaster B1	287 mph	7467 m	1730 miles	18000 lb	8 mg
German	Junkers Ju-88	269 mph	8200 m	1112 miles	2205 lb	3 mg
Italian	Cant Z1007	283 mph	7500 m	1367 miles	4409 lb	4 mg
Russian	Ilyushin DB-3F	255 mph	9000 m	2647 miles	3307 lb	3 mg
USA	Douglas A-20 (Boston)	342 mph	7391 m	1050 miles	2000 lb	5 mg
	Boeing B-17F (Flying Fortress)	299 mph	11400 m	1300 miles	8000 lb	9 mg
Japanese	Mitsubishi G4M2 (Betty)	272 mph	8950 m	1497 miles	2205 lb	2 cannon 4 mg

Fighters 1942

Nation	Type	Max. speed	Ceiling	Armament
British	Spitfire VII	408 mph	13106 m	2 x 20 mm 4 mg
German	Fw 190	408 mph	12000 m	4 x 20 mm 2 mg
Italian	Macchi C202	367 mph	13000 m	4 mg
Russian	Yakovlev Yak I	364 mph	12000 m	1 cannon 2 mg
USA	Bell P-39 (Airacobra)	368 mph	9784 m	1 37 mm cannon 4 mg
Japanese	Mitsubishi A6M (Zero)	332 mph	10000 m	2 cannon 2 mg

SECTION VI
The years of the holocaust
1943-5

The culminating targets for air power as the war moved into its final half were in Japan, but they had to wait while the overall Allied strategy was worked out in conformation with Anglo-American decisions which had been made when they formulated their initial plans at the beginning of 1942 during the Arcadia conferences. Before Japan could be attacked, her defences in depth, built upon the far outlying outposts seized in the initial offensive, had to be reduced, and that demanded an operation dominated by sea power and strongly influenced by the exercise of air power in advances that began from as far away as New Guinea in the south, India in the west and Midway in the east. However, prior to that, Germany was to be crushed, her armies defeated in the field with the aid of air power, her industry smashed by bombing and her U-boats' faltering stranglehold upon the sea lanes broken. Thus, on balance, air power tended to be more important over sea than over land, though it conditioned every warlike activity besides the economic and political considerations over which it threw an increasingly potent influence.

AIRCRAFT v SUBMARINES

The crisis of the Atlantic A/S battle came between February and May 1943, when the U-boats were committed to accepting heavy losses in order to penetrate strengthened convoy defences. Only seventeen Allied aircraft capable of operating in mid-Atlantic were available in February and, although the number had risen to 50 by May, this was still insufficient to fill the mid-Atlantic 'Gap'.

The employment of escort carriers on convoy escort duties swung the balance. USS *Bogue* was the first to see service in the 'Gap', but the first air-assisted kill by carrier aircraft was credited to Swordfish from HMS *Biter*, which sank *U-203* on 25

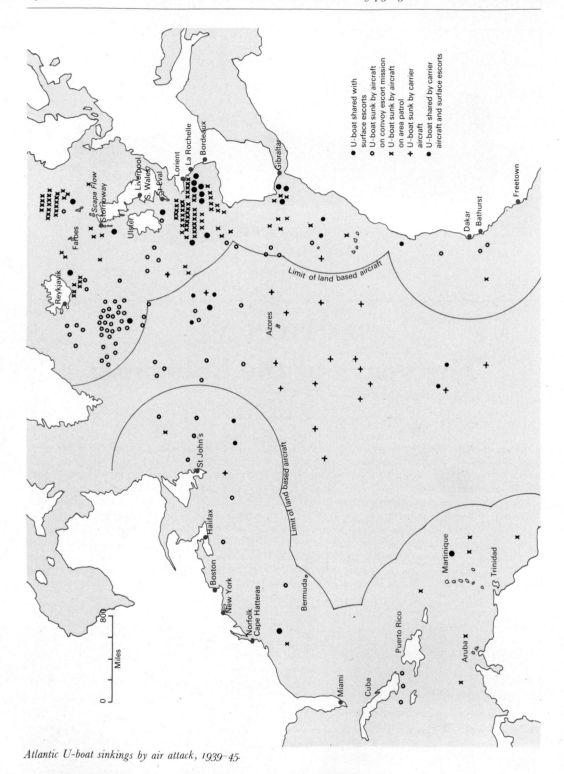

Atlantic U-boat sinkings by air attack, 1939-45.

April 1943. The carrier aircraft, aided by shore-based, very-long-range Liberators, denied the U-boats freedom of manoeuvre by day, preventing them from closing convoys on the surface or even from keeping in touch. Convoy losses fell from 72 merchant ships in March to 25 ships in April, while the U-boats lost heavily – fourteen to escorts (seven of them aircraft) and nine to patrol aircraft.

The Battle of the Atlantic was won in May 1943, when 36 U-boats were sunk in the Atlantic, 22 of them by aircraft. Of these aircraft kills, half were obtained by patrols in the transit areas – the Bay of Biscay and the Faeroe–Iceland passage. Equipped with 10 cm wavelength radar which gave a higher degree of bearing accuracy than the earlier ASV sets and, in a few aircraft, a powerful searchlight, the aircraft on patrol could locate and attack the surfaced U-boats by night and in bad weather.

The new A/S weapons claimed their first victims during May 1943. On 12 and 14 May, three U-boats were hit by air-launched acoustic homing torpedoes, and on the 23rd a Swordfish from HMS *Archer* sank *U-752* with rocket projectiles. The American homing torpedo represented a formidable advance, for no longer was absolute precision needed in the attack – once released in the swirl left by the diving U-boat, it would follow the noise of its prey's propeller. Between June and December 1943, carrier aircraft sank 25 U-boats in the Central Atlantic. Such was the scale of the air A/S effort, the transit time for U-boats between the Biscay bases and mid-Atlantic had been extended from three to five days in mid-1942 to up to twelve days by the end of 1943, and the crews were already exhausted by continual air alerts by the time they reached their patrol areas.

Beaufighters strafe a German convoy. Notice the barrage balloons.

In the campaigns against the Japanese and Italian submarine forces, the honours went to the Allied surface escorts and submarines, as the following table for the whole war shows:

Submarine Losses			
	German	Italian	Japanese
Air (solo and shared)	336	16	21
All other*	446	69	109

*Including those destroyed in air raids on ports.

MEDITERRANEAN AREA, 1943–5

From the beginning of 1943 Axis ability to take a decisive part in the air war over the Mediterranean area declined swiftly. The arrival of the British Eighth Army on the southern frontier of Tunisia brought Axis forces in that country under concerted air attack from two directions. Though individual German fighter units continued to take a heavy toll of Allied formations early in the year, the introduction of improved Allied air superiority fighters – notably Spitfire IXs – and the continual bombing by day and night of Axis airfields, steadily reduced resistance.

The first direct use of Allied fighter-bombers in battlefield support was made on 24 March 1943, when wave after wave of British fighter-bombers attacked the Axis anti-tank and artillery positions defending the Tebaga Gap on the flank of the Mareth line in Tunisia. Infantry and armoured vehicles were then able to pass through practically unscathed after what was the most effective use of tactical air power by the Western Allies thus far.

The sea routes to Africa were virtually closed to the Axis by Allied air and sea superiority, though during April 1943 a great force of German and Italian transport aircraft had been gathered in Sicily to continue supplying the forces in Tunisia. Between December 1942 and January 1943, for example, 19000 men and 4500 tons of stores were ferried. Against these activities, special Allied fighter patrols were established under the code-name Operation 'Flax'. **The**

Ju 52s caught in the Sicilian Narrows by USAF B-25 Mitchells.

The Me 323

first interception took place on 5 April, when US P-38s claimed eighteen transports shot down. Thereafter formations of Ju 52s, SM 82s, and giant six-engined Me 323s, were savaged regularly, while US heavy bombers raided the airfields in Sicily, claiming many others destroyed on the ground. By 22 April, when almost a complete formation of 20 Me 323s was shot down, total claims for transports destroyed had risen to over 400. While claims were frequently well in excess of actual losses, the cost to the Axis transport force, so soon after the Stalingrad disaster (see page 154), was crippling. The Allied air forces had gained complete air superiority and on 3 May the Axis ground defence began to collapse. Patrolling fighter-bombers prevented evacuation by sea; only a few personnel escaped by air.

The victorious Allies, their air forces now fully integrated to provide three major commands – strategic, tactical and coastal – prepared to move across to the north side of the Mediterranean in pursuit of their opponents. Escorted formations of US heavy bombers were already raiding Sicily and Sardinia by day, while RAF bombers attacked by night.

An exercise in the solo use of air power was begun on 7 June 1943, when a four-day series of concentrated attacks on the island of Pantelleria led to the island's capitulation to invading forces without a fight. A similar attack on Lampedusa achieved a surrender in one day from the demoralised Italian garrison. On 10 July 1943 Anglo-American forces made a major landing on the southern coasts of Sicily, aided by parachutists and protected by a constant air umbrella. While resistance on the ground stiffened, that in the air was demolished within days, and no great damage was done to ships of the invasion fleet by Axis aircraft. Yet, despite regular air attacks, it proved impossible to prevent the evacuation of a substantial part of the defending forces across the Straits of Messina to the mainland.

The first of the major allied landings on the mainland of Europe on 3 September in the far south of Italy was followed on 9 September by bigger Anglo-American landings at Salerno and coincided with **the last large-scale torpedo attack by the Luftwaffe** on the night of 8/9 September 1943, over 30 He 111s and Ju 88s attempting to strike at the British Fleet; but no hits were scored and at least twenty aircraft were shot down by the defences.

An extremely potent new weapon was used by the *Luftwaffe* on the day following the defeat of the torpedo-bombers. The Italian battleship *Roma*, on its way to surrender, was hit by a 3080 lb (1400 kg) 'Fritz X' guided bomb, released from high altitude by a Dornier Do 217. *Roma* was not, however, the first ship to succumb to guided missile attack, that doubtful honour having already gone to the

Ruhrstahl SD 1400 X radio-controlled bomb.

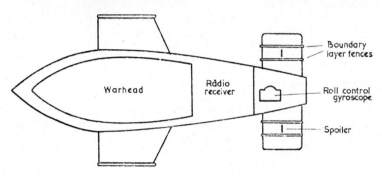

sloop HMS *Egret*, sunk on 27 August 1943 by an Hs 293 glider bomb, off the Biscay coast of Spain.

The first successful guided missile, the Henschel Hs 293, was a small tailless aeroplane which could be launched at a distance of up to 15 miles (24 km) from the target, allowing the launching aircraft (a Do 217, Fw 200, or Heinkel He 177) to remain clear of defensive gunfire while the bomb-aimer 'flew' the missile into the target. The 'Fritz X' was a simpler weapon, being an armour-piercing bomb with a tail incorporating aerodynamic control surfaces by means of which the bomb-aimer could correct the bomb's flight. It had no initial period of powered flight and thus the radio control was only a means of converting a wide miss into a near-miss or direct hit while the releasing aircraft had still to overfly the target.

Large numbers of Hs 293s were used against convoys in the Mediterranean and, principally, in the Atlantic, but only half a dozen merchant ships were sunk, in spite of attacks being made by as many as sixteen aircraft at a time, releasing their glider bombs at dusk. Both types of missile were finally defeated in the spring of 1944 by the Allied introduction of radio command jamming equipment aboard ships.

The last decisive Luftwaffe operations in the Mediterranean took place during late September 1943 over the Aegean area. On 13 September British forces landed on the islands of Kos, Leros and Samos, well within German-dominated territory and beyond the range of adequate air or naval support. A swift German reaction with all available air forces – including **the last successful use in daylight of the Ju 87 Stuka against the British** – was completely successful. All three islands were retaken by mid-October, with considerable British losses. US heavy bombers attacked airfields in Greece in support, but also suffered substantial losses to defending fighters. Thereafter a small but fierce air war was waged over the Aegean until mid-1944, as the Germans supplied and reinforced their garrisons there.

Allied Air Forces did much as they chose for the rest of the war after the remaining *Luftwaffe* fighter and fighter-bomber units were withdrawn in June 1944, leaving only a single night ground-attack *Gruppe* and some reconnaissance units, placing the defence of northern Italy in the hands of the recently formed air force of the new *Republica Socialista Italiana*. In June the Balkan Air Force was formed in Eastern Italy from RAF, Italian Co-Belligerent and Russian units, to aid Tito's partisans in Yugoslavia, but in July came the Warsaw uprising – with a call for aid from the Polish Home Army. From Italy RAF, South African and Polish heavy bombers and transports flew by night to drop supplies, but the range was great and the German defences strong. 93 sorties were made between 12 and 17 August, but seventeen losses were suffered, and the operation was called off, other than by Polish volunteer crews, which suffered further losses. Then, on 11 September, 107 US Air Force bombers tried dropping supplies from high altitude, but most drifted into the German lines. Only nineteen out of 1200 containers reached the Poles who surrendered soon after.

In Italy the war now was more than ever a ground-attack and close-support affair, all remaining fighter units being trained for the fighter-bomber role. Only over Yugoslavia was opposition in the air still met on any but the most occasional basis. Throughout the winter interdiction of the German supply lines in northern Italy continued unabated. On 9 April 1945 a concentrated air attack on the Eighth Army's sector of the eastern front was made by 825 heavy bombers, 234 medium bombers and 740 fighter-bombers and on 14 April a similar weight of attack was launched on the Fifth Army front in the west. Germany by then was in collapse, her armies everywhere in retreat, and a ceasefire took effect on 2 May.

STRATEGIC BOMBER OFFENSIVE

The introduction of new target location and marking devices at the beginning of 1943 – the 'Oboe' navigation aid, centimetric radar and special Target Indication bombs – resulted in the British Bomber Command attaining a satisfactory state of effectiveness due to improved guidance to the targets of the main bomber streams.

There were 738 'main force' RAF bombers, with an average lift of 2100 tons available for night raids, as well as 23 twin-engined Mosquitoes used for night target markings and daylight nuisance raids. The United States Eighth AF had 156 B-17s and B-24s ready to begin an offensive against the German aero industry and U-boat construction; the total lift of this force being about 230 tons. Against the bombers, the *Luftwaffe* could deploy 390 night fighters and 200 day fighters for the defence of Western Germany.

The first USAAF bombing attack on Germany was directed against Wilhelmshaven; 64 B-17s which attacked without fighter escort on 27 January 1943 hit the target and lost only three aircraft. A month later, seven B-17s were lost in an attack on the same target. The third attack on Germany inflicted serious damage on a U-boat shipyard in Bremen and only two of the 97 B-17s were lost. Such a contribution to the Allied anti-submarine war was extremely important.

Bremen was the scene of the Luftwaffe's first major success against the B-17s. On 26 April 1943, 107 bombers attacked the Focke Wulf factory and ran into fierce opposition, losing fifteen of their number to the Bf 109s and suffering damage to no less than 48 of the survivors. The first major strategic effect of daylight bombing was being felt by the *Luftwaffe* units outside the *Reich*, for fighters were now being transferred from the Eastern and Mediterranean fronts for the defence of the *Reich*.

Bomber Command opened the **'Battle of the Ruhr'** on 5 March 1943 with an attack on Essen, where 480 acres (192 ha) were destroyed or heavily damaged in one night. Essen, the home of the Krupp industrial empire, exerted a fascination on those responsible for targeting, and five attacks, involving 2070 sorties, were despatched thence between March and July 1944. Yet the city continued to function as a production centre in spite of the destruction.

The most effective raid during the Battle was that despatched to Barmen-Wuppertal on 29 May. Over 70 per cent of the 657 aircraft dropped their bombs within three miles of the aiming point and the damage covered over 1000 acres (400 ha). Duisburg, Aachen, Bochum and Düsseldorf also suffered heavily, but the total loss of production from the Ruhr was less than 10 per cent. The cost to Bomber Command was high: over 18 000 aircraft were despatched on 43 raids during the Battle of the Ruhr, and 872 failed to return while another 2126 were damaged. Bomber Command losses in June alone were 275 aircraft missing and 662 damaged. Not all were attributable to enemy action, but the **combined casualty figure was the highest of the war.**

The most spectacular feat of arms during the period was the destruction of two major dams, the Möhne and Eder, by a specially formed Lancaster squadron, on the night of 16 May. The bombers employed a novel weapon and technique for the attack and attacked at low level by night. In spite of the success of the mission, the effect on the industrial Ruhr's water supply was negligible.

Bomber Command came closest to achieving the object of Area Bombing between 24 July and 2 August 1943, when Hamburg was attacked by 3095 night bombers in four raids and 235 B-17s in two daylight raids. For the first time, Bomber Command employed 'Window' – a metallic chaff dropped from the aircraft which reflected the air warning and control radars on the ground as well as those of the night fighters, thus producing false 'echoes' which saturated the electronic defensive aids. The use of 'Window' produced a dramatic effect – only twelve out of the 741 aircraft which attacked Hamburg on 24 July were lost; on the basis of the previous 'main force' attacks on Hamburg, 48 aircraft could have been expected to be lost had the defences not been blinded. Two daylight attacks were made by B-17s and then came a second RAF **attack on 27 July which generated a horrifying phenomenon that was to be repeated only occasionally thereafter – the 'fire-storm'.** The high proportion of incendiary bombs dropped started fires which created convection currents with local wind strengths of up to 150 mph (240 km/h), providing draught for fires which reached temperatures of over 1000 °C (1832 °F). Over 40000 people died in Hamburg on 27 July – 13 per cent of the wartime total of German air-raid casualties. Apart from the high death toll and the devastation, the main

Hamburg – the fires of the city silhouette a Lancaster of the main force.

achievement of the raids was the dispersal of the work-force: by the end of August, only 35 per cent of the city's workers remained and two months later the figure had risen no higher than 70 per cent. Had this achievement been repeated against a handful of vital cities, then the area bombing campaign would have been justified, for German industrial output would have been seriously affected and the war brought to an earlier end. The confidence of the ruling hierarchy was severely shaken as well and nearly led to their collapse.

The first long-range fighter escort mission by Eighth AF fighters was flown on 28 July 1943, when over 100 P-47B Thunderbolts escorted B-17s from the Dutch frontier as the bombers were withdrawing from a raid on Kassel.

The strategic bomber forces scored significant victories on 17 August 1943, but at considerable cost. During the day, a two-pronged attack by 363 B-17s on Regensburg (Messerschmitt factory) and Schweinfurt (ball-bearings) scored damaging hits on the targets, but at a cost of 59 bombers. The 123 survivors of the Regensburg raid flew on to North Africa, where 55 B-17s were found to be damaged beyond the repair capacity of the newly established US Fifteenth Air Force. That night, 597 Bomber Command aircraft carried out **the first night precision bombing attack by the 'main force',** accurate marking being supplemented by radio instructions given by a 'Master Bomber', a new technique practised against a major target only ten days earlier. The target on this occasion was the rocket-weapon experimental station at Peenemünde, on the Baltic coast (see page 162 for development of these weapons). Severe damage was inflicted on the station, but the bombers also suffered heavily since this raid coincided with a change in *Luftwaffe* fighter control techniques. With 'Window' severely hampering the radar, the controllers now abandoned close control of the night fighters and, instead, broadcast to the fighters details of the bomber stream's route and target, when the latter became known. Each fighter was then left to find targets in the stream: with up to twenty bombers passing over a given point every minute, radar or visual location by experienced crews was not difficult. On this occasion, 40 bombers were destroyed and 32 others damaged – 12 per cent casualties – bringing Allied losses for the day to 99 'heavies' destroyed and over 100 damaged. Nevertheless, the German rocket programme was delayed – partly because of losses among technicians and plans – and a new kind of air warfare held back.

The most famous Eighth AF raid was that flown against Schweinfurt on 14 October 1943 – mainly because of the heavy losses sustained. Although P-47s had provided a round-trip escort to Emden on 27 September, the fighters could not carry the extra fuel needed to reach 400 miles (640 km) from their bases. Twenty-eight of the 291 B-17s were shot down before reaching the ball-bearing factories where the survivors inflicted severe damage on the targets. Another 32 were then lost on the way home. Of those that returned, only 93 were undamaged.

A new form of radio counter-measure assisted Bomber Command during its raid on Kassel on 22 October 1943. The German broadcast control frequency was monitored by German-speaking British operators in England and hoax messages to the night-fighter force were passed. The bombing of Kassel was effective, raising the second 'firestorm', but 42 of the 569 bombers were lost, mainly to fighters.

'The Battle of Berlin' was intended to mark the peak of the Area Bombing campaign. Air Marshal Harris had convinced the British Cabinet that if the USAAF joined Bomber Command in night raids on the German capital, then Berlin would be 'wrecked' and that at a cost of 400–500 aircraft the war would be won. In fact, this Battle, which lasted from 18 November 1943 until 24 March 1944, was a costly failure: the US Eighth AF was neither trained nor equipped for night bombing and the Schweinfurt losses had shown that unescorted day bombing was not a viable proposition; 581 Allied four-engined bombers were lost or damaged beyond repair in attacks on the city, the *Luftwaffe* having perfected their active defences. **At the end of the period Germany was producing more armaments than at the beginning.**

Sixteen major raids, involving 9111 sorties and sixteen 'nuisance raids', flown by 208 aircraft, were directed at the 883-mile^2 (1410 km^2) target. Although 48 factories were destroyed and 259 others damaged, the raids failed to inflict heavy casualties – less than 10000 – due to the vast size of Berlin, the strength of shelters and the efficiency of the civil defence authorities.

Nineteen raids were carried out against other German cities during the Battle of Berlin – Frankfurt-am-Main and Stuttgart four times each – for a total of 11113 sorties, from which 565 bombers did not return. In no attack did the damage inflicted approach that suffered by Hamburg or Kassel. During those months, in which Bomber Command lost 1146 night bombers, the German aero industry turned out nearly 9000 aircraft of all types.

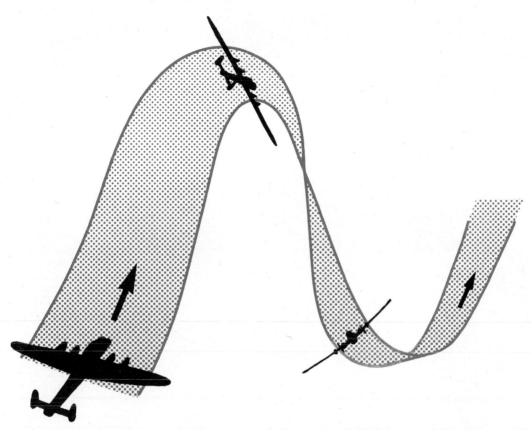

The 'Cork-screw'. By evading in elevation as well as azimuth the night-flying bomber rendered the task of the opposing night-fighter radar operator virtually impossible.

Bomber Command's heaviest individual defeat coincided with the end of the Area offensive. On 30 March 1944 an attack on Nürnburg inflicted relatively little damage, but the 294 German night-fighters airborne that night enjoyed their greatest individual victory, shooting down most of the 94 Lancasters and Halifaxes lost out of the 794-strong forces. Twelve more bombers were damaged beyond repair and 71 others less seriously damaged.

In 1944 the USAAF began a battle of attrition with the Luftwaffe, its strength in the European theatre being sufficient to permit the Eighth and Fifteenth Air Forces to adopt this policy. Over 2000 B-17s and B-24s operating from England and Italy would bomb factories and aircraft parks, while the P-47s, P-38 Lightnings, and the first P-51B Mustang Groups would find their 'killing ground' in the air around the bombers – a tactical policy paralleling the naval preference for convoy escort as a means of killing U-boats.

The first operation, on 11 January 1944, was a marked defeat. Bad weather in the Brunswick area prevented co-operation with the escort, and 60 of the 667 bombers were lost. The USAAF was not deterred and on 20 February the first sustained maximum effort offensive began – **the famous 'Big Week'.** Five attacks in six days attacked 26 aircraft factories, two as far distant as Poland, and cut

A B-17 over Messina.

production in the damaged plants by 20 per cent overall. Of the 3800 B-17s and B-24s despatched 228 were shot down, as were 28 fighters, but the *Luftwaffe* lost 355 of its 1000 front-line fighters and over 360 of its air crew, killed and wounded.

Only the superlative P-51 Mustang could provide round-trip escort to Berlin, and not until March were the two Fighter Groups ready for the 1150-mile (1840 km) mission. The Eighth AF made five daylight raids as its contribution to the 'Battle of Berlin', sending over 3000 bombers to attack individual targets within the city. On 6 March, 730 bombers with 796 fighters as escort attacked Berlin, but as fewer than 100 of the fighters could reach the target area the *Luftwaffe* was able to get through to the bomber 'boxes' and 69 were shot down – **the highest casualty toll for any Eighth AF mission.** *Luftwaffe* day-fighter losses were similar to those in previous months and the pilot-training organisation was unable to replace the lost men, many of whom were the highly experienced 'aces' of earlier campaigns outside the *Reich*.

The war had not been won by strategic bombing alone by the end of March 1944, when the priority for attack was shifted from Germany. Instead, the bombers were to prepare the way for the invasion of Europe, destroying the enemy's lines of communication in order to ease the task of the oldest of all war-winning arms – the soldier fighting on his enemy's territory.

Over a quarter of a million tons of bombs were dropped on 'transport' targets during 1944, not including the tactical air forces' contribution. Railways and inland waterways throughout Western Europe were virtually crippled with precision day and night attacks on specific targets such as viaducts and canal levees, as well as marshalling yards and repair workshops. Bomber Command continued its ever-increasing sea-mining campaign in German waters, and contributed greatly to the German supply difficulties in the Balkans by mining the Danube in the narrows of the 'Iron Gate', in Hungary.

The invasion of France in June 1944 involved the employment of the strategic bombers in tactical roles (see page 160) and also in the prosecution of the offensive against **the most important target of all – Germany's fuel industry.** Up to D-Day, only 11 718 tons of bombs had been intended for oil targets. **The most famous raid** was the US Ninth AF's low-level attack on Ploesti, in Rumania, on 1 August 1943. Only 123 of the 177 B-24s sent out from Libya had returned to base and the output of oil was diminished for only a short period. Towards the end of May 1944, the Allied bombers began an intensive day and night campaign and on 7 July the two USAAF Commands sent over 1000 B-17s and B-24s to four separate oil-producing plants in the Leipzig area.

The *Luftwaffe's* **first rocket-propelled fighters** were deployed but, limited in effectiveness by an endurance measured in minutes, the Me 163B did not provide the sought-after answer to the USAAF day attacks. **They achieved their first interception of a B-17 formation** on 16 August 1944, over Leipzig, but the rocket fighters did not enter service in sufficient numbers to become more than an occasional nuisance.

Bomber Command delivered its first large-scale daylight strategic raid on Germany on 27 August 1944, when over 200 Lancasters, escorted by Spitfires from French bases, attacked the synthetic oil plant at Meerbeck. No bombers were lost and all production ceased for two months.

Luftwaffe day fighter losses to the Eighth AF defences had now reached such proportions that the *Reich* was becoming indefensible, particularly after the loss of the French and Belgian radar sectors of the defence network to the invading armies. Aviation fuel production in Germany and its dwindling empire fell from 35 000 tons to 7000 tons between July and the end of September, further restricting the employment of the fighter units, as well as that of the armies – although the interceptor Groups had priority.

The destruction of the railway system around the Ruhr also resulted in a serious shortage of coal and coke from September. Indeed, from November, further bombing would have been unnecessary as the shortage of fuel for industry was beyond redemption.

Bomber Command never abandoned Area Bombing and right up to the end of April 1945 urban areas remained the main target, in spite of the increased accuracy of bombing and the Allied agreement that specific targets – oil and transport – were to have priority. **The final firestorm was raised at Dresden in mid-February 1945,** when 804 bombers attacked with devastating accuracy, killing over 100 000 people – **the largest number to die in any single city under air attack.** By any standards, the bombing of Dresden was an act of barbarism which achieved no strategic success whatsoever. So impotent was the German night-fighter force, only 27 aircraft rose to intercept and the *flak* claimed the three bombers that failed to return. **The first jet fighters were met by the Eighth AF** as early as September 1944, but not until 1945 were they encountered in appreciable numbers. On 18 March, the largest number to engage one raid – 37 Me 262s – shot down eight out of 1122 B-17s and B-24s attacking Berlin and lost none of their own number to the 632 escorting P-51D Mustangs. For some time past, a proportion of the escort had been used to interdict *Luftwaffe* fighter airfields and this procedure proved to be the most effective defence against the Me 262, which was vulnerable while taking off and approaching to land. In March and April, P-51s claimed over 70 jets shot down, most of them near their bases. Yet the German jets might have been decisive had priority been given to them as fighters instead of, as happened, bombers. Too late the change was made.

The strategic air offensive did not begin to succeed in its primary objective until after the invasion of Europe, by which time the Allied force included 1450 four-engined night bombers with an average 'lift' of 5250 tons of bombs, and over 3500 B-17s and B-24s carrying 6250 tons. Of the 1 782 191 tons of bombs dropped by Bomber Command and the two USAAF bomber Air Forces during the 69 months of war, 65 per cent was dropped during the last eleven months – **after the invasion which was to have been rendered unnecessary** according to the theories of Douhet, Trenchard and Harris.

The cost of their error was prodigious to both sides: Bomber Command lost 7449 night bombers in action and 47 130 aircrew killed on operations; over 8000 others were killed in training accidents and on non-operational flights. **Ten per cent of all British and Commonwealth war fatalities were sustained by Bomber Command.** The USAAF lost 8067 four-engined bombers, but the casualties which they and their escorts inflicted on the *Luftwaffe* were heavy (although not to the extent claimed by the USAAF at the time): the *Luftwaffe* lost 2012 day fighters and 1291 aircrew during the first six months of 1944 alone. Seventy German towns and cities had been subjected to area attack and the half-million tons of bombs had inflicted over 1 000 000 casualties, a third of them fatal, and destroyed 3 600 000 homes, leaving about 7 500 000 homeless. The *Reich* was a desert, but strategic bombing alone had not defeated the Nazi régime.

EASTERN FRONT, November 1942–May 1945

The greatest German airlift of all time began on 24 November 1942 in an effort to supply the encircled Sixth Army at Stalingrad. From the start the *Luftwaffe* command entertained serious apprehensions concerning the feasibility of this operation, advising a *Luftwaffe*-supported breakout attempt in preference. This was directly opposed to Hitler's policy of never giving up ground which had been won, and was turned down.

To supply the army at least 500 tons per day needed to be flown in, at a time when the weather was breaking and a vastly increased air transport requirement was manifesting itself in the Mediterranean. To carry out the operation two major bases were set up. At Tazinskaya eleven *Gruppen* of Ju 52s and two *Gruppen* of Ju 86s – 320 aircraft – began the lift with 300 tons on the first day. Bad weather then reduced deliveries over the next two days to only 65 tons per day. From Morosovskaya six bomber *Gruppen* and two transport *Gruppen*, with a total of 190 He 111s, began operations on 30 November, when total deliveries to the airfield of Pitomnik, within the Stalingrad perimeter, reached 100 tons. Support for the airlift was provided by fighters, a single *Gruppen* of Ju 87 'Stukas' and 'tank-buster' aircraft.

Some of the 36000 Il-2 'Shturmoviks' to be built.

The greatest quantity of supplies flown in during the lift totalled 700 tons, carried in 450 sorties in the period 19–21 December, but already the whole operation was threatened. On 16 December Russian forces broke through the Italian Eighth Army on the Don, and headed for Rostov – threatening the two airlift airfields. Evacuation was ordered on 23 December, but then cancelled, and at dawn on the 24th Russian tanks rolled on to the almost undefended Tazinskaya runways. 108 Ju 52s and sixteen Ju 86s were flown out under fire, but 60 transports were lost. At Morosovskaya the He 111s reverted briefly to their bomber role, joining the Bf 109s, the Ju 87s and the 'tank-busters' in a series of attacks on the Russian columns which inflicted heavy losses and brought them to a halt. A German counter-attack re-took Tazinskaya, but early in January 1943 both bases had to be abandoned, the Ju 52s moving to Ssalsk and the He 111s to Novocherkask. These new bases were 60 miles further from the Stalingrad area, and so deliveries were adversely affected. Only on 31 December, 1 and 4 January did more than 200 tons reach the besieged troops.

During January a second strip was prepared within the 'pocket' at

Gumrak, while small numbers of four-engined Fw 200, Ju 290 and He 177 aircraft were despatched to aid in the airlift. It was all to no avail. The despatch of the supplies themselves was badly organised, and frequently what was sent was unnecessary and space-consuming. On 10 January a major Russian assault began to reduce the perimeter, and on the 16th Pitomnik airfield fell. Six Ju 87s and a *Staffel* of Bf 109s had been operating from here, the fighters having claimed no less than 130 victories, 33 of them by one pilot, Fw. Kurt Ebener. The six remaining fighters were flown to Gumrak, but the strip was not ready, and five were destroyed while attempting to land.

Conditions at Gumrak remained bad when it did open, the last landings here being made during the night of 21/22 January. It, too, was then overrun, and thereafter only air-drops could be made. Gradually contact with the defenders was lost as conditions within the pocket worsened, and finally on 2 February von Paulus, the German commander at Stalingrad, surrendered. In the period 24 November–31 January 1943, no less than 490 German transport aircraft were destroyed.

The most costly air battle of all time was fought on 5 July 1943, marking the opening of Operation *Zitadel* against the Russian salient at Kursk. The German plan for the offensive included a massive air strike at dawn by 800 bombers, Stukas and 'tank-busters' (Henschel Hs 129B mounting a 37 mm armament) escorted by some 270 fighters. Aware of the German plans, between 400 and 500 Russian aircraft took the air before dawn in a gigantic pre-emptive strike, designed to catch the Luftwaffe aircraft still on their airfields.

German 'Freya' radar sets gave warning of the approaching onslaught,

Hs 129B close-support aircraft with 37 mm cannon for tank-busting.

and while all the bomber and ground-attack aircraft were got off the ground and away to prevent their destruction, the fighters 'bounced' the serried ranks of Russian aircraft, taking a terrible toll. For minimal losses they claimed 120 victories during this first clash of a record day, which was to end with their claims having reached 432. Next day 205 more victories were recorded.

Meanwhile the unscathed *Luftwaffe* bombed and strafed the Russian defences in wave after wave, raining down new SD-1 and SD-2 bombs – containers of small, air-bursting fragmentation bombs, which inflicted casualties on troops in the open. But the Russians, having allowed the initial offensive to burn up much of its power, began launching a series of strong counter-attacks on the flanks, the first of these, on 8 July, being broken up by **the first massed employment of the Hs 129Bs.**

As the German offensive began to fade, news was received of the successful Anglo-American landings in Sicily and this led to the withdrawal of many *Luftwaffe* fighters once the Kursk offensive came to an end. Thereafter the remaining *Luftwaffe* units in Russia were scattered all along the front to give direct support to the Army. This proved particularly frustrating in so far as the still-substantial bomber force was concerned, for no more concentrated bomber operations were to be undertaken in the East. The remaining Ju 88s, He 111s and He 177s were to operate in a purely tactical role.

The Russian air forces were growing in both size and quality. Kursk had seen the introduction of improved fighter aircraft of the Yak-9 and La-5 type, while experience and better training facilities were seasoning the Russian pilots. While never able

A Russian Yak-9 Fighter.

to equal the best of the German fighter pilots, the Russians were becoming able to take a growing toll of the others. The sheer numbers involved also allowed the Russians to swamp the opposition at times, and on some fronts they were able to operate virtually at will. They used many obsolescent aircraft by night to support the myriad partisan armies behind the German lines, but of strategic bombing they were totally innocent.

The critical air situation in the West and over Germany led to the withdrawal of German air units, mainly from the Northern and Central Russian fronts, in an attempt to prevent the Western Allies gaining complete aerial supremacy. It was at that point, on 22 June 1944, that the Red Army launched its greatest offensive of the war against the German Army Group Centre.

Shturmoviks attacking German armour on the open Russian steppe.

Critical in this campaign was the total Russian air superiority. So weakened by withdrawals to the West had been the air support of the Central front, that on 22 June *Luftflotte* 6 had only 40 fighters to provide cover against some 7000 aircraft in five Soviet air armies! Operating in great profusion, Il-2s, Yaks, Lavochkins and Pe-2s overwhelmed artillery positions, anti-tank guns, observation posts, headquarters and supply areas, the *Shturmoviks* also helping to reduce the remaining, outnumbered German tanks.

The Russian advance all along the front began to pick off Germany's allies everywhere; only the Hungarians would continue to support the Germans right up to the final surrender. A German withdrawal from the Balkans virtually put an end to Croat involvement, also removing the 'Southern shield'. And as if the *Luftwaffe* fighters did not already have problems enough, they now found themselves faced on frequent occasions by the powerful escorted bomber formations of the US Fifteenth Air Force from Italy and shuttle flights between East and West of the B-17s from the Eighth AF.

By the latter part of 1944 a line of sorts had been re-established to defend the Reich territory, but still the greater part of the *Luftwaffe* was retained for home defence and for the war in the West. In the East total strength stood at eleven *Jagdgruppen*, some sixteen *Schlachtgruppen*, plus a variety of reconnaissance and night ground-attack units.

The last battles in the East opened in January 1945, following a series of devastatingly heavy *Luftwaffe* fighter losses in the West (see page 166). Hitler decided that the remaining forces could be better employed against the Russians and diverted six *Jagdgeschwader* against them. Their presence on this front at the close of hostilities, coupled with the apparent retention of a considerable fighter force in the East – an impression created by the re-equipment of the *Schlachtgeschwader* with Fw 190s – led the Russians to claim subsequently that the Allied air offensive in the West and the Normandy invasion had not led to the withdrawal of significant numbers of *Luftwaffe* fighter units from the East. The fact remains that, in the vitally critical summer of 1944, they were not there. Denuded of their experienced leaders by the fighting in the West, most of the *Luftwaffe* pilots were now less experienced and well trained than their Russian counterparts. Thrown into action largely in a ground-attack role, they achieved little, and their losses were frequently as heavy as they had been in the West.

As to the bombers, by 1944 they were all but gone. The calls from all fronts for fighters and more fighters had led to the production of nothing else. Many bomber crews had been retrained, generally as night fighters, or to fly the new jet Me 262s. The few that remained in their original role were practically impotent, such support as could be given relying almost entirely on the fighter-bombers. Even these, as in the West, were restricted in their operations during the latter months of the war by the crippling shortage of fuel.

WESTERN EUROPE, 1943–5

As the war swung firmly in the Allies' favour during 1943 firm plans for an Allied invasion of Western Europe were laid, and the formation of a tactical air force similar to that in the Mediterranean area became paramount. A substantial proportion of the squadrons of Fighter Command came together in November to form the Second Tactical Air Force. At the same time the Headquarters of the US Ninth Air Force arrived from the Mediterranean to form an American tactical air force of similar size and composition.

The main British striking arm was to be the Hawker Typhoon fighter-bomber, carrying **either rocket projectiles – a new British development** – or bombs. Air cover and additional fighter-bomber strength was to be provided by Spitfire IXs and Mustangs by day, Mosquitoes by night. The force also included a strong reconnaissance element, both tactical and photographic, while the bomber group was equipped with Boston and Mitchell light bombers, and by growing numbers of Mosquito VI intruder fighter-bombers. The Americans used their P-47 Thunderbolts for fighter and fighter-bomber duties, backed by smaller numbers of P-38 Lightnings. Light bombing was carried out by Havocs and Marauders, while this force also included several reconnaissance units.

Initial operations were flown against rail targets, river bridges and airfields, while a considerable weight of attack (11000 tons in three months prior to June, 98000 tons eventually) was also directed on targets code-named 'No-Balls'. These were launching sites under construction in the Pas de Calais area, which Allied Intelligence sources knew to be for the recently developed V-1 flying bomb (see page 162). Against bridges the fighter-bombers of the tactical forces proved most economic, requiring an expenditure on average of only 100–200 tons of ordnance to destroy one such target, compared to 640 tons required by level bombers. These forces were frequently joined by the strategic bombers in attacks on communications targets throughout France and the Low Countries, the rail system receiving priority treatment with devastating onslaughts on railway marshalling yards and the immobilisation of 1500 out of 2000 locomotives in the French *Région Nord* – partly from low-level attack and partly lack of maintenance facilities. During May 1944 a systematic series of attacks on the coastal radar facilities was launched, coupled with assaults on fortifications all along the Atlantic and North Sea coastline.

One of the most cunning and carefully planned deception operations of the war was undertaken by a force of Lancasters during the early hours of 6 June 1944. These dropped 'Window' to an extremely accurate pattern to give the impression on the German radar that an invasion fleet was approaching the Pas de Calais. It helped (in conjunction with other measures) to persuade the German High Command that the Normandy landings were no more than a diversion.

The last phase of the anti-submarine war began with the Allied invasion of France. U-boats fitted with the new 'Schnorkel' air intakes for submerged cruising brought the battle back into coastal waters. Here they were within range of all shore-based aircraft which, in co-ordination with surface vessels, were able to provide massive protection for convoys and could swamp any area where U-boats were believed to be operating.

The Allied invasion of Normandy began before dawn on 6 June when waves of Anglo-American paratroops and glider-borne infantry dropped behind the coastal defence belt to attack special objectives.

On the first day few *Luftwaffe* aircraft were seen. The result of the continual attacks on airfields in the coastal region had been to force the withdrawal of their units into the interior. By evening, however, 200 fighters had been rushed to France from Germany, Norway and other areas, and they would soon be increased by the arrival of *Jagd* and *Schlacht* units withdrawn from Italy and the Eastern Front. From 7 June onwards the *Luftwaffe* appeared frequently, and many hard battles were fought over the beaches and behind. Allied air strength was overwhelming, however, and losses inflicted on the Germans were catastrophic, whole *Gruppen* being virtually wiped out on occasions. At night the remaining *Luftwaffe* bomber

B-17s lower their undercarriages to slow down while dropping supplies to the French Resistance.

Allied paratroops reinforce the airborne formations during the early hours of D-Day.

force appeared, but was shot down by night fighters and gunfire.

The first air-force units moved in to the bridgehead on 20 June, though at this stage some diversion of effort became necessary. For no sooner had the invasion got under way than **the first assault on England by unmanned missiles** was launched. V-1s from the Pas de Calais began to fall around London and the south-eastern counties. Bombers and fighter-bombers were diverted to attack the launching sites, while some of the Second TAF's high-performance fighters – newly arrived Hawker Tempests, some Mustang IIIs and the Meteor **(the RAF's first jet fighter)** were employed to help intercept and shoot down these robot aircraft.

The advent of unmanned, reaction-propelled missiles in the German armoury stemmed from the interest accorded to them after the Versailles Treaty had forbidden possession of bombing aircraft and heavy artillery. A V-1 (FZG-76 in German terminology) first flew at Peenemünde in December 1942 and was foreseen by some as an eventual replacement for bombers. Launching sites were being emplaced for an attack on London throughout 1943 – a programme that was delayed by sustained Allied air attacks against the sites and on various factories throughout Germany. Preparations for the offensive were incomplete when the Allies invaded Normandy and, therefore, when the first salvo was prematurely despatched on 12 June, a mere ten bombs could be launched of which only four reached England. Three nights later 55 sites got 244 missiles away and thereafter the struggle was on with some 190 launchings a day. The British response was to establish defended belts of anti-aircraft guns (eventually 620 heavy guns soon to be equipped with **the first radar proximity fuses** so that their shells automatically exploded within lethal distance of the target, 1762 light guns and 200 rocket projectors), zones of fighter aircraft and last ditch barrage-balloon zones. The bomb, powered by a pulse-jet unit, flew

The 'Gyro' Gun-sight. The radius of the 'diamonds' set at the wing span of the target provided the range of the target to the lead-computing sight, angular motion of the target being tracked by the pilot and resolved by the gyroscopes to give a deflection value for firing.

between 3000 and 5000 ft (900–1500 m) at speeds of 320–400 mph (512–640 km/h) to a range of 250 miles (400 km) and carried a 2000 lb (990 kg) warhead. It could not engage pin-point targets and was only suitable against built-up areas. Most were launched from ramps (8893) but they could also be carried by aircraft (1600). Barely 25 per cent reached their target and it was the AA gunners, as they became more practised, whose 74 per cent of all kills in a single valedictory week topped the list of kills. Yet in Britain 6184 people died while only 185 members of the German launching regiment were killed by retaliatory bombing attacks. The attacks died away when the advancing Allied armies captured the launching sites, but bombs continued to be launched against many European cities. Then, on 8 September, **the first of a new and more powerful rocket** – the A-4 – was launched against Paris. Ten hours later London became a target for two more. But **the city which received most V missiles** was the main Allied supply port of Antwerp with 11988 V-1s and the vast majority of 1766 V-2s fired against Continental targets after 11 October 1944. Altogether over 14000 people were killed and 24500 injured in this one city. **The first victory by a jet-propelled fighter** was scored on 4 August 1944 by an RAF Gloster Meteor which tipped a V-1 into the sea. **The most improbable V-1 kill** was scored by the turret gunner of a Royal Navy Grumman Avenger on anti-E-boat patrol at night in the Channel area on 11 July.

The first successful A-4 rocket (or V-2 as it was better known) was launched on 3 October 1942. With its one-ton warhead, peak trajectory of 60 miles (96 km), speed of 2200 mph

Attaching the wings to a VI.

(3520 km/h) and range of between 190 (304 km) and 200 miles (320 km), it was thoroughly inaccurate as well as being temperamental. Out of 1600 launched against England only 1115 arrived and many of these only fell within an 11-mile (17 km) radius of the aiming point. Yet A-4 was a terror weapon, the harbinger of a new epoch in air warfare though situated only on the periphery of this history.

The massive overall strength of the Allied air forces allowed many diversions without undue cost to the effort in Normandy. For **the first of many occasions Bomber Command's heavy bombers were employed in a massed tactical assault** on German defences at Caen on 7 July – an attack with enormous morale impact but one whose deep craters later caused serious difficulties to advancing land forces in the devastated area.

The most celebrated German counter-attack , which began at Mortain on 7 August against the Americans, drew in nineteen squadrons of RAF rocket-firing Typhoons, flying 294 sorties to fire 2088 rockets and drop 80 tons of bombs. Though fighter-bomber pilots claimed over 80 armoured vehicles destroyed these were grossly exaggerated since the rockets had only a minute chance of killing the target. The main effect of the attacks was in destroying 'soft-skinned' support vehicles carrying fuel and ammunition and in preventing most logistic movement by day.

The defeat of the Germans in Normandy led to their pell-mell withdrawal to the Low Countries and the *Reich* frontier – harried all the way by air attacks against which *Luftwaffe* attempts at defence brought only more losses upon itself with little reward.

A major Allied airborne operation was launched on 17 September in an effort to end the war before winter arrived. A complete Anglo-American airborne corps was dropped by parachute and glider at Grave, Nijmegen and Arnhem with the intention of capturing vital bridges that would allow the Allied spearheads to pass

V-2 rockets ready for launching.

straight through Holland and plunge direct into northern Germany. The first two bridges were taken, but inclement weather restricted the build-up and the presence of German armoured units in the Arnhem area frustrated the paratroops (who, by necessity, could not have landed medium tanks by air) and prevented relief columns getting through in time.

Air power was demonstrated once more as a complementary weapon to the land battle. It could not prevent the successful German defence and local attacks, and following the capture of the Nijmegen bridge, though the *Luftwaffe* strove with everything it had, its efforts to destroy the bridge were futile – despite **the first major use of Messerschmitt Me 262 jet fighter-bombers.**

As autumn weather arrived, the Allied advance petered out, allowing gains to be consolidated, units to be rested, and the squadrons of the tactical air forces, which had frequently fallen beyond range of the front during the swift advance, to be brought up to new airfields, closer to the front. The British and Canadians concentrated on clearing the Belgian and Dutch coastal areas, and particularly the difficult polder country around the Scheldt estuary that had to be swept clean of Germans before Antwerp's vital port facilities could be utilised. These operations, including the invasion of Walcheren Island, involved the breaching of the sea dyke at Westkapelle by Bomber Command Lancasters with 12000 lb (5455 kg) bombs on 3 October.

Further south French and American aircraft neutralised and aided the gradual mopping up of German garrisons still holding out in the French ports, a few of these remaining until the end of the war. Weather during the autumn and winter of 1944/5 was particularly hard, greatly reducing aerial activity at this time.

The last offensive by the German Wehrmacht depended far more on the neutralisation of their enemies' air power by bad winter weather than the ability of the *Luftwaffe* to achieve local air superiority on merit. Because of the technical decline of its equipment, due to earlier mismanagement by Göring, Ernst Udet and elements in the aircraft industry, the *Luftwaffe* was outclassed in nearly all departments besides being outnumbered.

By careful husbandry, 500 sorties were possible on 16 December 1944, the first day of the offensive into the Ardennes, and for a while the ground attack swept all before it, under low cloud that denied the Allied tactical air forces the chance to fly in any numbers. On 23 December a spell of fine weather dawned, allowing massive tactical air strikes, backed up by attacks from the strategic bombers, to hit the Germans hard. By Christmas Day all were halted, and on 27 December they began withdrawing.

During November and December *Luftwaffe* losses approached 100 in a day on several occasions and on 24 December reached a peak with 106 pilots being reported killed, wounded or missing, with even more aircraft destroyed or badly damaged. Despite this, Operation *Bödenplatte* was planned and became:

The biggest Luftwaffe operation in the West during 1944–5. Launched before dawn on 1 January 1945, some 900 fighters and fighter-bombers attacked Allied airfields, mainly in the Second TAF area. Generally the Allies were taken by surprise, though some fighters were in the air on early patrols. Widely differing results were achieved and sources do not agree on the final figures. Allied losses are generally reported at just below 150 aircraft destroyed, with about 80 more damaged – in no way a mortal blow since some of the aircraft were not even operational types and most were destroyed on the ground; few pilots were lost. Within days most units were fully up to strength again.

For the *Luftwaffe* the story was much more serious. **The second heaviest losses ever suffered in a single day by this air force** occurred during the 'great blow', for not only were losses to Allied anti-aircraft and fighter defences severe, but as the German aircraft returned

A B26 hit by flak over Toulon.

over heavily defended areas of their own front at low level, they were fired on by 'friendly' *Flak*. The German gunners took the heaviest toll of all. Personnel casualties totalled 255, including nineteen unit commanders; total aircraft losses are unknown, but for the whole operation are estimated to have reached at least 300. Hereafter, little of the *Luftwaffe* was seen over the Western front during January and February 1945 since most aircraft had been transferred to the East (see page 159).

The only tactical use of the V-2 occurred during mid-March 1945, when 11 missiles were fired at the vital Ludendorff Railway Bridge over the Rhine at Remagen. Area bombardment weapons were unsuitable for the task and the American bridgehead was built up without delay.

The most successful large-scale Allied airborne operation was undertaken early on 24 March, in co-ordination with a water-borne crossing of the Rhine on the British front. 903 American and 669 British transport aircraft and glider tugs, towing 1326 gliders or carrying paratroops, were escorted by 679 US Ninth Air Force and 213 Fighter Command fighter aircraft; 1253 more fighters from the US Eighth Air Force patrolled over German territory, while 900 more from the Second TAF gave cover to the drop and landing zones. When it is considered that the Anglo-American air forces could put at least 3000 bombers into the air at this time in addition to these aircraft, and that these numbers took no account of the substantial forces available in Italy and southern France, some idea of the preponderance of Allied air power at this time can be gained. Against it the *Luftwaffe* still managed some last kicks, though with little effect, and the war came to an end with jet aircraft pointing the way to the future. Long after the Germans, **the first operational use over the front of Allied jet aircraft** was made by a single RAF squadron of Gloster Meteor jet fighters making ground attack sorties shortly before the fighting ended.

By the evening of 4 May 1945 action over most of Germany had virtually ceased, and on 7 May Unconditional Surrender in the West took place.

At this late stage in the war, with Japan still in contention, the revolution in aircraft performance compared with those at the beginning and in mid-term could be recognised – as comparison between the tables on page 85 and 140 with that given below will show.

Bombers – 1945

Nation	Type	Max. speed	Ceiling	Range with max. load	Max. bomb load	Armament
British	DH Mosquito IX	397 mph	11 000 m	1370 miles	5000 lb	—
German	Heinkel He 177	303 mph	7900 m	3107 miles	2205 lb 2 missiles	2 cannon 6 mg
Russian	Petlyakov Pe-8	280 mph	8850 m	3730 miles	8818 lb	2 cannon 4mg
USA	Boeing B-29	357 mph	9700 m	3250 miles	20 000 lb	1 cannon 10 mg
Japanese	Yokosuka (Frances) Y-20	367 mph	10 120 m	2728 miles	2200 lb	1 cannon 1 mg

Fighters – 1945

Nation	Type	Max. speed	Ceiling	Armament
British	Gloster Meteor III	493 mph	13410 m	4 cannon
German	Messerschmitt Me 262	541 mph	11450 m	4 cannon
Russian	Yakovlev Yak 3	403 mph	10800 m	1 cannon 2 mg
USA	North American Mustang P-51D	437 mph	12771 m	6 mg
Japanese	Nakajima Ki 84 (Frank)	427 mph	10500 m	2 cannon 2 mg

Bridge on the Burma–Thailand railway dropped by B-24 attack.

THE FAR EAST, 1943-5

The Supply War over the Mainland

The air war in Burma was quickly established as one in which supply was the main strategic consideration. The JAAF was not strong and its most destructive raid was a surprise attack on the main 'Hump' airfield in Assam, where nine Dakotas and twenty fighters were destroyed or badly damaged on 25 October 1942. And the rapid introduction of radar-equipped night fighters brought a Japanese night-bombing offensive against Calcutta to a sudden end in January 1943. British bomber operations, for their part during the Arakan campaign in 1943, were nearly all in support of the Army and **pioneered a new technique** of bombing targets hidden by the jungle canopy and indicated by artillery smoke shells.

The only strategic bombing target in Burma was Rangoon, the main entry port for Japanese supplies. Against strong opposition USAAF B-24s by day and RAF Wellingtons and Liberators by night attacked the harbour area, warehouses and railway marshalling yards. Far more effective were the B-24 minelaying operations off Rangoon and Moulmein, first undertaken in February 1943.

The second most bombed target in Burma was a rail bridge south of Mandalay, no less than 543 tons of bombs being dropped on it in 1943, 337 USAAF bombers scoring eighteen hits to put it out of action for a total of eight months. Yet five other bridges survived nearly 500 tons without damage.

The first heavy bomber unit to be based in China arrived in March 1943, but its first mission was not flown until 4 May as the B-24s had first to freight their own fuel, spares, personnel and bombs over the 'Hump' from Calcutta. Also in March, the USAAF units in China became the Fourteenth Air Force, commanded by Chennault, who had previously been subordinate to the India-based Tenth Air Force.

The JAAF made a serious attempt to disrupt the 'Hump' air traffic in October 1943, intercepting the unarmed transports *en route* after raids on Kunming and Yunnanni airfields had failed with heavy losses. Eight C-46s were shot down in the fortnight up to 27 October, but on that day a dozen JAAF fighters attacked what they took to be a formation of C-87 Liberator transports; Liberators they were, but actually B-24s engaged on a freighting run whose gunners destroyed eight Ki 43 'Oscars' before the latter realised their mistake.

The first joint American-Chinese air units entered combat in November 1943 and were immediately used in support of the Chinese Army defending the Changsha sector. Previous Chinese Air Force operations had been severely limited by the lack of aircraft and the few operational units had been based in north China.

Operations which depended almost entirely on air supply were the penetrations by 'Chindits' to disrupt Japanese lines of communications. In north Burma 9052 men and 1359 mules were flown into two jungle clearings by glider and Dakota between 5 and 11 March 1944. Like a smaller 'pilot' operation a year earlier, the operation failed in its object although the USAAF and RAF air support was completely successful, flying in over 1200 tons of supplies and evacuating many sick and wounded. **The last Japanese offensive in Burma** began in March 1944, after the 'Chindits' had been flown in behind the Japanese lines. The Third Allied Tactical Air Force defeated the Japanese attempt to win air superiority in February 1944, thanks in large

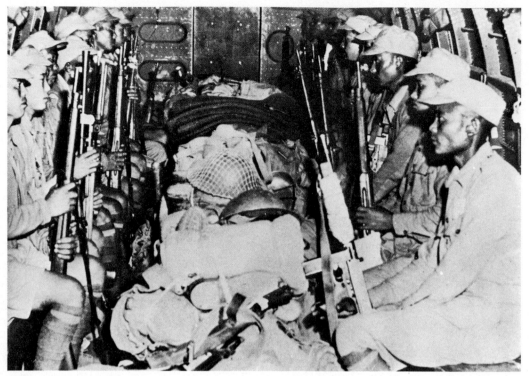

Operation 'Grubworm' in early 1945 when two complete Chinese Army divisions were flown from Burma to China to defend Kunming against the last Japanese offensive.

measure to the activities of **the first Spitfire squadrons to operate in Burma,** but this did not prevent the Japanese Army from besieging the vital Allied base of Imphal and advancing on Kohima – the nearest rail terminus. RAF close-support aircraft bombed to within 100 yd (90 m) of their own front lines to hold the enemy, flying from the airstrips within the Imphal perimeter.

Air supply was again the key to victory. Allied transports and bombers flew in 18 300 tons of supplies and 12 622 reinforcement into Imphal between 1 April and 23 June 1944 and evacuated over 10 000 wounded. Allied attacks on Japanese transport resulted in the besiegers facing starvation by the time that they began their precipitate retreat. In sharp contrast was the Allied siege of Myitkina: Chinese troops around the city were supplied entirely by air between May and August 1944.

The cumulative effects of the attack on Japanese shipping in the South China Sea, mainly by USN submarines but with an ever-growing Fourteenth AF contribution, forced the Japanese to open a major offensive in China in April 1944, the object of which was to drive a corridor through Honan and Kwangsi provinces to Indo-China, to open a rail link to South-East Asia via Hanoi. The axis of the advance cut through the line of Fourteenth AF airfields. American and composite units inflicted heavy losses on the JAAF and the Japanese Army,

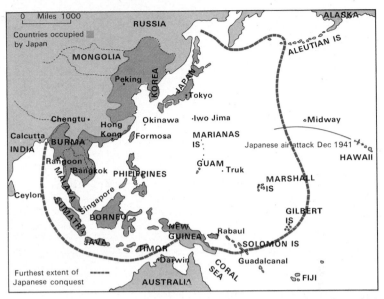

The Pacific Theatre of War showing the Japanese expansion and the bases from which the air assault on Japan was launched.

but the former still managed to provide effective close support and the battle-weary Chinese Army gave way.

The crisis for the Fourteenth AF came in May 1944. Less than 3000 tons of fuel had reached Kunming for the Fourteenth AF in April, and rickety transport in China resulted in delays of over a month between arrival at Kunming and receipt at the forward airfields. Consumption was heavy during the Japanese offensive and after another poor delivery in May, the units in the east were so short of fuel that B-25 operations had to be halted. Over 10 000 tons of fuel were delivered for Chennault in June 1944, but this had come too late and took too long to be moved forward to allow the bombers to be able to stop the Japanese from forcing their way through.

The corridor provided a 'killing ground' for the fighter-bombers and bombers of the Fourteenth AF, which moved to new airfields which paralleled the axis to landward and seaward. Japanese traffic was bombed and strafed whenever the weather permitted, the JAAF proving powerless to prevent the attacks.

Guided bombs were used for the first time in Burma on 27 December 1944, when USAAF B-24s scored hits on a railway bridge with 'AZON' bombs. The bombardier could make only left/right corrections – *Az*imuth *Only* – to the bomb's flight so that the weapon was best suited to targets with greater length than breadth, such as bridges and ships in harbour, both of which were attacked with great success. The strategic air forces extended their raids into Thailand in 1944, bombing Bangkok and the railway into Burma. On 5 June 1944 **the first Boeing Superfortress (B-29) mission** had as its target the Bangkok railway workshops.

The prime necessity for bomber operations from China was that they should be self-supporting. B-29 bases were built at Calcutta and Chengtu, at vast expense, and a separate air supply organisation was formed to carry all fuel and material to China; certain air stores which were in short supply had to be flown all the way from Casablanca by the Twentieth Bomber Command transport echelon.

The first B-29 arrived at Calcutta on 2 April 1944, having flown out via Britain and Libya. The first arrivals were immediately pressed into service as transports, some of them being stripped of combat equipment to carry seven tons of fuel, compared with only three tons in the standard aircraft.

The first B-29 raid on Japan was timed to coincide with the invasion of Saipan (see page 179), the purpose of which was the acquisition of B-29 bases closer to Japan than Chengtu. Sixty-seven B-29s, each loaded with four 500 lb (230 kg) bombs, left the Chengtu airfields on 15 June 1944 for a night attack on the steel works at Yawata on Kyushu, 1550 miles (2480 km) distant. Seven B-29s were lost and ten had to turn back, most of them with the engine defects which were to plague operations until the end of the year.

The first successful raid by Twentieth BC was a daylight attack on the steel works at Anshan, in Manchuria. Sixty-five out of 95 B-29s bombed the primary target without loss, but one of a pair attacking Chenghsien was damaged by AA fire and then finished off by JAAF fighters. **The B-29s' first victory** was scored on the next mission from China, a night-fighter being shot down during an ineffective incendiary raid on Nagasaki on 10/11 August – a raid which coincided with the equally unsuccessful attack on Palembang (see page 173).

The JAAF instituted ramming attacks on B-29s on 20 August, when two were destroyed by a single fighter in daylight over Yawata. Two more B-29s were destroyed by enemy action and ten were lost 'operationally' out of 88 despatched.

Two more missions to Anshan were flown in September, and improved bombing accuracy resulted in the production loss of nearly half a million tons of steel to the Japanese – **the greatest contribution made by Twentieth Bomber Command.**

Increased fuel deliveries in late September and early October enabled the Command to schedule over 280 B-29 sorties from Chengtu in October 1944. The Joint Chiefs of Staff required the B-29s to support the invasion of Leyte, and on 14 October 104 aircraft dropped 650 tons of bombs on a JNAF airfield on Formosa, the raid coinciding with attacks by Task Force 38 carrier strikes (see page 182). Another, smaller raid on Formosa two days later was followed by the first of five raids on aircraft factories at Omura, Kyushu, where more than five months' production was lost due to the bombing.

The first successful fire-raising attack by B-29s was directed against the city of Hanchow and was the only mission undertaken in direct support of land operations in China.

Overall the B-29 strategic offensive from China bases was a failure. Over 41 000 tons of stores had been flown into Chengtu in ten months to mount 1045 B-29 sorties on fourteen missions to Kyushu and Manchuria. Only 700 aircraft bombed their primary targets, 400 of them being forced to use radar for aiming, so that less than 600 tons of bombs were known to have been dropped on the briefed targets identified by the bomb-aimer. The raids on Formosa and Hanchow were more successful, but they were not what the B-29 had been deployed for and the results did not justify the diversion of so much fuel from the Fourteenth Air Force – over 6000 tons during the crucial period during the summer of 1944.

The JAAF made only two attempts to raid Chengtu, both in September 1944, but two day-fighter groups (144 aircraft) and a night-fighter squadron were tied down for the defence of the bases, whereas the Japanese air forces withdrew only 115 fighters from overseas for the defence of Kyushu. One hundred and forty-seven B-29s were lost from all causes up to the end of January 1945, the majority due to non-combat causes.

The Sumatra oil refineries were the most important left to Japan by the end of 1944. The Borneo oil installations had been bombed and shipping attacked since 1943, but the remoteness of Palembang from British bases had prevented attack, apart from one unsuccessful B-29 raid. In January 1945, a Royal Navy carrier force delivered attacks on the two main refineries and reduced the output by two-thirds; nearly 140 JAAF aircraft were destroyed in exchange for 25 carrier aircraft. **The operation was the Royal Navy's greatest contribution to the victory in the Far East,** coming at a time when Japan was already suffering from a severe fuel shortage.

The last Japanese offensive in China opened in April 1945, the objective being Chihkiang. Two B-25 squadrons and four fighter squadrons provided all the air support for the Chinese Army during the 51-day campaign, the 80 aircraft flying over 3200 sorties, firing nearly four million rounds of 0·50 in ammunition and dropping 95 tons of bombs in this vital period while the Chinese Army held firm.

The overland route from Burma to China was re-opened in February 1945 after the capture of Ledo. But deliveries via the 'Ledo Road' during the first three months came to only 55 546 tons, 40 293 tons of which was accounted for by the weight of the vehicles themselves! The 'Hump' airlift brought in 55 286 tons in June alone, and the peak of over 71 000 tons was reached the following month.

The B-29s returned to China in March 1945 for two minelaying missions over the Yangtse River, but the 22 sorties took off from Luliang, a Fourteenth AF base. The last Twentieth BC raid was a low-level night incendiary attack on Singapore's main oil fuel depot on 29 March. After this, the aircraft were transferred to the Marianas, the base for the culminating B-29 offensive against Japan as the advancing Allies closed in on the heart of the Empire.

THE DESTRUCTION OF THE JAPANESE EMPIRE

The Japanese evacuation of Guadalcanal in February 1943 left the Allies in firm possession of good bases in the south-west Pacific. The pressure on Port Moresby had been reduced and, with the full commitment of local Japanese air strength to support of the Guadalcanal campaign, the Allied air forces in New Guinea were able to go over to the offensive. USAAF B-17s continued to attack Rabaul, but rarely were sufficient aircraft available to provide the number of bombs needed for effective bomb patterns. **The first daylight mission** was not flown until 5 October 1942; and the greatest number of B-17s in any operation was 30, which went out on 9 October. The results against shipping were particularly poor and so, in an attempt to improve accuracy, selected B-17 crews made low-level attacks on ships in Rabaul harbour, scoring hits on their first moonlight attempt on 23 October. Fully developed, and practised by more suitable aircraft, **skip-bombing tactics such as these became the most effective form of anti-shipping attack by Air Force aircraft.** At the same time, the effectiveness of low-level attacks on airfields was much improved by the use of **parachute-retarded fragmentation bombs** – 'para-frags' – which prevented the bombs from ricochetting past the target and then exploding under the releasing aircraft. Douglas A-20 Havoc attack bombers used this weapon for the first time against Buna in September 1942.

The Allied advance on Buna took the form of several thrusts, all through jungle and mountain terrain, and the columns were supplied almost entirely from the air, by parachute, free drop, or from the many small airstrips hacked out of the bush by engineers accompanying or preceding the troops. Australian Wirraways spotted for artillery shoots during the siege, and these were the most effective direct-support missions since air-ground liaison was generally unsatisfactory, due largely to the inexperience of the pilots in working closely with the Army. As during the build-up, **the greatest contribution was made by the supply aircraft, which delivered nearly 2200 tons** of rations and supplies, including vehicles and two batteries of medium artillery.

The Japanese Army had not abandoned hopes of reaching Port Moresby overland and even as Buna was under siege the main base in New Guinea – Lae – was reinforced and Wewak and Hollandia were occupied.

However, the push towards Port Moresby was stopped at Wau by a small Australian force which had been supplied entirely by air since June 1942, and which was now further assisted by the delivery of 2000 men in two days. Wau was also the scene of severe air fighting, from which the USAAF and RAAF emerged victors, P-40s and P-39s claiming 24 out of 48 JAAF aircraft shot down, without loss to themselves, on 6 February alone.

Nevertheless, wildly optimistic claims by JAAF fighter and bomber crews led the Japanese command to believe that the Allied air forces were seriously weakened, and a convoy of eight slow transports escorted by eight destroyers and strong fighter patrols was sent to Lae on 28 February 1943.

The 'Battle of the Bismarck Sea' opened on 2 March with attacks by sixteen B-17s which dropped bombs from 6500 ft (1950 m) to sink one transport. The following day, RAAF Beauforts, Beaufighters and A-20 Bostons joined USAAF B-25s and A-20 Havocs in a series of co-ordinated low-level attacks, with two waves of B-17s attacking from medium level. Six more transports were sunk by the bombers, as well as four destroyers. The Japanese fighters fought fiercely, concentrating on the B-17s, but the P-38 cover and bomber gunners destroyed twenty, for the loss of three P-38s and a B-17. The one remaining transport was sunk after nightfall by American motor torpedo boats.

This victory ranks with the destruction of the Guadalcanal-bound convoy in November 1942 (see page 137) as a decisive stage in the war in the south-west Pacific. Thereafter the Japanese adopted a defensive strategy in New Guinea, which was intended as an outpost for the main base at Rabaul. JAAF losses since 5 January totalled 98 aircraft and 38 pilots and the units had to be returned to Japan to reform. In their place came less well-trained air regiments from Manchuria, ferried by carrier to Truk, Caroline Islands, and then flown down to Rabaul. Lacking over-water navigation experience, these units suffered severe non-combat losses in transit.

The first operational jet fighters – Messerschmitt Me 262s tackle a formation of B17 Flying Fortresses.

The Japanese Navy made a major error of judgement in mid-March 1943 in believing that the situation in the south-west Pacific could be remedied by the commitment of the best available aircrew to Operation 'I-Go'. 96 fighters, 65 dive-bombers and a dozen torpedo-bombers were disembarked from the four serviceable carriers, making 370 JNAF and 200 JAAF aircraft available to neutralise Allied positions on Guadalcanal and New Guinea. But although the Allies possessed 850 aircraft in the Solomons and over 500 in Papua they scored but 39 victories (representing only 6 per cent Japanese losses), whereas their interceptors lost the same percentage to the escorting 'Zeros'. Japanese non-combat losses were high, however, and cost over 100 aircraft, many from the carrier group, for no significant returns.

The most important casualty was the Fleet Commander, Admiral I Yamamoto. Believing that a major victory had been obtained, he flew from Truk to Bougainville on 16 April, only to be intercepted by an 'execution squad' of fourteen P-38s from Guadalcanal – a mission flown at 360 miles (576 km) range for this specific purpose on information obtained through knowledge of the Japanese codes.

The Allies made the first moves for an offensive in New Guinea in July 1943 seizing offshore islands to provide fighter and light-bomber bases to support the assault on Lae. The Fifth AF bomber force had been built up since March, and although the main effort was directed at the Lae and Wewak areas, a Darwin-based B-24 group undertook a diversionary strategic strike against the oil refinery at Balikpapan on 13 August. Eight of the nine aircraft which attacked returned from the 17-hour mission – **the longest yet flown by**

B-24 Liberators attack the oil refinery at Balikpapan in the course of a seventeen-hour mission from Australia.

Allied strategic bombers. Japanese aircraft losses began to pile up so that, with nearly 600 aircraft destroyed in two months, **the summer of 1943 became a disaster for the Japanese air forces.**

In the Central Pacific, the first new ships of the rejuvenated USN carrier fleet made their début on 1 September 1943 with 275 offensive sorties against Marcus Island, 999 nautical miles from Tokyo, the purpose being diversionary activity while Baker Island was occupied to provide a reconnaissance flying-boat base within range of the Gilbert Islands, **the first objective of the forthcoming Central Pacific amphibious offensive.** Aware of the implications of the increasing tempo, the JNAF fought back but to little avail, losing ten aircraft in October for every enemy aircraft downed.

Again the Japanese Navy landed the best of its air units on 1 November, 173 aircraft being flown from the carriers at Truk to Rabaul. The US Navy kept its carrier aircraft embarked and on the same day two carriers struck at Bougainville airfields.

Three days later, the same two carriers, *Saratoga* and *Princeton*, crippled the Japanese Fleet at Rabaul with incredible economy of effort: only 23 TBF Avenger torpedo-bombers and 22 Dauntlesses were available, but they put out of action six cruisers and two destroyers, in spite of intense flak and the attentions of some 70 fighters. Five of the escorting F6F-3 Hellcats were shot down, as well as five dive-bombers, but this was a small price to pay for the achievement.

A follow-up strike by five carriers on 11 November was less successful, one destroyer being sunk and another damaged by the 148 bombers. On this occasion the escort outnumbered the interceptors by 127 to 68, but only six 'Zeros' were claimed, while 13 USN aircraft were lost. But when 41 JNAF dive- and torpedo-bombers, escorted by 68 fighters, attempted to attack the American carriers they failed to score any hits and only ten dive-bombers returned to Rabaul – **the first occasion on which a Japanese carrier-plane strike had failed to score a hit.** Eighty-six of the 192 air crews had been killed, losses which forced the Japanese carrier fleet to begin again the process of rebuilding its air groups at a time when they were badly needed to intervene against American advances.

Rabaul was effectively neutralised by the invasion of Bougainville. The encirclement was completed by landings on New Britain and on islands off New Ireland for the purpose of building further air bases; but Rabaul was never cleared out, the Americans preferring to leave the garrison to 'wither on the vine', subjected to constant air attack.

The cost to Japan in the south-west Pacific was enormous. No fewer than 2935 JNAF aircraft were lost in this area between August 1942 and February 1944 while the JAAF lost over 1000 in 1943 alone. As these figures represented more than a third of the total number of combat aircraft produced during the same period, the Japanese air forces were having great difficulty in maintaining their strength, let alone expanding to meet the ever-increasing Allied commitments on many fronts. American losses in the New Guinea and Solomons campaigns were at least as high as those of their enemy, but American production was able to make good material losses many times over and, more important, American air-crew casualties were light, thanks to the great efforts put into the recovery of downed crews.

The first amphibious operation of a series which was to sweep north-west to the Home Islands of Japan began when the US Fast Carrier Task Force struck at airfields in the

The aircraft carrier USS Sangamon *about to be hit by a Kawasaki Ki 61 Hien fighter during a 'Kamikaze' suicide attack off Okinawa, 4 May 1945.*

Marshall Islands in November 1943 and provided cover against a sortie by the Japanese Combined Fleet. Then they struck at the Gilbert Islands until D-Day, 20 November, when six escort carriers with 147 aircraft between them took over the close support and protection role. Japanese torpedo-bombers were active every night from 20 November, and in their first attack, at dusk on D-Day, one scored a hit on the light carrier *Independence*, putting her out of action. No night-fighters were available, but a Grumman TBF Avenger fitted with anti-shipping radar scored **the US Navy's first carrier night-combat victory** during the night of 26/27 November. Remorselessly the Americans seized footholds in the Marshall Islands while demolishing Japanese air and sea forces.

The American carrier strike on Truk on 17 February 1944 was one of the most effective strategic air operations of the war. Attacks on the three airfields destroyed or damaged 265 out of 370 JNAF aircraft. With only AA fire to oppose them, waves of bombers then attacked shipping in the lagoon by day and night until the late forenoon of the 18th. The nine carriers launched 1250 sorties during the operation and for the expenditure of 400 tons of bombs and the loss of only seventeen aircraft, sank ten assorted warships and 33 auxiliaries and merchant ships, totalling 200 581 tons, and damaged nine more warships. Eleven more ships were sunk by Fifth AF and AirSols aircraft during February, adding further to the Japanese transport problem that was desperate in the south-west Pacific. The Truk pattern of attack was repeated over Palau on 30 and 31 March 1944, with Hellcats sweeping aside JNAF fighters to achieve clear skies for the strikes plus **the innovation of using 78 minelaying aircraft** to block the exits of the main anchorage to prevent shipping from escaping. Twenty-six auxilliaries and merchant ships were sunk, totalling 107 000 tons.

Nowhere was the lack of fully trained crews more serious than in the Japanese carrier fleet. The destruction of the 1st Carrier Division's Air Group at Rabaul and in the Marshalls and the 2nd Cardiv's at Truk, forced the JNAF to form new units for both in January and March 1944, while a completely new 3rd Cardiv's Air Group was formed in February. Although new types of bombers were being delivered – the Yokosuka D4Y 'Judy' dive-bomber and the Nakajima B6N 'Jill' torpedo-bomber as well as updated models of the 'Zero' – the aircrew could not be given sufficient training in their use before the nine carriers of the three divisions were brought together at Tawi-Tawi in the Philippines in mid-May 1944.

Japanese plans ignored the lessons of previous carrier strikes by splitting their forces. At Pearl Harbor, Colombo, Rabaul, Truk and Palau the carrier fighters had swept away the land-based opposition, allowing the bombers to wreak havoc, achieving **concentration at the decisive point.** To make matters worse for the Japanese, the US carriers possessed numerical superiority as well as the offensive initiative, for there were fifteen fast carriers with 895 aircraft, eight escort carriers with 196 aircraft for close support of the landings on Saipan, and another five escort carriers with 135 aircraft in reserve at sea; over 100 replacement aircraft were at hand aboard transport carriers.

Saipan was invaded on 15 June 1944, just nine days after the invasion of Normandy, half the world away. **The fifth and last great carrier battle** began four days later, when the nine carriers of the Japanese Fleet launched four strikes, comprising 373 aircraft, and 33 floatplane and carrier-borne reconnaissance and shadowing missions. Their Guam-based aircraft made the first contact with the US Task Force 58, but a strike from the island was scattered as it was forming over the island, 33 Hellcats destroying 40 Japanese aircraft. Only two of the Japanese carrier strikes flew straight to TF 58's position, where they were met by up to 100 of the 200 Hellcats on Combat Air Patrol (CAP). A few of the aircraft from the other two strikes also attacked the American carriers. The CAP shot down 120 of the enemy, but 53 broke through to attack the ships. It was at this point that the JNAF pilots' lack of training was demonstrated, for although four carriers were near-missed by bombs and torpedoes, the only hits were on two battleships, neither of which was seriously damaged. Those returning Japanese aircraft which made for Guam were slaughtered over the island: in one mid-afternoon scrap, 54 were destroyed or damaged beyond repair by 41 Hellcats. Raiders which elected to return to their ships found two less – the large carriers *Taiho* and *Shokaku* had been torpedoed by submarines and both sank during the afternoon of 19 June. This action, known as **the Great Marianas Turkey Shoot', was the most decisive defensive air battle of all time.** The American defences had destroyed 243 shipborne aircraft and 58 from Guam, for the loss of fourteen Hellcats and a Dauntless, plus minor damage to only four ships.

A Hellcat closes in for the kill.

Admiral Raymond Spruance, commanding the Fifth Fleet, was afterwards criticised for the defensive strategy that had won such a brilliant victory, his critics preferring to have seen him conduct the sort of slogging match which had cost the US Navy so dearly in the four previous battles. He delayed the American *riposte* until the late afternoon of 20 June, and the 131 Avengers, Curtiss SB2C Helldivers and Dauntlesses did not attack until near sunset. Forty 'Zeros' met the strike and destroyed twenty American aircraft, but lost all but fifteen to the 85 escorting Hellcats. One carrier, *Hiyo*, was sunk

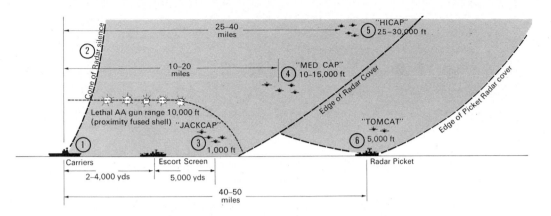

Fleet Air Defence 1944–5.   *1 Carrier controlling defence.*   *2 Cone of radar silence.*
    3 Last-ditch fighter defence.   *4, 5 and 6 Outer defensive fighter patrols.*

Japanese torpedo attack on the damaged carrier Yorktown *at Midway.*

and three others were damaged, and two tankers also sunk. Returning in the dark to their carriers, 340 miles away, 80 aircraft with 209 crewmen ran out of fuel or crashed on landing. Of the crews, 101 were rescued before dawn and 59 thereafter by destroyers, submarines and flying boats. Yet even after these losses, TF 58 still possessed over 700 aircraft while the Japanese were left with only 35 carrier aircraft and fifteen serviceable floatplanes.

Carriers supported the successful invasions of Guam and Tinian. However, loss of the Marianas was to hold greater significance for the Japanese than the breaching of their defensive network and the destruction of their carrier-borne air force. For, even before the fall of Saipan and Tinian, USAAF engineers were surveying airfield sites, and the construction of five B-29 airfields was begun immediately, just 1500 miles (2400 km) south of Tokyo.

The last major attempt by the Japanese to use conventional forms of attack against the fast carriers lasted from 10 to 16 October 1944. Task Force 38, with sixteen carriers, entered the South China Sea to strike at Formosa and Okinawa, whence most of the air reinforcements for the Philippines would come. Large number of Japanese aircraft were shot down by the Hellcats over Okinawa and Formosa, and even at night the Japanese were unable to strike back as effectively as they were wont, for the light carrier USS *Independence* had been fitted out and armed as a night carrier, carrying a squadron of night-fighter Hellcats. Over 400 Japanese aircraft attempted to attack Task Force 38, but their only successes were two torpedoed cruisers and superficial damage to the carrier *Franklin*. At the end of the week, the JNAF admitted the loss of 492 aircraft and the JAAF lost over 150 in the same period. At the same time, US Navy losses were heavier than ever before, but their 2·8 per cent loss rate in the course of 3800 sorties was well within the replacement capacity of the eleven ferry carriers which accompanied the tanker force.

The invasion of Leyte Island on 20 October 1944 sparked off the Japanese Navy's last desperate throw to turn the Americans back. Few Japanese air attacks occurred up to 24 October, but by the 24th the JNAF and JAAF had 396 aircraft available in the Philippines and over half of these approached the beach-head to have 66 shot down by the fighters from the escort carriers. Meanwhile, the Japanese Fleet was detected and attacked by 150 bomber sorties, but with discouraging results. Although the monster battleship *Musashi* was sunk, only one other ship was forced to turn back. Five battleships and seven heavy cruisers continued while the air battle went on elsewhere and the naval battle was resolved by conventional ship versus ship combat in Surigao Strait.

The Battle of Samar was the only occasion in the Pacific War in which battleships engaged carriers, an action that lasted just over two hours and in which the Japanese battleships and cruisers succeeded in sinking only one carrier and severely damaged another two. In fighting back, the carriers' aircraft, assisted by those of another Group, sank three heavy cruisers and damaged all the other major units for the loss of nearly 50 fighters and torpedo-bombers out of fewer than 200 attacking.

The Japanese provided another major tactical surprise during this action – the introduction of the planned aircraft suicide attack. The first carrier victim was the large escort carrier *Santee*, hit by a 'Zero' which dived through the flight deck and set her on fire.

A 'Zero' attempts to shake off a Wildcat over Leyte Island.

The first ship to be sunk by suicide attack was the escort carrier *St Lo*, the only one of her group to have escaped shellfire damage earlier. Every one of the five 'Zeros' in this attack inflicted damage on the five carriers, leaving only one fully operational.

The possibility of the Japanese adopting suicide tactics had been foreseen by the RAF as early as 1931, and there had been examples of this form of attack from Pearl Harbor onwards, by pilots of damaged aircraft and by occasional determined individuals. Not until after the Battle of the Philippine Sea, when the carrier air groups had been expended for no returns, was any attempt made to organise and harness this ultimate expression of the warrior creed. For the pilots the likelihood of return from a conventional attack on American carriers was already slight and the prospects of success slender; the pilots of the 'Special Attack Corps', more commonly known as 'Kamikaze', would certainly die, but in doing so they would have a better chance of achieving a hit, eliminating as they did all bomb-aiming errors. Although there had been marked reluctance on the part of the Naval Staff to employ suicide tactics, the failure of dive- and torpedo-bombers off Formosa and off Leyte on 24 October removed most doubts and the début of the Kamikaze attack was an outstanding success.

Sustained Japanese efforts cost the US Navy dear. Seven fast carriers were hit and damaged by Kamikazes, which also sank seven and damaged 23 other ships up to 12 December. By mid-November, 80 USAAF P-38s were on Leyte, but not until Marine Corps fighters arrived on 3 December was there a suitable anti-Kamikaze or night-fighter force available. The Marine Corsairs also acted as an anti-shipping striking force, routing two Japanese reinforcement convoys off Leyte.

Even before the Leyte campaign was settled, the first moves were made to capture an air base beach-head on Mindoro Island, 300 miles (480 km) further north. Thirteen fast carriers and six escort carriers provided support up to 16 December, the day after the landings, when Leyte-based fighters took over. **Effective measures by the fast carrier force,** improvised during the short rest period, resulted in few suicide aircraft reaching the ships up to the evening of 14 December, and none thereafter. **The 'Big Blue Blanket'** of Hellcats spread over Luzon claimed 270 aircraft destroyed in three days. Only two ships were badly damaged by Kamikazes and two assault craft sunk.

Not until 29 December were Mindoro-based fighters able to take over defensive patrols from the Leyte groups, and in the interim six more ships had been sunk and seven others damaged by air attack.

The most effective Kamikaze attacks of the war occurred during the approach to and invasion of Luzon, at Lingayen Gulf, on 9 January 1945. Fewer than 100 suicide aircraft took off between 3 and 9 January, but 34 scored hits, sinking one escort carrier and damaging four others. Bad weather had prevented TF 38 from keeping the airfields under full surveillance, although over 3000 sorties were flown during the period. Great damage was inflicted on the Clark Field complex by 132 B-25s and A-20s which attacked at low level on 7 December.

The most daring raid by the fast carriers took place between 10 and 22 January, when fourteen fast carriers with 926 aircraft (578 of them fighters) operated in the land-locked South China Sea, striking at shipping between Indo-China and Formosa. Over 300 000 tons of shipping was sunk, half of it on the 12th, but not until the 21st was the force found and attacked by Kamikazes, which damaged two carriers and a destroyer.

The first carrier strikes on Tokyo were part of the pre-invasion offensive for the assault on Iwo Jima (19 February). Under the command of Spruance and Mitscher, Task Force 58 launched 2761 sorties on 16 and 17 February, concentrating on the destruction of aircraft and aircraft factories in the Tokyo Plain. Bad weather limited the effectiveness of the operation, but over 200 aircraft were destroyed in air combat and more on the ground, for the loss of 60 USN aircraft to AA and fighters – **the heaviest casualties since 1942.**

The last great invasion was that of Okinawa, on 1 April 1945. Support for the landings came from seventeen American and four British fast carriers and eighteen American escort carriers, with over 1900 aircraft between them. Against this force the Japanese possessed about 6000 aircraft in all areas. But many of their pilots had barely completed basic training, and the true value of the air forces was less than the figures suggest.

Task Force 58 sustained heavy casualties during preliminary strikes on Japan on 18 and 19 March. The JNAF employed Kamikazes and conventional dive-bombers against the carriers, and it was the latter which inflicted the most spectacular damage, putting *Yorktown* out of action until July and *Franklin* for the remainder of the war, the two ships losing 824 men dead and 534 wounded between them. The JNAF admitted the loss of 161 of the 193 aircraft sent

B-29s on the way out from Japan.

Fire bombs on their way down.

against TF 58 on the two days, and another 38 were lost on 21 March, when an attempt to launch manned rocket-bombs at the carriers was defeated by Hellcats.

The Kamikaze offensive reached its peak during the three-month Okinawa campaign. No less than 355 suicide sorties were launched on 6 April alone, outnumbering the 341 dive- and torpedo-bombers committed on the same day. Twenty-eight direct hits were scored by suicide aircraft and six ships were sunk off the beaches. Defending fighters and AA fire claimed 327 victims. In all, 1900 JNAF and JAAF suicide aircraft were despatched, sinking 26 ships and damaging 164 others, including eleven carriers. Allied carrier aircraft destroyed 1434 aircraft and shore-based USMC and USAAF fighters accounted for another 607, out of 4135 enemy aircraft lost in combat. Only 74 American aircraft were shot down in air combat, and 367 destroyed by AA fire in attacks on Okinawa and Kyushu; overall losses from all causes amounted to 740 Allied aircraft, compared with 6810 Japanese.

The carriers' last operations took them to Japan in mid-July, and there they remained until 15 August, when Japan surrendered. Fifteen USN and four RN fast carriers roamed at will off the east coast of the Home Islands, their aircraft destroying what remained of the Imperial Japanese Navy and the Japanese merchant marine. The railway system and the airfields came under attack, but there was little airborne opposition as the Japanese had dispersed most of their aircraft to save them for opposing the B-29 raids and to throw back the expected invasion. In spite of the heavy losses earlier in the year, the Japanese still possessed about 5000 front-line aircraft in August 1945, and 5350 more were available for Kamikaze operations.

THE ASSAULT ON JAPAN

The first B-29 arrived on Saipan on 12 October 1944. Like the Twentieth Bomber Command in India, the Twenty-first BC in the Marianas was part of the independent Twentieth US Air Force, but based as it was in the Pacific, the Command was under the operational control of Admiral Chester Nimitz, the Commander-in-Chief of the US Pacific Fleet.

Supply was no obstacle to operations from the Marianas as it was from China. Although Guam is over 6200 miles (9920 km) from San Francisco, the US Navy had complete control of the Pacific and sufficient cargo tonnage to meet all the demands for fuel, stores and ordnance. **The 7000 tons of freight carried by a single Liberty ship was the equivalent of 2650 1000-mile (1600 km) round trips by C-46s on the Chengtu 'Hump' route.**

The first American aircraft to fly over Tokyo since April 1942 was an F-13 reconnaissance aircraft which carried out a completely successful photographic mission on 1 November 1944.

The Japanese aircraft industry was the prime target of the first phase of the offensive on Japan, the Nakajima factory near Tokyo being attacked on 24 November. Eighty-eight of the 111 B-29s actually bombed Japan, but owing to cloud and strong high-level winds, only 24 found and bombed the primary target. Approximately 125 enemy fighters attempted to intercept and one B-29 was brought down by a ramming attack, but the only other loss was due to fuel shortage.

Seven more raids were delivered on Japan up to the end of 1944, all directed either at the Nakajima factory or the Mitsubishi factories at Nagoya. Only the latter were seriously damaged, the aero-engine output being reduced by 25 per cent; four B-29s were shot down and 31 damaged by fighters, out of 71 attacking Nagoya.

The Japanese struck back at the bombers' base, making seven attacks between 2 November and 2 January. Nineteen B-29s were destroyed or damaged beyond repair and 35 suffered repairable damage; the Japanese lost nearly half of the 80 fighters and bombers which attacked. The raids had staged through Iwo Jima which was already under continuous attack from Seventh Air Force B-24s, but after a particularly damaging JNAF raid on Saipan on 7 December, 62 B-29s unloaded 20000 lb (9100 kg) of bombs each on Iwo in a combined attack with 102 B-24s which dropped only 4000 lb (1820 kg) each.

The Marianas B-29s first inflicted major damage on Japan on 19 January 1945, in an attack on the Kawasaki aircraft and engine factory outside Tokyo. Sixty-two B-29s dropped 155 tons of bombs which reduced Japanese aero-engine production by an eighth and aircraft by nearly a fifth. On the following day, Major General C LeMay USA took command of Twenty-First BC to rectify the Command's previous indifferent performances. However, the eight missions against Japan between 23 January and 4 March did not inflict great damage on the main targets, although bombers making incendiary attacks on urban areas at Kobe, Nagoya and Tokyo destroyed rather less than two square miles of these secondary targets. The carriers of TF 58 which struck at the Tokyo area on 16 and 17 February (see page 184) inflicted more damage in a single raid on the oft-bombed Nakajima factory at Musashino than the B-29s had achieved in six missions.

The most devastating bombing attack of the war was delivered against Tokyo on the night of 9/10 March 1945. Three Wings sent 334 B-29s to drop napalm and 'conventional' incendiaries on 12 miles^2 (19 km^2) of the most built-up city in the world, where the roof area constituted half the total area. So concentrated was the bombing and so inflammable the target that nearly 16 miles^2 (25 km^2) were burnt out and over a quarter of a million buildings destroyed. Japanese casualties exceeded 124000 dead and injured and a million people were made homeless. Bombing from under 10000 ft (3000 m), instead of from well over 20000 ft (6000 m), 14 B-29s were shot down by AA fire and another 42 were damaged; the bombers were carrying no ammunition for fear of firing on one another, but all the attempted night-fighter interceptions failed.

Osaka, Kobe and Nagoya shared Tokyo's fate during the nights that followed, with 1261 B-29s making four attacks up to 20 March. Better fire precautions than those in Tokyo prevented similar outright destruction, but 330000 buildings were destroyed and over 16 miles^2 (25 km^2) gutted in the three cities. The lavish use of 9365 tons of fire-raising bombs in the five attacks left the Twenty-First BC with an acute shortage of napalm and oil bombs.

Successful and less costly in aircraft was the minelaying offensive which began on the night of 27/28 March with 92 B-29s dropping nearly 1000 mines in the Shimoneseki Straits, between Kyushu and Honshu. The Japanese had still not yet developed an antidote to the magnetic mine and the acoustic mine, while the pressure mine which was first used in May 1945 was at that time unsweepable by any navy. As the offensive gained momentum, so great

Only the modern concrete Japanese buildings survived incendiary attacks by B-29s in the spring of 1945.

tracts of inland and coastal waterways became unusable, not only around the Home Islands, but also as far afield as the north-east coast of Korea. Japanese losses to air-laid mines reached 85 ships of 213 000 tons in May 1945. **Two years were needed to make Japanese waters safe for navigation after the war,** such was the extent of the four-month campaign.

The last oil tanker reached Japan in April 1945, and thereafter the country was entirely dependent upon its accumulated stocks. Storage tanks were hit as 'targets of opportunity' during industrial and urban raids by B-29s, but only one B-29 mission had as its primary target an oil installation up to the night of 26/27 June. Then B-29B aircraft, equipped with 'Eagle' precision blind-bombing radar and armed only with two machine-guns in the tail, made 1095 successful night sorties up to 14 August 1945, dropping over 9000 tons of bombs, of which 1225 tons fell on the oil storage targets, destroying over 750 000 tons of fuel oil.

What RAF Bomber Command had failed to do against the solidly built, well-prepared and disciplined German cities, the US Twentieth Air Force succeeded in achieving against the densely packed Japanese cities. Highly accurate bombing at heights below 10 000 feet had not been effectively opposed by either AA or night-fighter defences and only 136 of the 6960 B-29s taking off had been lost: had the defences equalled the efficiency of those of Germany during the winter of 1943/44, then 353 would have failed to return. Japanese civil defence was poor, particularly in view of the

A load of jellied petrol incendiary bombs for a single B-29 Superfortress.

inflammable nature of the buildings, and the population had been given no inkling of the nature of the whirlwind that was to be reaped, so that discipline broke down during and after the attacks.

Daylight precision attacks on individual aero-industry factories were undertaken throughout the period. The Japanese dispersed their machine tools and assembly areas to the countryside, but these movements cut production and the new factories could not reach the output attained in the long-established works. **The last of the daylight precision raids** saw 625 B-29s in seven separate formations unload 3708 tons of bombs on empty shells of factories.

The B-29s delivered fire raids on 58 secondary cities between 17 June and 14 August. With a city per Wing per raid only three re-strikes had to be flown. Over 62 miles² were burned out and 12 cities were more than 70 per cent destroyed; on the night of 1/2 August part of a force of 853 B-29s destroyed 95 per cent of

The most thorough job of destruction achieved by aircraft – 95 per cent of the city of Toyama was burned out on the night of 1/2 August 1945.

the old city of Toyama – **no other city sustained damage even approximating the extent suffered by Toyama, relative to its size.** The cost of this small-town fire raising campaign was negligible – only one B-29 was lost to enemy action out of over 8000 dispatched, 66 were damaged, and 18 lost through non-combat causes.

All of the 58 target cities had their industries, and by July 1945 their production had fallen to 38 per cent of the 1944 peak. The isolation of Japan from overseas sources of materials had caused an overall reduction, an example of what could be achieved without interference from bombing was the 83 per cent production achieved by one unbombed city – Hiroshima.

Five Japanese major cities had been deliberately avoided since January 1945. Kyoto, Hiroshima, Niigata, Kokura and Nagasaki were quarantined in order that they might be virgin targets for the atomic bomb which would become operational in the summer. At the insistence of H H Stimson, the US Secretary of State, Kyoto was deleted from the list as it was a cultural centre with little military significance.

Twelve training missions by the special 509th Composite Group involving 38 aircraft made attacks on targets separate from those of the 'main force' on four days, the weapon dropped being a 12000 lb (5450 kg) high-capacity blast bomb with ballistic qualities similar to those of the atomic bomb, the fissionable material for which arrived at Tinian on 26 July, ten days after **the successful test of the first atomic bomb** at Alamogordo.

Hiroshima's suspended sentence came to an end at 0815 on 6 August 1945, when the six-ton 'Little Boy' was released from B-29 'Enola Gay', flown by Lieutenant Colonel Paul Tibbets, 31600 ft (9480 km) above the city. After release, Tibbets pulled the B-29 round in a fighter-like diving turn to clear the area before the atomic bomb detonated 50 seconds and 15 miles (24 km) away, a mile above Hiroshima. Exploding with the force of 20000 tons of TNT the bomb's blast and fireball destroyed 4·7 miles^2 (7·5 km^2) of the city centre, the 49000 buildings comprising two-thirds of the urban area. Personnel casualties were afterwards assessed at 71379 dead and over 68000 injured.

Although greater casualties and more widespread destruction had been inflicted by conventional bombs in individual attacks on German and Japanese cities, these had involved hundreds of bombers and thousands of bombs. Hiroshima was obliterated by a single bomb, dropped by a single bomber. Three days later Lieutenant Colonel Sweeney, flying 'Bock's Car', took off for Kokura. Cloud prevented the briefed visual attack from being made and Sweeney accordingly proceeded to **the alternate target – Nagasaki.** Here, too, cloud obscured the target, which was approached using radar until a convenient 'hole' was found and the 'Fat Boy' dropped visually at 1100 on 9 August.

The geography of Nagasaki prevented a disaster on the scale of Hiroshima. High ground protected some districts from fire and blast, and destruction was restricted to 1·45 miles^2 (2·3 km^2). The exact loss of life is not known but ranged between the official Japanese figures of 25700 dead and 23300 wounded to the American estimate of 35000 dead and 65000 wounded.

The last bombing attacks on Japan were delivered by carrier aircraft from the ships that had checked the advance of the Japanese in the Coral Sea, and in the Pacific and had then made possible the capture of the islands which were to be used to bring Japan within range of the well-supplied Twenty-First Bomber

Hiroshima after the debris of 6 August 1945 had been cleared away.

Command. In six months, shipborne aircraft had dropped 7000 tons of bombs on the islands, compared with the same amount by B-24s and B-25s operating from Okinawa, and 147000 tons of bombs and the equivalent of 40000 tons in the two atomic bombs had been dropped by Twentieth and Twenty-First BCs.

Royal Navy Supermarine Seafire fighters scored the last air-combat victories before the cease-fire on 15 August. Escorting a strike in the Tokyo Bay area, eight Seafires were attacked by a dozen 'Zeros' and shot down eight of their assailants for the loss of one Royal Navy fighter.

The air offensive did bring the war to a premature close, but the end for Japan had been in sight by October 1944, when the invasion of the Philippines cut her off from her main sources of raw materials. Even after over 27000 B-29 sorties by the Twenty-First BC and all the casualties of the Okinawa campaign, the Japanese still had 5300 aircraft available for use for suicide missions, as well as 5000 conventional aircraft in service and 7000 in reserve. The air offensive's major contribution was its prevention of those forces from being larger. It made unnecessary the loss of life which would have accompanied an invasion of the Home Islands. **Lord Trenchard, General Douhet and all their disciples had been right** – though none had envisaged a weapon with the power of those dropped on Hiroshima and Nagasaki, and without which their visions would have been but pipe-dreams.

Over 300 different types of aircraft saw service during the Second World War, the principal antagonists producing over three-quarters of a million airframes during the six years. In some cases, production far outstripped the ability of the air force concerned to bring the aircraft into action. For example, in 1944 the German aircraft industry produced 39807 airframes while the *Luftwaffe* lost 20010 aircraft, but such were the shortages of pilots and fuel, the front-line strength at the beginning of 1945 was only 10 per cent of the surplus.

Country		Aircraft Produced	Aircraft Lost	Remarks
Britain	1939–45	128775	45000	**Combined British-US figure: losses in the European theatre amounted to 33770 aircraft, of which over 15500 were destroyed in 1944. US losses world-wide from all operational causes came to 22600 aircraft.**
USA	1940–5	272000	22600	
USSR	1941–5	158218	47000+	
Germany	1939–45	118778	50000	
Occupied countries		8139		
Italy	1940–3	*c* 11000	4000	
Japan (Navy)	1941–5	32422	10370	
Japan (Army)	1941–5	28000	*c* 8000	
		757000+	164000+	

The United States provided over 45 000 aircraft of all types to her Allies, the Soviet Union being the somewhat graceless recipient of 14 000 modern aircraft which gave her designers an insight into advanced Western techniques. Russia was the most prolific producer of individual designs, with no fewer than 36 736 single-engined Yakovlev fighters of four types and 36 163 Ilyushin Il-2 ground-attack aircraft in two major variants. Aggregate loss figures are difficult to ascertain, the various Services using different criteria, but it is believed that the following data are reasonably accurate in respect of production.

The 'Top Twenty' military aircraft types between 1939 and 1945 were:

Ilyushin Il-2 Shturmovik'	USSR	s/e ground attack	36 163
Messerschmitt Bf 109	Ger.	s/e fighter	35 000
Supermarine Spitfire/Seafire	UK	s/e fighter	22 884
Focke-Wulf Fw 190	Ger.	s/e fighter	20 001
Consolidated B-24 Liberator	US	4/e bomber	18 188
Yakovlev Yak-9	USSR	s/e fighter	16 769
Republic P-47 Thunderbolt	US	s/e fighter	15 660
North American T-6 Texan	US	s/e trainer	15 094
North American P-51 Mustang	US	s/e fighter	14 819
Junkers Ju 88	Ger.	t/e multi-purpose	14 676
Hawker Hurricane	UK	s/e fighter	14 231
Curtiss P-40 Kittyhawk/ Warhawk	US	s/e fighter	13 738
Boeing B-17 Flying Fortress	US	4/e bomber	12 723
Grumman F6F Hellcat	USN	s/e fighter	12 272
Vickers Wellington	UK	t/e bomber	11 461
Petlyakov Pe-2 (NATO – 'Buck')	USSR	t/e ground attack	11 426
Mitsubishi A6M 'Zero' or 'Zeke'	Japan	s/e fighter	10 938
Douglas C-47 Dakota	US	t/e transport	10 926
North American B-25 Mitchell	US	t/e bomber	10 521
Vought F4U Corsair	USN	s/e fighter	10 447

Six per cent of the types produced accounted for over 43 per cent of the numbers produced world-wide.

Note: Although over 20 000 Polikarpov Po-2 trainer biplanes were built in the Soviet Union, the majority were constructed between 1927 and 1937.

Boeing B-29 Superfortresses of the USAF over Korea late in 1951 come under attack by a North Korean MiG 15. An escorting Republic F-84 Thunderjet attempts to drive the interceptor off.

Left to right: Ernst Udet, Germany's second ranking ace of the First World War, with Adolf Galland and Werner Mölders, first great German ace of the Second World War, who had achieved 115 confirmed victories by the time of his death on 22 November 1941.

The most successful fighter pilots of the Second World War, by nationality, were:

Country of origin		Aircraft credited destroyed in combat
Australia	Wing Commander C R Caldwell	$28\frac{1}{2}$
Austria	Maj Walter Nowotny	258
Belgium	Major Count Ivan Du Monceau de Bergendal	8
Bulgaria	Lieutenant Stoyan Stoyanov	14
Canada	Flight Lieutenant G F Beurling	$31\frac{1}{3}$
China	Colonel Liu Chi-Sun	$11\frac{1}{3}$
Czechoslovakia	Second Lieutenant Rotnik Rezny	32
	Flight Lieutenant K Kuttelwascher	18
Denmark	Group Captain K Birksted	$10\frac{1}{2}$
Finland	Lmsti Eino Juutilainen	94
France	Captain Marcel Albert	23
Germany	Major Erich Hartmann	352
Hungary	Second Lieutenant Dezsö Szentgyorgyi	34
Italy	Magg. Adriano Visconti	26
	Capitano Franco Lucchini	26
Japan	Warrant Officer Hiroyoshi Nishizawa	87
Netherlands	Captain C Vlotman	4
New Zealand	Wing Commander C F Gray	27·7
Norway	Captain Svein Heglund	$14\frac{1}{2}$
Poland	Wing Commander S F Skalski	21
Rumania	Captain Prince Constantine Cantacuzene	60

Country of origin		Aircraft credited destroyed in combat
South Africa	Squadron Leader M T St J Pattle	51 approx.
UK	Group Captain J E Johnson	38
USA	Major Richard I Bong	40
USSR	Colonel Ivan N Kozhedub	62
Yugoslavia	Lieutenant Cvitan Galic	36

A paradox in the evaluation of the part played by the 'Aces', whose combat contribution is sometimes denigrated because of over-sensationalism accorded their deeds, is high-lighted by research which shows that, during the Second World War, they tended to claim between 35 and 55 per cent of all confirmed victories while making up for less than 1 per cent of all operational fighter pilots. Clearly they played an important part in the task of gaining air supremacy without which other air operations were seriously impeded – though, as has been shown, the gaining of air supremacy depended largely upon other factors and actions as well. Obviously the Aces set a supreme example in skill, sustained courage and leadership as the pre-eminent arbiters of the actual fighting in the sky – as opposed to those who direct operations from the ground.

The main product of air attack on land warfare – chaos on the lines of communication.

The most effective pre-emptive strike ever carried out. Israeli Mirage IIICJ fighters streak in for an early morning surprise attack on an Egyptian airfield in the Cairo area, 5 June 1967.

SECTION VII
Confrontation, Cold and Limited Wars 1945–

The advent of the atomic bomb persuaded the United States of America's Government that the best hopes for peace lay in the deterrent power of this weapon, a conclusion that led to the creation of their Strategic Air Command in March 1946, with truly global responsibilities and, in 1947, the grant of autonomy to their Air Force from the Army. A strength of 70 groups by 1950 was proposed, including five to be equipped with the mighty new B-36, **the first truly intercontinental bomber,** a six-engined aircraft which could operate at over 40 000 ft (12 000 m) carrying a large bomb-load. In an atmosphere of mutual mistrust in which Soviet Russia feared this massive build-up of American power there occurred:

The first major hostile act of the Cold War by which the Russians sealed off the land routes to the $2\frac{1}{2}$ million inhabitants of Berlin in the American, British and French zones of the city. 4500 tons of food and fuel per day would be required to keep the city going – vastly more than had ever been required in any wartime airlifts. To meet the challenge vast fleets of air transports from all available sources and air forces were gathered in Western Germany to operate the biggest airlift in history until then. During the fifteen months that it was maintained, from 26 June 1948 to 30 September 1949, 2 343 313 tons were carried in by 277 264 Allied flights. Even Sunderland flying-boats landing on the lakes were used and a large number of chartered civil transports also took part. The failure of the Russians to starve out the city was a major diplomatic defeat made possible by superb Allied organisation and air traffic control. Despite the numbers of aircraft involved, and the difficulties and dangers inherent in having to keep to tightly defined air corridors, the level of safety achieved was quite remarkable. In 50 000 sorties, for example, the RAF suffered just four fatal accidents. At peak periods, Gatow airfield in Berlin was handling 580 aircraft per day.

The pattern of Soviet policy, coupled with the Communist victory in China in 1949, led the West to put off any thoughts of reducing their forces to normal peacetime levels, and air forces were much enlarged and equipped with much more powerful aircraft.

The B-36 strategic bomber was matched with a Republic RF-84 to produce a parasitic inter-continental reconnaisance system.

The new generation of jet bombers which began appearing in the 1950s were designed to outfly rather than outfight the latest jet fighters. In the United States the eight-engined Boeing B-52 Stratofortress was designed to replace the B-36, while in Britain the four-engined Vickers Valiant was followed by the delta-winged Avro Vulcan and the crescent-winged Handley Page Victor. In due course they would carry the hydrogen bomb that was first tested by the Americans in 1952 and first dropped in 1956 by a B-52. The Russians who had neglected the development of strategic heavy bombers during the Second World War, copied an American B-29 that had force-landed in Mongolia after a raid on Japan, and put it into production at the Tupolev factories. Thus when Russia's own atomic bomb was developed, the initial force built up to deliver it was also equipped with virtually the same aircraft as the USAF and RAF were initially operating. The announced intention of these bomber forces was the application of a deterrent to war, but faced by the prospect of unthinkable and unacceptable mass destruction each side merely implemented more subtle and limited ways of furthering their political aims, short of global atomic war.

The formation of guerrilla armies to fight against the Japanese occupation forces in South-East Asia during the latter years of the Second World War posed the old colonial nations with problems after the conclusion of hostilities. As the Dutch, French and British returned to their respective colonies of the East Indies, Indochina and Malaya, they were faced by nationalist elements determined to drive them out. Air power was called upon to support armies in underdeveloped terrain, but the air forces were diverse in both equipment and method.

In the East Indies, and Java, an Indonesian Republic had been proclaimed in August 1945 by Dr Sukarno and his followers. Some two dozen abandoned Japanese aircraft were taken over, but there were only five qualified pilots, rendering this force practically powerless. During November 1945 fighting broke out and RAF aircraft made attacks while Dakotas flew in additional troops.

Several RAF aircraft were shot down by ground fire, but no aerial engagements took place until the Dutch arrived in spring 1946, bringing with them a substantial air force.

Fighting broke out on a wide scale in July 1947 when Indonesian airfields were bombed and eight aircraft destroyed on the ground by the Dutch, and continued sporadically until December 1949, when the new Republic was recognised. Thereafter the Dutch aided in setting up an Indonesian air force with their own aircraft, leaving the majority of these behind when they withdrew.

Typical jungle terrain of the East Indies, with a British Scout helicopter at a radio relay site in Sarawak during the confrontation with Indonesia in the 1960s (see page 207).

In Indochina the French *Armée de l'Air* units were forced to equip with captured Japanese Nakajima Ki 43 fighters, until Spitfire IXs arrived from France. The aircraft carrier *Dixmude* arrived to undertake **the first French carrier aircraft strikes ever made** with SED Dauntless dive-bomber strikes on 2 April 1947, and subsequently to cover amphibious landings along the coast and deliver strikes on Vietminh strongholds. Later in the year this carrier transported more Spitfires and Ju 52 transport aircraft from France, before covering a paratroop assault on the Vietminh headquarters in Tonkin during October 1947.

But the Vietminh began forming and training divisions of Vietnamese troops in China after 1949 and these allowed the Vietminh gradually to gain control of the mountains and forests, while the French Union forces retained the flat countryside of the coastal plains – part of a relentless process in which the Eastern people began to assert themselves against those of the West.

In Malaya initial air strength available to support the British ground forces in 1948 against the Communist Malaya People's Liberation Army included two squadrons of Spitfires, one of Beaufighters, one of Sunderland flying boats, two of Dakota transports, one photo-reconnaissance unit, and a flight of Auster light aircraft. Early strikes on bandit camps were made and in April 1949 the guerrillas took to the jungle.

Late in 1949, the carrier *Triumph* launched a strike against the guerrilla bases and at the same time Lancaster heavy bombers arrived to bomb jungle areas suspected of housing guerrilla camps.

The first operational use of helicopters was made by the RAF during May 1950, when Westland-Sikorsky Dragonflies undertook casualty evacuation duties from jungle clearings, the first Casevac Flight being formed the following month. **The first defoliant spraying for anti-terrorist purposes** was undertaken by the RAF at this time, Austers and Dragonflies carrying out these duties to reduce cover for ambushes, and as part of a crop-denial plan aimed at the guerrillas. The Austers were also active marking targets and spotting for strikes by other types. **The first use of jet aircraft against guerrillas** occurred in December 1950, when Vampires replaced the remaining Spitfires.

The first major aerial confrontation after the Second World War came about as a result of **the first failure to contain the cold war** and **the first test of the United Nations' ability to control world events.** On 25 June 1950 Communist-controlled North Korean forces invaded the US-aided South. As the ill-equipped South Korean army fell back everywhere, the US first evacuated their advisers and their families with transport aircraft from Japan. These were attacked on the ground by aircraft of the small Russian-equipped North Korean Air Force, and in consequence fighter cover was provided. **The first combat of the war occurred** when F-82 Twin Mustangs of the USAF shot down three Yak 9 fighters over Seoul and **the first engagement involving American jets** took place that same afternoon when F-80C Shooting Star fighters shot down four of eight Il-10s over Kimpo.

American intention to aid the hard-pressed South was approved by the United Nations, and early assistance from other countries was forthcoming.

An initial shortage of jet fighters, coupled with their limited range, resulted in large quantities of war surplus P-51 Mustangs being put back into service by the USAF, RAAF, South African Air Force, and by the new Republic of Korea Air Force as it was formed. Carriers of the US Navy were in position offshore to add weight to the assault, joined in July by a Royal Navy carrier. During the early attacks great use was made of napalm and strafing, and to a lesser extent – due to the presence of North Korean armoured vehicles – of rocket projectiles. Against the massed use of troops frequently made by the Communists, the most effective weapons proved to be newly developed air-bursting fragmentation bombs, and the aircraft's own guns. Meantime elements of the US Strategic Air Force were called in with their B-29s to bomb interdiction targets well behind the lines, and also to attack Northern industrial targets. The assaults of the fighter-bombers caused the North Koreans to restrict most of their movement to the hours of darkness, and here the Americans could do little. By September the North Korean Army, starved of supplies, had been held and a United Nations' counter-offensive, spearheaded by an air and sea invasion of Inchon on 15 September, rolled them back in defeat. By November 1950 almost the whole of North Korea had been occupied, the United Nations' intention being to defeat the Communists totally. But at this stage Chinese aircraft began to intervene at the front. On 1 November MiG 15 jet fighters of Russian manufacture were seen for the first time and **the first jet versus jet combat in the world** took place on 8 November when F-80Cs met the new MiG 15s over the front, Lieutenant Russell J Brown shooting one down. Already it had become apparent that the older piston-engined fighters were more vulnerable to hostile ground fire than the jets, but the arrival of jet fighters on the North Korean side made their early replacement even more desirable. The MiGs outperformed in most respects every fighter type available to the United Nations including the North American F-86A Sabre. A wing of these aircraft, rushed over from the States, made **the first encounter between opposing swept-wing jet fighters** on 17 December 1950, the result again being in the Americans' favour when Lieutenant Colonel Bruce H Hinton shot down one MiG.

Fighter performance in Korea

Nation	Type	Speed	Ceiling	Armament
Russian/Chinese	**Mikoyan Mig 15**	**683 mph**	**15540 m**	**3 cannon**
USA	**North American F-86F (Sabre)**	**670 mph**	**15000 m**	**6 mg**

A massive counter-attack was launched by newly arrived Red Chinese divisions, and the United Nations forces were thrown back. By the end of January 1951 the Chinese had re-taken the South's capital, Seoul, and might have gone further had not the overwhelming level of UN air support reduced their rate of advance. But even this advantage was threatened as the retreat continued and the airfields from which the Sabres operated were overrun, forcing them back to bases in Japan. The MiGs began to appear in growing strength over the battlefield and started taking a toll of the fighter-bombers. Growing numbers of US jet fighters arrived in South Korea, the USAF sending in more F-80s, reinforced by F-84 Thunderjets. To replace the RAAF Mustangs came British-built Gloster Meteor 8s, whilst the US Navy had introduced its new Grumman F9F Panther and McDonnell F2H Banshee fighters.

North American F-86 Sabre fighters on an advanced airfield in Korea.

While the training and experience of the UN pilots generally allowed them to hold their own, it was quickly clear that none of these aircraft could match the performance of the MiG; all were swiftly relegated to fighter-bomber duties and the air-to-air combat left to the F-86s. In May 1951 the battlefront settled down to trench warfare as a preliminary to armistice negotiations. The air war therefore assumed an artificial format:

● The MiG 15s were based mainly on airfields across the Yalu river, on Manchurian territory, from whence they possessed the range only to protect the industrial and depot areas of the north (subsequently to be known to UN pilots as 'MiG Alley'), and not the battlefront further south.

● In their efforts to control the use and strength of the MiGs over the northern part of the country, the Sabres were not permitted (for political reasons) to pursue the MiGs beyond the Yalu river, into Manchurian or Chinese air space and were not allowed to attack their airfields there.

● Unless the Communists could construct and occupy airfields further south, they could in no way interfere with the UN fighter-bombers over the battlefield. Provided that the Sabres could, when necessary, keep the MiGs in check, UN bombers and fighter-bombers could smash these new airfields as they were constructed, before they could be fully occupied and used.

So, while the main UN air forces concentrated on ground-attack duties in direct support of the armies, the Sabres flew regular patrols up to the Yalu to bring the MiGs to battle, on occasions also escorting B-29s and fighter-bombers to hit supply, transport, new airfield, or industrial targets there. But since the MiGs were always present in greater numbers than the Sabres, and protection of the elderly and vulnerable B-29s was impossible in every case, the loss of five of these bombers during October 1951 led to their relegation to night operations.

Russian, Chinese and East European aircrew operated the MiGs, as well as Koreans, and it was noticed by the Sabre pilots that as soon as one batch had gained combat experience, they were replaced by a new, inexperienced batch, for the latter to acquire their baptism of fire also. Only rarely did the Communists attempt to use their air power offensively, as on 30 November 1951, when an attack on UN-held offshore islands was made by twelve Tupolev Tu-2 twin-engined bombers, sixteen Lavochkkin La-9 piston-engined fighters and sixteen MiGs. The Sabres were ready for them, claiming eight Tu-2s, three La-9s and a MiG without loss. The better training and experience of the American pilots – particularly the large number of Second World War veterans – enabled them to gain an early ascendancy over the Communists. Fighter tactics differed from earlier wars in that, at the height and high speed at which it was necessary for the Sabres to operate if they were to hold their own over the MiGs' home territory, the day of the big formation was over. They operated in basic formations of four because concerted operations by formations much more than double this size were found to be impracticable.

The best month of the war for the Sabres proved to be June 1953, when 77 and eleven probables were claimed. Exchange pilots from the RAF, RCAF, USN, and USMC, also operated with the USAF Sabre units during this period. When the war ended on 27 July 1953, UN aircraft had claimed 900 Communist aircraft shot down, 811 of these being MiGs. From this total the Sabres had claimed no less than 829 for a loss of 78. Total UN aircraft losses in air combat were 139, although the number lost to ground fire was very much greater. **The**

most successful fighter pilot of the war was Captain Joseph McConnell Jr, credited with the destruction of sixteen MiGs.

The Korean War marked **the first use of helicopters to recover shot-down pilots from within enemy territory,** but usually they were employed for supply and casualty evacuation duties on a large scale for the first time.

The festering guerrilla wars elsewhere continued to stimulate air operations in support of anti-guerrilla armies.

In Indo-China the real test came in 1953 when, in order to improve their supply routes to the south, the Vietminh crossed western Tonkin, marching towards Laos and Thailand. On 20 November 1953 a massive landing by 13 000 French paratroops was made in the Dien-Bien-Phu valley, astride the Communist route into Laos. This base was to be entirely air-supplied, allowing columns to be despatched on 'seek and destroy' missions, with light tanks, guns and other equipment airlifted or parachuted in. For 5½ months 4 per cent of the French Union troops tied down about half the Vietminh forces – five divisions – in this area. Steadily, however, the Communists encircled the base. The dense jungle prevented napalm, which had proved the most effective air-support weapon in the low coastal areas, from being of much use. The rainy season also restricted the level of air support which could be given. Despite this, less than 100 transport aircraft – mainly C-47 Dakotas, but also a few C-119 Flying Boxcars, flown mainly by American civilian pilots, brought in 6410 tons in 6700 sorties. Air support was provided by 150

Armée de l'Air *Grumman Bearcats in Indo-China, protected against enemy infiltrations by barbed-wire entanglements.*

combat aircraft which made 3700 close-support sorties. In reply the Vietminh built up a weight of light anti-aircraft fire around the perimeter which exceeded anything veteran French air crew had met in Europe during 1944–5. Forty-eight French aircraft were shot down and 167 more were damaged, forcing the survivors to fly higher and press their attacks home less determinedly. A further fourteen aircraft – mainly transports – were destroyed on the ground within the fortress by enemy fire. Gradually the out-numbered ground forces were compelled to give way and were deprived of the air-landing zones. The fortress finally fell on 7 May 1954 with the loss of 13 000 troops, after a siege of 56 days.

In Malaya, by 1952, the security forces were getting on top of the guerrillas. For propaganda purposes, **the first 'sky-shouting' with loud-hailers** was undertaken during November 1952 by Austers, and later by Dakotas and Valettas. Early in 1953 Royal Navy S-55 helicopters arrived, undertaking troop carrying, SAS paratroop dropping, and Casevac sorties. These aircraft even proved capable of carrying light guns, greatly expanding the support of troops by helicopter within the British forces. Lincolns continued to bomb jungle areas with a significant lack of success and, in July 1953, a trio of USAF B-29 Superfortresses joined in for a brief period. This war was won by land forces marginally aided by air power and ended by political means – as was the case in all subsequent confrontations in Indonesia and Malaysia throughout the 1960s.

AFRICA

In Africa aircraft were repeatedly used against terrorist or guerrilla forces. **In Kenya** the RAF was employed against the Mau Mau (1953–5) to attack this force of terrorists in its jungle hideouts. **In Algeria** the French became involved in widespread fighting, which flared up in 1955. Unlike other major colonial wars, this was not fought in a jungle-clad countryside, but among barren, craggy mountains and the desert areas of the interior. Against the 'Fedaheen' in their mountain hideouts, the *Armée de l'Air* soon discovered jet fighters to be far from ideal, so elderly F-47D Thunderbolts were sent to Africa to replace Vampires in these activities.

The first major use by the French of helicopters was made during this fighting, large numbers, mainly of American manufacture, being used to carry troops to trouble-spots, evacuate casualties, supply garrisons, etc.

FORMOSA

Only sporadic air actions took place between Communist and Nationalist forces in China from the close of the Second World War until the evacuation of the Nationalist troops from the mainland to Formosa in 1948, but in due course the US re-equipped the Nationalists with modern aircraft. There were a number of clashes over the Formosa Straits, one of which saw **the first use in aerial combat of air-to-air guided weapons.** On 24 September 1958, six Nationalist F-86F Sabres, armed with heat-seeking Sidewinder missiles, and eight other Sabres fought twenty MiGs. Ten MiGs were claimed as shot down, four of them believed to have been destroyed by the missiles.

The most intensive outbreaks of air warfare since the Korean War have taken place within the air space of three relatively small zones of conflict and are, in themselves, classic examples of limited non-nuclear wars that have overstepped the Cold War threshold. The areas concerned are:

● The Middle East, centred on the Israeli-Arab confrontation.
● The Indian sub-continent and the enmity between India and Pakistan.
● Vietnam and the struggle by the North for domination of the South.

The latest of these conflicts have provided important pointers to the future of air warfare.

THE ISRAELI-ARAB CONFLICTS, 1948-76

When Arab forces first attacked Israel during June 1948, Egyptian air attacks were desultory due to the small numbers of aircraft available. **The first Israeli air action against Arab aircraft** occurred on 3 June when Modi Alon in an Avia C 210 intercepted and shot down two Douglas Dakota transports which the Egyptians had converted to bomb Tel Aviv. By 1949 Israeli fighters had claimed fifteen victories, including Egyptian Spitfires and Fiat G 55s, a Harvard belonging to Syria – newly independent of the French – a number of RAF Spitfires and Tempests, and a Mosquito, all ostensibly 'mistaken for Egyptian aircraft' over the Suez Canal Zone.

A typical escalation situation set in as peace of an uneasy nature descended and both sides purchased whatever aircraft were suitable and available at a reasonable price. But in September 1955 an Arab agreement was reached with Czechoslovakia, and the supply of Russian MiG 15s and MiG 17s began. To redress the balance, the Israelis managed to purchase from the French 24 Dassault Mystère IVA fighters, together with Ouragan fighter-bombers from the same 'stable'. Tension mounted when, on 26 July 1956, Egypt nationalised the Anglo-French owned Suez Canal. The French and British despatched troops, RAF Valiant and Canberra jet bombers and two fleets with aircraft carriers, to Cyprus and Malta, while the French, extremely sympathetic to the Israelis, sent 36 more Mystères for their air force.

With Anglo-French plans complete, Israel, on 29 October, unexpectedly launched a full-scale attack on Egyptian forces in Sinai, following a succession of Arab guerrilla attacks. That there was prior collusion, at least between France and Israel, is hardly in doubt. Before this attack began 36 French *Armée de l'Air* Mystères and 36 F-84F Thunderstreaks had landed at Israeli bases to provide cover for these while the Israelis struck.

The initial attack was spearheaded by a paratroop drop on the Mitla Pass as Israeli columns began a sweep through Sinai. Meanwhile, on 30 October the French and British presented an ultimatum to both sides to withdraw from 10 miles (16 km) each side of the Suez Canal, or it would be occupied. The Israelis, still many miles to the east, happily agreed, but the Egyptians refused.

An Anglo-French air attack, initially at night, bombed the four main Canal Zone air bases. Twenty MiG 15s and twenty Il-28 jet bombers intended for Syria, but still in Egypt, were flown to the spot, accompanied by some Egyptian MiGs, but when the Il-28s landed at Luxor, they were spotted and destroyed on the ground by French F-84Fs from Israel. RAF bomber attacks, still flown at night due to the presence of the MiGs, continued for two more nights, but as several airfields were seen by air reconnaissance to be still intact, the attack was taken up in daylight by aircraft from British and French carriers, and by

Royal Marines prepare to embark in naval Whirlwind helicopters off Port Said. November 1956.

Venoms, Canberras and F-84Fs from Cyprus. Between 1 and 6 November 260 Egyptian aircraft were destroyed on the ground for the loss of seven Anglo-French aircraft, all to ground fire. On 5 November an Anglo-French paratroop force dropped on Port Said, aided by 'Cab Ranks' of carrier fighter-bombers from both navies. Next morning the main force landed by sea and helicopter, three more RN fighters being lost while supporting them.

Operations ceased on 7 November, the United Nations resolving to establish a peace force and a ceasefire. The Israelis meanwhile had occupied Sinai after desultory air fighting with casualties of twelve Israeli and ten Egyptian machines. The sole Anglo-French loss in air-to-air combat was an RAF photo-reconnaissance Canberra shot down over Syria by a MiG 15 when undertaking a reconnaissance sortie.

Guerrilla warfare was uppermost for the next nine years, the next clash in the air not coming until 1965; **the biggest of this 'inter-war' period** occurring on 7 April 1967, when Israeli Mirages claimed six Syrian MiG 21s shot down. By June 1967 the air forces of both sides were considerably bigger than in 1956. **The Israelis** possessed 196 combat-worthy fighters – all French – and they also

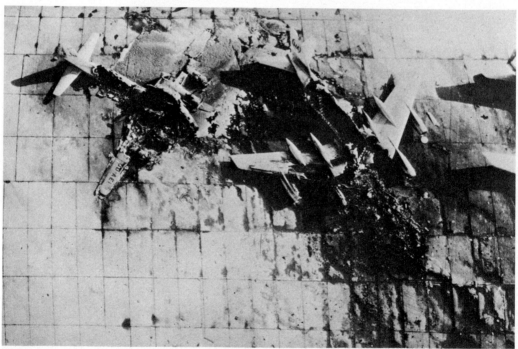

Aftermath of an air strike by Israelis on Cairo airport in 1967 showing airliners destroyed.

had 25 Vautour light bombers, 35 transport aircraft, 22 helicopters, and some American Hawk surface-to-air guided missiles. **The Arab League** nations – Egypt, Syria, Jordan, Iraq, Lebanon and Algeria – possessed about 700 fighters, including 66 Hunters, and 110 medium bombers, plus 146 transports, 79 helicopters and at least 30 Russian SA 2 guided anti-aircraft missiles.

The most successful pre-emptive air strike ever launched came from the Israelis at dawn on 5 June 1967 to open the 'Six Day War'. Mystères and Ouragans attacked airfields and radar stations in Sinai. Cairo, the Canal and Nile Delta bases were attacked by Mirages and Super Mystères, while the Vautours hit bases in the distant southern regions of Egypt. Later in the day the Israeli aircraft went out again to attack bases in Jordan, Syria and Iraq. By midday 100 Arab aircraft were claimed destroyed, and when night fell claims stood at 240 Egyptian, 45 Syrian, 16 Jordanian and 7 Iraqi aircraft destroyed, 30 of them in the air. The Israelis had flown nearly 1000 sorties, losing about twenty aircraft, only one of them (a Vautour) in air combat.

A new weapon employed during this attack was the 'Concrete Dibber' bomb. Dropped on runways, this had a delayed initial fall to prevent it exploding beneath the delivery aircraft. Its slow initial drop was then greatly accelerated by rocket power, driving it deep below the concrete, its explosion being delayed until this point to allow maximum destructive effect on the runway surface.

Israeli land forces thrust into Sinai, their attack supported by armed Magister light jet trainers which were subsequently transferred to join Mystères and Ouragans in supporting an advance into Jordan.

While the Sinai and the West bank of the River Jordan were being occupied, other Israeli troops had also advanced into Syria, backed by a paratroop landing behind the Syrian lines on the Golan Heights. In six days, for the loss of 31 aircraft, the Israeli air forces destroyed 353 Arab aircraft – 43 per cent of the total available – several tanks and much other equipment.

Again there was a reversion to a desultory guerrilla and frontier struggle in which the air forces were expanded and frequently engaged, the Israelis claiming 114 Arab aircraft shot down against a loss of about 25 during the next six years. Following a retaliatory strike on Beirut airport by Israeli helicopter-borne commandos, during which a number of airliners were blown up, the French put an embargo on the delivery of further arms to Israel. But to make good this loss, the US elected to deliver McDonnell F-4E Phantoms and A-4D Skyhawks to Israel, to counter growing deliveries of Russian aircraft to the Arabs. A series of Israeli air strikes deep into Egypt in 1973 raised their claims to around the 150 mark for Arab aircraft destroyed in a period which saw the extensive use by both sides of air-to-air missile armament. The Israelis used the French Matra weapon, and then US Sidewinders; the Arabs employed a Russian copy of the Sidewinder. By October 1973 the Israeli establishment included 128 Phantoms, nearly as many Skyhawks, and 55 Mirages, plus other older types. Egypt alone had over 600 Russian fighters, including the latest models of the MiG 21, Su 7, and some Russian flown Mach 3 MiG 25s. Syria had 75 Su 7s and many MiG 21s, Jordan 30 F-104As, 45 Hunters, while Libya had twelve Mirages and Iraqi had more of these aircraft on order. Added to this the Egyptians had installed a missile system to protect their forces in the Canal Zone, including 70 SA 2 and 65 SA 3 sites, SA 6 and 7 mobile launchers, and new, mobile ZSU 23-45P batteries comprising quad radar-guided 23 mm anti-aircraft cannons.

Ground defences won a significant victory when, on 6 October 1973, 'Yom Kippur', an Israeli Holy Day, the Arabs launched an attack on two fronts. While fighting raged on the Golan Heights in the north and the Israeli defences on the Suez Canal were overrun, the Israeli air force, trying to attack enemy air bases, suffered heavy losses, believed to amount to 80 aircraft during the first week and 38 in the second. Ninety-five of these fell to the guns and missiles, only a few in combat.

During the subsequent fighting, however, Israeli pilots began to learn the various tricks for avoiding the larger SA 2 and 3 missiles, though many aircraft returned with their rear fuselages damaged by the smaller, heat-seeking SA 6s and 7s. Once fully mobilised, the Israelis counter-attacked in the north, retaking the Golan Heights, advancing into Syria, and crossed the Suez Canal on 15 October with the initial aim of destroying the SA missile sites to leave the Israeli air force free to hold air superiority and accomplish ground-attack duties. In combat the Israeli fighter pilots maintained their mastery, and at the end of the second week Arab losses were believed to have been:

Egypt	113 of 580
Syria	149 of 240
Iraq	21 of 200

The war had swung firmly in Israel's favour when a UN instigated armistice brought it to a halt. By this time US observers considered total Arab losses to have been some 440 aircraft, about 25 of them brought down by Hawk missiles. And during the initial period of the armistice, while negotiations continued, there were frequent outbreaks of fighting, particularly in the air, until, at the end of 1973, Israeli claims included 248 Egyptian and 221 Syrian aircraft, 30 of these since the armistice had come into force. This air war had proved much more difficult for Israel than those of the past. MiG 25s, making high-speed reconnaissance passes over the country at high level, had proved impossible to intercept, though a Tu-16 bomber, attempting to launch stand-off bombs against Israeli towns, had been caught and shot down before it could do any damage.

A major reappraisal became necessary as the arms race went on. With threats of less American support in the future, the Israelis began developing their own aircraft industry and placed in production a re-engined development of the Mirage, the Kfir. Jordan has revitalised her air force, receiving Northrop F-5E Tigers, while Egypt, having fallen out with Russia, sought arms and aircraft from the United States, Great Britain and France.

Above all, the devastating effects of anti-aircraft fire, particularly at low level, have to be taken into account for the future, and with it a reassessment of the nature of fire support that can be given to land forces, with the possibility that artillery must do much that aircraft once did.

INDO-PAKISTAN CONFLICTS

The Sidewinder/Sabre combination was employed again in 1965, when war broke out in early September between India and Pakistan. Both sides made conflicting claims in a territorially indecisive confrontation, but the highly trained Pakistan Air Force more than held its own, though outnumbered by the much larger Indian Air Force. Claims by both sides for aircraft destroyed on the ground, and for those shot down by ground fire, were greatly exaggerated, but air-combat claims were not unreasonable. Thirty-six claims were made by the Pakistanis, all but five by Sabre pilots, while the Indians claimed 73 for a loss of 35. The Pakistani claims were a mixture of Sidewinder and gun victories, but it was reported that there were considerably more tight-turning dog fights and deflection shooting than had been the case during the Korean War. **The most successful jet combat currently on record** occurred when Squadron Leader Mohammad Allam in a Sabre claimed five Indian Hunters shot down in one engagement; the Pakistanis subsequently announced the names of all the Indian pilots shot down. Against the Sabre the Gnat proved to be the most successful Indian fighter.

As soon as the three-week war was over the usual escalation pattern appeared, both countries building up their armed forces from all possible sources. By 1971 Pakistan had added Canadair-built Sabre 6s plus three squadron of MiG 19s obtained from the Chinese and one of Mirages bought from France. The Indian Air Force was greatly strengthened by a large number of MiG 21 fighters, most of them assembled in India, Sukhoi Su 7 fighter-bombers, home-designed HF-24 Marut fighter-bombers, plus the

First in action over North Vietnam, the Mach 1·8 MiG 21 'Fishbed' is in service with a dozen 'non-aligned' nations, including India, as here, where over 250 of these relatively uncomplicated and lightweight interceptors have been built under licence.

older types still in service. Also available by this time was the Indian aircraft carrier *Vikrant,* with Sea Hawk fighters and Breguet Alizé anti-submarine aircraft.

Air clashes developed again during November 1971 followed by all-out hostilities on 3 December. The larger forces involved led to Pakistan claims of 104 Indian aircraft destroyed, 50 of them in air combat, against an admitted loss of 54. The Indians claimed 94 with Pakistan admitting the loss of only ten in the air with several on the ground. But this war was one more test of the combat merits of American and Russian aircraft. Pakistani/US F-104As engaged Indian/Russian MiG 21s for the first time – apparently not to the advantage of the Pakistanis – while MiG 19s fought against both MiG 21s and Su 7s.

VIETNAM

The longest war in American history can be reckoned to have started in February 1965, when regular units of the People's Army of the Republic of Vietnam gave open support to the guerrilla forces of the Viet Cong in South Vietnam, and the US air forces began to strike at targets in the Communist North.

The air forces of the Republics of South Vietnam, Cambodia and Laos were armed in 1960 mainly with obsolescent attack, trainer and transport types, suitable for Counter Insurgency (COIN) operations against small-scale guerrilla activities until it became obvious, as Laos and then South Vietnam failed to check the spread of Communist control, that Communist activities were not on a small scale.

The first American air units to serve in South Vietnam arrived in mid-1961 and consisted of US Army helicopter squadrons which were to augment the Vietnamese Air Force (RVNAF) troop lift capacity. US military advisers were already flying alongside RVNAF pilots, coaching the Vietnamese air crew but not allowed to fire on the guerrillas. The rule was relaxed in 1961 to permit the American personnel to fire 'in self defence' – in other words, provided that the enemy fired first. Air operations were mainly in support of Army bases and in protection of re-supply convoys, whose routes led through jungles and mountains which favoured ambushes.

In spite of greater American participation, corruption, indolence and treachery prevented effective action against the Viet Cong even after the fall of the original *régime* in 1963 and the emergence of the former Air Force commander, Marshal Ky, as the new President. North Vietnam was the principal source of arms for the Viet Cong, the 'Ho Chi Minh Trail', by-passing the well-guarded border between the Vietnams by way of Laos, whose eastern portion was controlled by the Communists. But the US Government refused to allow air interdiction of the Trail through Laos, permitting supplies to be delivered without check to the Viet Cong.

The first bombing raid on North Vietnam was launched by aircraft from two US Navy carriers, on 5 August 1964, in retaliation for reputed attacks on a USN destroyer in territorial waters off North Vietnam on 2 and 4 August. Sixty-four aircraft attacked three fast patrol boat bases and a major oil-fuel storage area, losing two aircraft but destroying eight FPBs and most of the oil-fuel tanks. The incident did not lead to an immediate escalation of the war, except that the USAF increased its fighter-bomber and tactical-bomber commitment. Nine aircraft were destroyed on a major airfield near Saigon by Viet Cong guerrillas in November while, over the target areas, Viet Cong heavy AA machine-gun and small-arms fire not only forced the US bombers to release from greater heights but claimed several victims each month.

The bombing of North Vietnam began in earnest following a North Vietnamese Army (NVA) ground attack on a US Army base. The US Government gave approval for limited, retaliatory strikes on nominated targets in the southern 'Panhandle' of the country. On 7 and 11 February, in monsoon weather, 182 carrier aircraft plus a rather smaller number of USAF and RVNAF machines attacked barracks and NVA camps, inflicting considerable damage.

Operation 'Rolling Thunder' – a strategic air offensive intended to force the North Vietnamese to negotiate – began on 18 March 1965. US Navy and Air

By swift manoeuvring, a pair of Republic F-105 Thunderchief fighter-bombers manage to avoid an SA-2 guided missile over North Vietnam, 1967.

Force tactical bombers were to begin by bombing military and transport targets in the 'Panhandle' and then gradually move the bombing line north towards Hanoi; once the capital was threatened, it was hoped the North Vietnamese would be ready to sue for peace on US/South Vietnamese terms. Had the US Government been prepared to mount an unrestricted bombing campaign, or even had it been confronted with a democratic country in which public opinion would sway the leadership, this policy might have worked. In the event, the American President imposed crippling restrictions on his air forces for fear of incurring adverse world opinion, while the Communist régime in the North held fast with an iron discipline on the populace, whose sufferings were exploited by propaganda which eroded the American public's support for their Government.

To the pilots, the bombing restrictions were incomprehensible. The detailed instructions as to targetting referred to above were extended to include the fusing of the bombs, time on target, ordnance load and even, on occasion, the direction of attack. Built-up areas were to be avoided at all costs, providing sanctuaries in which the North Vietnamese could store *matériel* and build their AA defences. The rules of engagement were rigid: motor transport could only be attacked while on the move in open country, and then only if on or within a prescribed distance of roads or tracks: the result was that vehicles moved only by night and parked in full view in villages during the day. Enemy aircraft could not be attacked on their airfields – long established as the primary targets in any battle for air supremacy – and were not to be engaged in air combat before positively identified.

The North Vietnam Air Force (NVNAF) scored its first success on 4 April 1965, when four MiG 17 'Fresco' fighters bounced a flight of USAF F-105D Thunderchiefs and destroyed two. Following this incident, the F-105 missions were provided with a top cover of USAF F-4C Phantoms.

USMC EF-10B Skyknight electronic support aircraft arrived at the same time and these were immediately pressed into service over the 'Panhandle', accompanying the 'out-country' USAF strike aircraft and jamming the enemy gunnery fire control radar.

The first American aircraft to be lost to a guided missile was a USAF F-4C, shot down south of Hanoi on 24 July 1965. As early as 5 April, a reconnaissance aircraft from a carrier had photographed a Surface-to-Air missile (SAM) site under construction, but although the US Seventh Air Force and Seventh Fleet proposed an immediate joint offensive against the site before Russian-built SA-2 'Guideline' missiles could be emplaced, Washington forbade any pre-emptive action. The ban was lifted after the loss of the F-4C, and 55 USAF F-100 Supersabres and F-105s attacked the SAM site responsible three days afterwards. The missiles claimed none of the strike aircraft, but four were shot down by AA gunfire.

The increasing effectiveness of the AA defences forced the American air forces to accelerate the development of electronic equipment for detecting, identifying and jamming warning and control radars. Miniaturisation of components allowed equipment to be fitted in external pods on fighter-bombers and attack aircraft which could be used specifically for AA and SAM warning and suppression in support of a strike. The 'Wild Weasel' (USAF) and 'Iron Hand' (USN) divisions were armed with anti-radiation missiles which homed on the emissions from radar transmitters. The North Vietnamese countered by using the radar intermittently and for short periods, in order to draw the anti-radar missiles' fire and then leave them with no source on to which to home. Only when a SAM was fired was the target-illuminating radar used for long enough to allow a 'Shrike' missile to find the radar. American pilots found that the 'flying telegraph poles' could be evaded by flying at low level or, provided that the SAM was seen in time, by taking violent evasive action at the last possible moment.

The 60–70 MiGs of the NVAF posed no great threat, compared with that of the SAMs and AA guns, but USAF and USN Airborne Early Warning aircraft patrolled off the North Vietnamese coast, watching for NVAF airborne activity and listening in on the fighter control radio frequencies. As soon as MiGs were known to be airborne, the AEW aircraft broadcast warnings to the strikes.

NVAF fighters: a camouflaged MiG 17 and a silver MiG 21.

The US Navy was far better equipped for the campaign over North Vietnam than the US Air Force. The latter had seen its role as a deterrent force; thus, the F-105 fighter-bombers of Tactical Air Command were intended primarily for the delivery of nuclear weapons in the sophisticated setting of a European war of short duration. In Vietnam these Mach 2·1 aircraft were obliged to carry up to 6000 lb (2730 kg) of 'iron bombs' which had to be delivered accurately on to a visually identified target at speeds which was well within the performance limits of the Mach 0·95 MiG 17 and the AA fire control radar-aided predictors. By contrast, the US Navy's day-attack workhorse was the Douglas A-4 Skyhawk which weighed less when carrying full fuel and 8000 lb (3640 kg) of ordnance than an empty F-105! The A-4's night and bad-weather partner was **the Grumman A-6 Intruder – the best attack aircraft of the war.** Equipped with radar linked to a bombing and navigational computer and flown at low level, the A-6 was the only aircraft capable of achieving the demanded level of accuracy during the worst of the monsoon season and the only one allowed to release its bombs 'blind'. On 22 December 1965, over 100 USN aircraft made a day strike on a power station near Haiphong, inflicting 'serious damage'; on the night of 18 April 1966, two A-6s each dropped **thirteen** 1000 lb (454 kg) bombs on the same power station, virtually destroying it – not one bomb fell outside the perimeter fence!

Douglas Skyhawk 'Tinker Toy' light attack aircraft, each loaded with nine 250 lb (112 kg) retarded bombs, taxi out for a strike from USS Coral Sea.

The US Navy also enjoyed the advantage of secure bases close to the target areas. The 'Yankee Station' for the carriers was within 100 miles (160 km) of the Vietnamese coast, whereas the F-105s were based in Thailand, their closest airfield being 480 miles (768 km) in a straight line from Hanoi. The F-105s were obliged to adopt a 'Hi-Lo-Hi' flight profile, flying out at high level and descending for the approach to the target and subsequent withdrawal, and then climbing out to meet a Boeing KC-135 Stratotanker to refuel for the return to base. The US Navy also maintained tanker aircraft over the Gulf of Tonkin, but these were for emergency use rather than essential to the success of the mission.

The cost of the bombing of the North was high. By the end of 1967, over 670 US aircraft had been shot down by AA guns, SAMs and MiGs. The US Navy's share came to 52 per cent of the casualties, but the carrier aircraft were flying over 65 per cent of the missions. The USAF's heavier proportion of losses was largely attributable to the long distance to friendly bases: a hit by a small-calibre projectile on an aircraft crammed with fuel and hydraulic lines and electric wiring could result in it 'bleeding to death' in minutes, far from its land base though perhaps within distance of a carrier.

A deeply disturbing aspect of the 'Rolling Thunder' campaign was the American fighters' failure to achieve the air-to-air combat results expected with sophisticated weapons'

McDonnell F-4B Phantom II.

The airborne KC-135 tankers were essential for USAF strikes on North Vietnam by the F-105 strike aircraft.

systems. Nearly 50 Air Force and Navy aircraft were shot down, compared with 110 North Vietnamese, a 2·3:1 ratio, which fell far below the Korean War MiG : Sabre average of over 9 : 1. The US Navy, which had lost more aircraft than it had shot down during the first five months of 1968 and had failed to obtain a kill with the 50 Sparrow and Sidewinder missiles fired thereafter, decided that its pilots' training was deficient and instituted a 'Top Gun' dog-fighting course as early as September 1968. The three years of the 'Top Gun' course produced some first-rate leaders and marksmen, who averaged 23 MiGs shot down for every two carrier aircraft, whereas the USAF, who did not copy the Navy until October 1972, managed only a 2:1 victory ratio.

The combat rescue helicopter units did much to maintain the morale of the strike crews. Helicopter-carrying destroyers inshore off North Vietnam and bases in northern Thailand and Laos provided rescue facilities over most of the North – **the first pick-up took place only 20 miles (32 km) from Hanoi,** on 20 September 1965. These operations often provoked minor battles, with first the downed pilot's formation providing him with close support, relieved by the Douglas A-1 Skyraiders escorting the helicopters, and then by the helicopters' own guns.

The development of helicopters received a massive impetus from the 'in-country' war in the South. The Communist domination of the poor-quality overland lines of communication forced the extensive use of air transport, and the helicopter became a 'flying truck', the ubiquitous Bell UH-1E ('Huey') Iroquois being used to carry an infantry assault squad apiece, while the Boeing Vertol CH-47 Chinook could outlift the fixed-wing C-47 Dakota, still in service as a tactical transport and, incredibly, as a night gunfire support aircraft.

Time-exposure photograph of an AC-47 Dakota 'Dragon Ship' providing night saturation support gunfire on the outskirts of Saigon.

The vulnerability of helicopters to ground fire was demonstrated early in the war. Relatively slow-moving when cruising, the approach to the hover and the actual landing reduced the speed to the point where the helicopters were easy prey for rifle and light machine-gun fire. With up to 200 helicopters involved in a single assault, flying in close formation in successive waves, individual aircraft were unable to take radical evasive action. **Total American helicopter losses in Vietnam amounted to approximately 3000 machines.**

Armed helicopters progressed from the airborne assault aircraft, with light machine-guns mounted in the doorways, to the custom-built AH-1 'Huey Cobra', armoured against small-arms fire and armed with wire-guided anti-tank missiles and a gun turret mounting combinations of 'Gatling'-type machine-guns and grenade launchers. The original purpose of the armed assault helicopters was to provide suppressive fire during a landing, but so useful were they that further missions, such as escorting road and river convoys, were also imposed upon them.

The US Army attempted a radical approach to providing helicopter bases in thick jungle. A 10-tonne 'bomb' was released from a heavy-lift helicopter flying at about 9000 ft (2700 m) and the resulting explosion cleared trees and undergrowth, the debris of which could be used to fill in the vast crater. **Defoliation** was widely practised to deny the Communists the protection of the jungle canopy: transport aircraft sprayed vast areas with chemicals to create new deserts in which genetic mutations of plant-life are reported now to abound.

The bombing of the North, attacks on the 'Ho Chi Minh Trail' and the heavy scale of support for the Army and Marines in South Vietnam failed to prevent the Communists in the South from increasing their ability to wage guerrilla war or to deter the Government in the North from continuing support.

The bombing of the supply routes was successful only in that it forced the Communists to move more slowly, using vast numbers of porters to carry the loads down through Laos and, in the South, out of Cambodia, which served as a port of entry for supplies.

North Vietnam was divided into 'Route Package Areas' for the purpose of targetting strikes. Transport systems remained at the top of the list, bombed and strafed not only by carrier and Vietnam-based tactical strike aircraft, but also by the gigantic Boeing B-52. Flying 2500 miles (4000 km) from Guam to drop upwards of 15 tonnes of bombs on carefully selected target complexes, the strategic bombers inflicted severe damage but were not used for raids on the more politically sensitive targets in the well-defended Red River area.

In the 'Iron Triangle', an area embracing the cities of Hanoi, Haiphong and Thanh Hoa, oil fuel became a priority target in mid-1966, and by the end of the year most of the storage sites and rail and water fuel tankers had been destroyed, forcing the Vietnamese to disperse their fuel storage sites underground and to build an oil pipeline system. Oil imports through the port of Haiphong fell to a twelfth of their June 1966 level, and the fuel was now delivered in drums, instead of in bulk. Electricity generating stations also came under attack, those in built-up areas being restricted to aircraft armed with 'Smart' bombs, such as the television-guided 'Walleye'. The North's generating capacity was very seriously reduced.

There was no coherent strategy discernible in the bombing policy up to the summer of 1967. The US Secretary of Defence, Robert MacNamara, was responsible for the day-to-day conduct of the war, and his system for determining the effectiveness of the bombing was based on the number and weight of bombs **allocated** to categories of targets, not the number **hitting** the targets – a preoccupation which may have its origins in the experiences of Colonel R S MacNamara as an Air Transport Command statistician, at one time attached to the 'Hump' Route organisation.

The key to the North Vietnamese war effort was the port of Haiphong, through which virtually all the weapons from the Soviet Union passed. Washington refused to allow direct attack or mining, but did authorise the USN and USAF to attempt to seal off both Haiphong and Hanoi from the remainder of the country. Bridges were destroyed, railway ferry slipways damaged and river dredgers sunk. (By the end of October, silt banks in Haiphong harbour mouth closed the port to ships drawing over 22 ft (6·7 m).) The first signs of victory were orders on 25 August 1967 instructing all non-essential civilians to leave the

18 tons of bombs are released by a Boeing B-52D on a Vietnam target.

two major cities. This was followed by an obvious increase in the size of the storage areas in Haiphong, where the difficulty in unloading from ships and then distributing the imports resulted in 200 000 tons of military stores being stacked in the open by October. These splendid targets were in the city limits and therefore not cleared for attack. Instead, the pilots had to go on with their attacks on heavily defended, rebuilt bridges.

The potential and limitations of the isolation campaign were best illustrated by the effectiveness and activity of the defences in the Iron Triangle. On 21 August 1967, 80 SAMs were fired at US Navy aircraft; nine days later rather fewer were fired on the first of seven days' unbroken strike activity. By the end of the fifth day the North Vietnamese batteries had run out of SAMs and AA ammunition. For the succeeding two days the naval aircraft briefed for AA suppression were diverted to the main targets. Three days of bad weather followed, during which the carrier aircraft did not cross the coast; when they did return, they were greeted by the usual storm of AA and SAM fire, enemy stocks having been replenished.

The 1967 holiday bombing 'stand-down' for the Christmas, Western New Year and Vietnamese New Year were expensive political gestures, the Communists using the time available to move ten times the stores normally seen in the open on strike days. Monsoon weather in January permitted visual attacks on only three days and the A-6 Intruders alone were unable to stem the rush of war supplies into South Vietnam.

The longest continuous battle of the War was the siege of the US Marines jungle base at Khe Sanh. This major offensive outpost was encircled in January 1968 and remained so for another five months, while the Communists tried to win another prestige victory which would have the same world-wide impact as that at Dien Bien Phu, 14 years earlier. The situation was, however, completely different: instead of under-equipped paratroops with inadequate artillery and air support, the Communists were faced with a well-armed garrison who called upon the aircraft of the USAF, RVNAF, USMC and US Navy to provide all stores, close support, area support, and

The door-gunner of a UH-1 'slick' gunship provides covering fire for an assault force landing in paddy fields.

interdiction of enemy lines of supply. Helicopters and fixed-wing transports flew in ammunition and food and flew out wounded, even though the enemy penetrated to within 50 yards of the aluminium matting airstrip on occasion. Marine and Navy attack aircraft (the latter from up to five carriers) provided really close support with guns, rockets and bombs, while B-52s dropped loads of up to 70000 lb (32000 kg) on suspected stores and bivouac areas in the surrounding country side. The Communists acknowledged defeat in June 1968.

The failure of American policy in Vietnam was brought home to the US Government by the initial success of the 'Tet Offensive' in January 1968. But American air power was the major factor in the defeat of the offensive, for the Viet Cong and NVA had no real answer to aerial attack when caught in the open and committed to a stand-up action.

Peace talks between the United States and North Vietnam had begun shortly before the 'Tet' onslaught, the Communists' hope being to make political capital out of the success of their troops. As this was swiftly nullified, the North Vietnamese intransigence weakened and Washington ordered the cessation of bombing north of the 'Panhandle' as a demonstration of American willingness to come to a just settlement. Bombing of military installations north of the border and of the 'Ho Chi Minh Trail' continued after the cessation order on 31 March, but on 1 November **all bombing of North Vietnam was halted.** US air power had drastically reduced the North Vietnamese capacity to support the War, but this had been achieved at a cost of 915 fixed-wing aircraft.

During the next two years, the anti-Communist forces in South Vietnam gained an ascendancy, using fire-power and mobility to prevent the guerrillas and regular troops from rebuilding their strength. The hitherto inviolable sanctuaries in Cambodia and Laos were raided by helicopter-borne troops and ground columns in 1970 and 1971, these incursions destroying supply dumps and training camps. From time to time, retaliatory strikes were delivered against selected targets in North Vietnam, the first such occasion being 2 May 1970. During this period, the bulk of American and Allied ground troops were withdrawn and the Army of the Republic of Vietnam (ARVN) and the (RVN) Air Force were re-trained and given confidence by achieving unaided victories. By the end of 1971, **South Vietnam was emerging as the victor.**

North Vietnam was rebuilt between 1968 and 1971, the anti-aircraft defences taking high priority. New SA-3 'Goa' missiles, with longer range and better low-level capability, supplemented the SA-2s, improved warning and control radars were installed, and the fighter force converted all its units to the MiG 21. But, as in the Middle East, the MiG 21 enjoyed relatively little success, due mainly to the inexperience of the NVAF pilots at that date.

The lull came to an end on 26 December 1971, when North Vienamese occupation of the vital central plain of Laos, added to the obvious insincerity of the North Vietnamese delegation at the Paris talks, forced the United States Government to order the resumption of the bombing of the North. The carrier and land-based aircraft struck at the well-known transport targets and the SAM defences, but losses were heavier than up to 1968, in spite of improved stand-off weapons, electronic defensive systems and new aircraft types. Yet, in spite of their losses, the American aircraft soon began to make a decisive contribution to the reduction of the North. Again the Communists were faced with the prospect of defeat on all fronts.

In desperation, the North Vietnamese committed their Army to a full-scale invasion of the South, on 2 April 1972. The reconstructed ARVN fought tenaciously, but what saved the country was **the massive scale of air support** provided by the RVNAF, the USAF and the USN whose pilots at last had a conventional enemy to attack in the open – an enemy, furthermore, who lacked any air cover and was out of range of his long-range SAM batteries. Aircraft of all types slaughtered the Communists – men and tanks – while the fixed and rotary-wing transports supplied the ARVN in the field.

The most advanced Russian AA weapon to be deployed was the infra-red homing SAM-7 'Grail' – carried and fired from a bazooka-type launcher by a foot soldier. Although effective against helicopters, it was not particularly successful against heavier, faster attack aircraft, many of which were equipped with decoy flare dispensers.

As the Communist invasion reached its high tide in the first week of May, President Nixon at last authorised the closure of the port of Haiphong by aerial minelaying. **On 9 May 1972, carrier-based A-6 Intruders carried out the most effective strikes of the war.** The thousands of magnetic, acoustic and pressure mines they laid sealed off all the major ports for the duration of the conflict, isolating North Vietnam from its principal supplier, except by the lengthy air supply route via India and Burma.

The last bombing halt in response to the familiar North Vietnamese demand of 'stop the bombing and we'll start talking' lasted from 23 October until 18 December, with a single break on 22 November, when very heavy raids were delivered by B-52s as well as the tactical strike aircraft.

The much-extended American patience snapped in mid-December 1972. In an all-out attempt to 'bomb the Vietnamese to the conference table', even the B-52s were employed to attack **all** targets associated with the war effort, irrespective of location. The North Vietnamese fought back desperately with SAMs and MiG 21s; in spite of massive electronic counter-measures support, 17 B-52s were shot down by SAMs for which they provided ideal targets as they flew straight and level at 37000 ft (11 100 m). But the MiG 21s did not fare so well, losing two of their number to B-52 gunners and failing to down any of the bombers. A 36-hour Christmas Day truce was, as usual, violated by the North Vietnamese and intensified bombing began again on the 28th. Three days were sufficient – by 30 December Hanoi and Haiphong had ceased to be effective military centres or useful supply bases and the North Vietnamese were ready to sue for peace on their own terms.

Unrestricted bombing of military targets had at last brought to an end the War against North Vietnam. The political leadership had shown irresolution up to the spring of 1972, fearing the ultimate escalation of actually winning. The conduct of the pilots flying over the North was in marked contrast: in spite of being put at risk without the prize of victory as incentive, dedication and morale remained high – even as they dodged SAMs fired from residential areas or fought with MiGs whose airfields they were not allowed to bomb.

Against the chilly background of the Cold War numerous small wars have produced minor yet significant incidents in air combat. For example:

In Katanga in 1960 the UN formed forces from many nations, including India, Ireland, Denmark, Norway and Sweden. Towards the end of a protracted struggle, in late December 1961, Katangese gendarmes fired on UN forces, and fighting broke out again. **Next day the most important UN air action of the war** took place when six SAAB J-29Bs strafed Kolwezi airfield several times. More attacks were made over the next five days, Katanga's air force was virtually wiped out on the ground and shortly thereafter peace was restored.

In Nigeria in 1968, Biafra broke away and hostilities commenced. Initially the Biafrans managed to acquire some Douglas B-26 light bombers and mercenary pilots, but Nigeria was supplied by Eastern Europe with 12 An 12s, 10 MiG 17s, six MiG 15 trainers, and six L-29 Delfin jet trainers/ground-attack aircraft, soon followed by more MiG 17s and six Ilyushin Il-28 jet bombers. Dornier Do 28s were also acquired. These aircraft were flown by Egyptians and a number of British and South African mercenaries. Early attacks by the B-26s destroyed several MiGs on the ground, the Biafrans also using a Fokker F 27 Friendship airliner as a bomber.

Gradually the Biafran aircraft were lost, but in March 1969 eight little Swedish-built MFI-9B Minicon light aircraft arrived with some Swedish pilots led by Count von Rosen. In a number of daring strafing attacks with rockets and machine-guns, these tiny aircraft destroyed a considerable number of Nigerian MiGs, Il-28s and other aircraft on the ground, virtually gaining control of the air by the end of June. But early in 1970 the starving remnants of the Biafran population surrendered what was left of their territory.

The final stages of the war in Biafra, as in the Congo in 1961 and Angola in 1976, saw the extensive use of airline transports chartered by the International Red Cross Organisation for the evacuation of refugees.

One of the most ridiculous wars was that which broke out in 1969 between Honduras and El Salvador, following a disputed World Cup football match between the two countries! On this occasion Honduras employed F4U-5 Corsairs, El Salvador using F-47D Thunderbolts and F-51Ds. Apparently some eight Honduran and four Salvadorean aircraft were shot down, about half of them during dog fights.

Overall looms the threat of total nuclear war waged by combinations of all three services. The following tables give samples of aircraft performances in the 1970s.

Bombers 1970

Nation	Type	Speed	Ceiling	Range	Max Load	Armament
British	H-S Vulcan Mk 2	620 mph	20 000 m	3000 miles plus	21 000 lbs	—
Russian	Tupolev Tu-16	587 mph	13 000 m	3975 miles	19 800 lbs	7 cannon
USA	Boeing B-52	630 mph	16 800 m	8000 miles	65 000 lbs	1 multi-barrel cannon or 4 mg

Fighters 1970

Nation	Type	Mach No.	Speed	Ceiling	Armament
British	BAC Lightning	2.2	1450 mph	18 000 m plus	2 cannon 2 missiles
Russian	Mikoyan MiG-21	1.8	1320 mph	17 000 m	2 cannon 2 missiles
French	Dassault Mirage III	2.2	1460 mph	17 000 m	2 cannon 3 missiles
USA	McDonnell F-4E Phantom II	2.3	1500 mph	19 000 m	1 multi-barrel cannon 8 missiles

The development of nuclear arms produced smaller tactical weapons that could be delivered by light bombers and even fighter-bombers, while air-to-air refuelling increased the range of such high-performance aircraft considerably. **Intercontinental guided ballistic missiles** with nuclear warheads supplemented both sides' bomber arsenals during the late fifties/early sixties, while the nuclear-powered submarines capable of firing such missiles whilst submerged provided a new factor in the game of deterrent and counter-deterrent, terror and counter-terror.

As improved defensive systems rendered the ageing intercontinental bombers vulnerable, stand-off guided missiles were developed which were carried by the bombers to within range of the target, these weapons then being launched at a safe distance from possible dangers. Following this came the next advance – the use of the big bombers at low altitude to avoid radar detection.

The most important but least publicised activity of both sides during the Cold War has been the unceasing watch on one another's activities. Air reconnaissance has been the Western Alliance's principal method of reaching behind the 'Iron Curtain', beginning with high-altitude photographic missions at the time of the Berlin Airlift.

Deep penetration of Soviet airspace was not possible until the mid-1950s, when one of the most remarkable of all strategic aircraft entered limited service. The Lockheed U-2 was a single-engined, straight-wing jet aircraft which owed much to the high-performance sailplane, possessing a long-span high-aspect-ratio wing and a light structure. Able to reach altitudes of 90 000 ft (27 400 m), it could then shut off its engine and glide down to about 60 000 ft (18 300 m) where it was still above the ceiling of current interceptors, relight the engine and climb back up again. Using this technique, the U-2 progressed across the USSR from bases in the United Kingdom, Norway, Turkey and Pakistan, concentrating its attentions on the Soviet ballistic-missile industry and collecting atmospheric samples in the vicinity of nuclear and thermo-nuclear test sites.

The veil of secrecy surrounding these operations was dramatically broken in May 1960 when the Russians at last managed to bring down a U-2 with a guided missile. A major diplomatic confrontation was followed by cessation of the U-2 flights over the Soviet Union, and the aircraft were switched to flights over the People's Republic of China and Cuba, where a socialist régime hostile to the United States made necessary surveillance closer to home. It was the photographic evidence of the construction of strategic missile bases in Cuba, gathered initially by U-2s and latterly by US Navy tactical reconnaissance aircraft, that led to the 'Cuba Confrontation' between the United States and the Soviet Union in the autumn of 1962.

An epochal advance in technology had meanwhile made redundant the penetration of heavily defended airspace by manned aircraft. On 4 October 1957, the Soviet Union launched the first orbiting satellite into space. By the early 1960s, both of the major powers were launching reconnaissance satellites equipped with cameras which covered not only the visible spectrum but also the ultra-violet and infra-red, in addition to being capable of picking up electronic emissions. Multi-channel communications satellites and weather-watching stations round out the current military use of space, for the first Strategic Arms Limitation (SALT) Treaty forbade the use of nuclear weapons held in earth orbit. It remains to be seen whether this agreement will be honoured.

Electronic reconnaissance has been the most continuous aerial surveillance activity. Long-range aircraft flying in international or friendly airspace have probed the other side's radar networks and listened to his communications chatter. Loaded with electronic listening gear, Lockheed P-2 Neptunes, Martin P-4M Mercators, Boeing RB-47 Stratojets and a variety of RAF aircraft have flown around the land and maritime borders of the Communist 'bloc', occasionally straying too close and being shot down by fighters. These monitoring operations have also been undertaken by Soviet aircraft flying not only from Russia, but also from Cuba and Egypt, supplementing the ever-present 'spy trawlers' which are stationed in international waters around the coasts of the Western democracies.

Aircraft with a Future

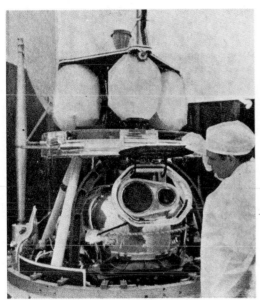

The interior of an orbiting satellite showing its cameras.

The Lockheed YF-12A or SR 71 Reconnaissance Aircraft.

The VTOL Hawker Siddley Harrier.

Appendix
Trends and Prospects

Nothing that has appeared in recent years and wars suggests that the manned aircraft is unable to play its traditional roles in war. The human eye is still required for confident identification of targets, whether they be on the ground, at sea or in the air. Electronic identification can be counterfeited by the enemy and equipment prone to malfunction can leave a friend without his electronic 'password'. In combat over North Vietnam, American fighters habitually closed to within visual range (under 2 miles (3·5 km) before firing radar-guided missiles with a range in excess of 10 miles (6·5 km), simply to ensure the identity of the target.

The potential of modern strategic reconnaissance was revealed in the 1973 War when the Israeli Army went over to the offensive, driving across the Suez Canal into Egypt into a weak sector of the defences, 6600 ft (2000 m) wide, that was revealed by US Air Force Lockheed SR-71 reconnaissance aircraft flying at Mach 3·5 (35 miles – 56 km – per minute) at 90000 ft (27000 m) and uninterceptable by the Egyptian or Soviet Air Forces. The Egyptian High Command was unaware of the extent of the penetration of their own territory, Israeli air support of the column having prevented any tactical reconnaissance, until the Egyptians' Russian advisers produced photographs taken by satellites in orbit outside the earth's atmosphere. The Americans and Russians maintain such satellites for surveillance and the range of their sensors – optical, infra-red, active radar – make camouflage difficult, whether by artificial means or by the presence of cloud. In conditions of total war, orbiting reconnaissance vehicles could be destroyed by weapon-carrying satellites, but in time of uneasy peace it is tacitly accepted that destruction of a satellite would constitute an open act of war.

The need for precision attacks has led to the retention of the manned bomber capable of delivering missiles, guided free-fall bombs or mines. (Although strategic and tactical ground-to-ground nuclear missiles have largely usurped the area bombardment role.) Penetration of the enemy's defensive system can be attempted at low level, in order to take advantage of the 'gap' under the early-warning radar cover, or by using electronic counter-measures to jam warning radar and the fighter direction and missile fire-control radars. A major disadvantage of the high-power jammer is that its position can be fixed by direction-finders and current fire-control systems are being built with filters and suppressors which minimise the effect of interference which is not specifically directed at individual radars.

The gap under the radar was first filled by the US Navy in 1944/5 to deal with Kamikaze aircraft approaching at low level. Later a very powerful set was carried by converted Lockheed Constellations, fitted out as airborne radar stations which patrolled sea areas which could be used by enemy aircraft approaching to attack the USA and its overseas bases. From the operations of these and carrier aircraft over North Vietnam stemmed the Airborne Warning and Control Station (AWACS) requirement which could provide surveillance, warning, fighter and missile control and strike direction over

THE AIR DEFENCE LAYOUT OF A SOVIET ARMY GROUP

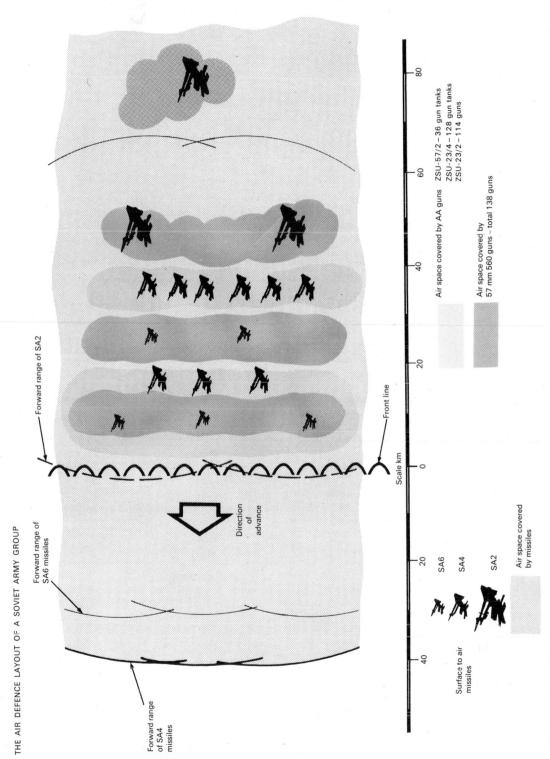

Forward range of SA2

Forward range of SA6 missiles

Forward range of SA4 missiles

Front line

Scale km

Direction of advance

ZSU-57/2 – 36 gun tanks
ZSU-23/4 – 128 gun tanks
ZSU-23/2 – 114 guns

Air space covered by AA guns

57 mm 560 guns – total 138 guns

Air space covered by

SA6
SA4
SA2

Surface to air missiles

Air space covered by missiles

Acknowledgement International Defence Review

vast areas; with a ground-level horizon range of 245 miles (392 km) and a 15 000-ft (4500 m) horizon range of 300 miles (480 km), an AWACS at 30 000 ft (9000 m) over each of Hamburg and Regensburg can monitor take-offs and landings from airfields in East Germany and the western areas of Poland and Czechoslavakia. Such surveillance capability vastly improves identification of 'hostiles', for it can be taken for granted that aircraft detected taking off from enemy bases are indeed enemy, and with a data link feeding interception instructions from the AWACS' computer to the friendly fighters' fire-control computers, the fighters can take full advantage of the 100-mile (160 km) range of the air-to-air missile, six of which can be fired at different targets in a single engagement by aircraft such as the US Navy's Grumman F-14 Tomcat.

The first use of AWACS by the Soviet Union in a war occurred during the Indo-Pakistan War in December 1971, when a Tupolev 'Moss' was used to direct Indian Air Force attack aircraft to make accurate night raids on targets 230 miles (368 km) from the controller, conning the Canberras and converted transports past Pakistani night-fighters.

No completely adequate tactical transport has yet been designed to replace the Douglas Dakota, hundreds still being in service in 1975, carrying an infantry platoon, a modest three and a half tons of supplies, or armed with rapid-fire machine-guns for night counter-insurgency operations. Later aircraft have shown improvements in load-carrying capacity, overall performance and short-field operations, but few of these propeller-driven tactical transports have possessed the ease of operation and lack of complication that has made the Dakota the supreme supplier of forward areas.

Airborne assault has been revolutionised by the troop-carrying helicopter. Furthermore, troops landed by helicopter can also be evacuated by helicopter. Yet fixed-wing transports are still needed to deliver troops by parachute at any great distance behind the main front. Slow-flying helicopters and paratroop transports are vulnerable to ground fire and fighters, though this can be minimised by the rotary-winged craft using its manoeuvrability and following the nap of the ground while, by dropping at low level at night, the larger fixed-wing transport can avoid fighters and visually aimed AA gunfire. **Airborne assault can still only succeed in areas where air superiority is assured** and close air support is available to make up for the almost inevitable weakness in airborne artillery and armour.

Tactical air support is an extension of the artillery arm, with the aircrew acting as observation post and battery, to reach targets out of reach of guns or which are difficult to hit with guns, or even to substitute for a shortage of guns. However, the hazards of modern close air support as vividly highlighted by the fatal experiences of low-flying Israeli Air Force machines in 1973 show that considerable effort has to be given over to the suppression of the mobile 23 mm and 57 mm AA batteries – which leads to a reduced load being delivered on primary targets.

Long-range ground–air missiles can be evaded, and air–ground missiles can be fired from outside the envelope of gunfire and short-range missiles. Using 'smart' bombs, with television guidance or infra-red, or even homing on to the reflection of a laser beam of the target, the launch aircraft can deliver an accurate, albeit expensive, weapon in relative safety. Tackling the problem more directly, the USAF decided in the early 1970s to develop a heavily armoured aircraft for use over the battlefield. Built around a 30 mm 'Gatling-gun' cannon with a rate of fire of over 4000 rpm, the A-10 has been designed to survive in this most hostile environment, carrying up to 12 000 lb (5450 kg) of ordnance as well as the gun, though, unlike most contemporary attack aircraft, it has little capacity for self-defence against fighters.

Tactical Reconnaissance (TAC/R) over the front lines is as hazardous as close support, and several Western armies have introduced 'remotely piloted vehicles' (RPVs) – short-range, unmanned aircraft which can take photographs optically or outside the visual spectrum. Small in size and operating by day or night at low altitude, the RPV is a difficult gun or missile target. In addition to its reconnaissance function it would appear to have an application as a low-cost reusable ordnance delivery vehicle. Longer-range TAC/R behind the lines is still undertaken by manned fighter-type aircraft, but the air crew's knee-pad-aided memory and camera has had to be supplemented by high-definition radar and the infra-red scanner, such is the speed of the single pass that is all that is tactically possible over the target.

A drone missile fitted for trials with a 'Maverick' TV-guided 'smart' bomb.

The idea of Army support aircraft operating close to the front line, from unprepared strips, is an attractive concept, though not entirely practical, for operational and logistic reasons. Modern jet aircraft burn considerable quantities of fuel, and a fuel load of three tons for 40 minutes at low level is a reasonable figure; add a ton of bombs to the fuel load, and the aircraft will need four tons (3640 kg) per sortie. Whether the stores arrive by truck or, ideally, by helicopter, this represents a major diversion of tactical load-lifting capacity, particularly if there are several detached VTOL units. Only the most basic aircraft maintenance facilities exist for maintenance at a forward site, and aircraft must be returned to the main base for major repairs or component replacement – assuming that they can be flown out. Jet efflux on take-off and landing erodes grass or bare earth surfaces, posing an engine debris ingestion problem and rendering the site vulnerable to detection. Once detected, the site is liable to attack, and the provision of defences requires further dispersion of resources. Co-ordination between detachments is difficult with temporary communications in peacetime; in war, when concentration, not dispersal, is essential if the initiative is to be retained, it is doubtful whether the air forces operating VTOL aircraft would allow the major units to be dispersed.

The most promising application of the VTOL attack fighters is in the shipborne role, used either in the interceptor/light attack role against shadowing aircraft or surface warships, or as a close-support aircraft with an amphibious assault force. The Royal Navy was given authority to order a naval variant of the Hawker Siddeley Harrier for deployment aboard its *Invincible*-class anti-submarine cruisers, which will constitute the only form of fixed-wing aircraft carrier with the Royal Navy in the 1980s. Similar ships are under construction for the Soviet and US Navies, the latter designating them 'Sea Control Ships'. None of the three classes have catapults or arrester gear, but by using a short take-off run for their VTO aircraft the latter's inherently short range can be slightly extended and the aircraft given a worthwhile load.

    The major user of VTOL aircraft in the 1970s is the US Marine Corps, which deploys its AV-8 Harriers in squadron-sized units which can be lifted to the scene of action aboard helicopter carriers (LPH) and then operate from the ship close inshore, until the aluminium mat Short Airfield for Tactical Support can be built ashore. STOL operations from the SATS, supplied by the LPH's medium-lift helicopters provide the USMC with an invaluable **organic air support arm** for action outside the main battle area, as amply demonstrated in Vietnam.

The armed helicopter is also part of the LPH's offensive contribution. Firing optically guided missiles at ranges of up to 13 000 ft (4000 m), the helicopter can take full advantage of terrain to remain unobserved, but it is difficult to employ effectively against targets that are partially concealed and well protected in a close battlefield environment.

The submarine remains the principal threat at sea and aircraft are essential to the defence of trade. The nuclear submarine, with underwater speeds of up to 30 knots, can now evade the ASW ships by running away, so that it can only be caught by a long-range weapon – the best of which is an air-launched homing torpedo or nuclear depth-charge released by a manned or remote-controlled vehicle. The sonar-equipped helicopter can operate either defensively or offensively against the submarine, hovering while it uses its detection and localisation equipment and 'jumping' to maintain a favourable position.

Two or three helicopters working together are a formidable ASW team, with one or two holding contact while the other jumps ahead of the submarine, thus maintaining contact until the kill can be made. Embarked in ships down to destroyer size, the ASW helicopter can also be operated off merchant ships with suitable decks and support facilities. Fixed-wing aircraft from shore bases or carriers have a better area surveillance capability than the helicopter, as well as a higher transit speed and longer range, so that they are necessary for direct support of shipping and the reinforcement of threatened areas. An interesting feature is that the principal land-based ASW aircraft of the mid-1970s are derivations of civil-airliner designs, only one of which – the RAF's Nimrod – is a propeller-less jet. In spite of the wide armoury of sonic, magnetic, atmospheric sampling and electronic aids at the disposal of the long-range maritime-patrol aircraft, **the submarine still has the advantage,** for it is vulnerable only when it exposes itself by choice or by accident. With deep-diving submarines not needing to surface to charge batteries or check geographical positon, the opportunities for detection before they attack are few.

The most essential lesson of air warfare is that its evolution is dynamic. A nation wishing to maintain a viable military or naval air force cannot afford to fall behind in either technology or tactics. Although in wartime the conditions exist for the evolution of an effective force, in peace the armed forces are subjected to economic and political pressures which can result in the stultification of development. The world's first air force – the RAF – provides a sad example of this subordination to economics and politics: the English Electric Canberra jet bomber entered service in 1951 and was not superseded until the mid-1970s; some Canberra units were re-armed in the late 1960s – alongside the H-S Buccaneer, an aircraft which had first seen embarked service with the Royal Navy six years before its first employment with the RAF. Set in an earlier context, this is the equivalent of the RAF using a mixture of 1917 DH-4s and 1930 Hawker Harts as light bombers in 1941 – except that the gap between the 120 mph (190 km/h) DH-4 and the 320 mph (510 km/h) Douglas Boston was less than that between the Mach 0·83 Canberra and the Mach 2·2 McDonnell Douglas F-4M Phantom FGR.2.

Air supremacy is not a condition to be attained and thereafter exploited – it needs to be maintained by the unrelenting effort of all concerned in the defence of their alliance, politicians no less than the professional men-at-arms and supporting industries.

Select Bibliography

This Bibliography does not attempt to be fully comprehensive because the works dealing with Air Warfare are so many. It therefore concentrates upon the most important sources and those mainly consulted by the authors, some in their private possession. There are many more besides to which reference was made, including those official histories not mentioned below. Also the following periodicals not mentioned in the Bibliography were consulted: *Air Pictorial*; *Royal Air Force Flying Review*; *Cross and Cockade Journal*; *Air Enthusiast*; *American Aviation Historical Society Journal*; *Aero Album*; *Flight*.

Anon	*The Rise and Fall of the German Air Force.* *1933–45.*	Air Ministry. 1948
	Reports of the US Strategic Bombing Survey for the European and Pacific theatres.	
Authors, various	*Aircraft Profiles.*	Profile Publications 1965–72
	International Defence Review.	Interavia
	US Naval Institute Proceedings.	U.S.N.I.
Bekker, T	*The Luftwaffe War Diaries.*	Macdonald. 1966
Bowyer, M J	*2 Group RAF.*	Faber. 1974
Brown, D	*Carrier Fighters.*	Macdonald. 1975
	Carrier Operations in World War II. (2 vols).	Allan. 1974
Carel, P	*Hitler's War in Russia.* (2 vols).	Harrap. 1963
Collier, B	*Air Defence of the United Kingdom.*	HMSO. 1954
Craven, W and Cate, S	*US Army Air Forces in World War II.* (7 vols).	University of Chicago Press. 1954–8
Cynk, J	*History of the Polish Air Force. 1916–68.*	Osprey. 1972
Douhet, G	*Command of the Air.*	1921
Freeman, R	*The Mighty Eighth.*	Macdonald. 1970
Futrell, R F	*The United States Air Force in Korea. 1950–1953.*	Duell, Sloan & Pearce. 1961
Gamble, C F S	*Story of a North Sea Air Station.*	Spearman
Gibbs-Smith, C	*Aviation.*	HMSO. 1970
Girbig, W	*Six Months to Oblivion.*	Allan. 1975

Green, W and Fricker, F	*The Air Forces of the World.*	Macdonald. 1958
Goldberg, A	*A History of the U.S. Air Force. 1907–57.*	Van Norstrand. 1957
Harris, A	*Bomber Offensive.*	Collins. 1947
Hess, W R	*Pacific Sweep.*	Doubleday. 1974
Hoeppner, E von	*Deutschland Krieg in der Luft.*	1920
Hotz, R (Ed)	*Aviation Week and Space Technology.*	McGraw Hill. 1964–73
Irving, D	*The Mare's Nest.*	Kimber. 1964
Jones, H A and Raleigh, W	*The War in the Air.* (6 vols)	Oxford University 1922–37
Jones, N	*Origins of Strategic Bombing.*	Kimber. 1975
Krivinyi, N	*World Combat Aircraft.*	Arms & Armour. 1973
Lamberton, W	*Fighter Aircraft of the 1914–18 War.*	Harleyford. 1960
Lawazabal, J S	*Air War over Spain.*	Allan. 1974
Lee, A G	*No Parachute.*	Jarrolds. 1968
Mason, F and Windrow, M	*Battle over Britain.*	McWhirter Twins. 1969
Morison, S E	*History of US Naval Operations in World War II.* (14 vols)	Boston. 1962
Morris, A	*Bloody April.*	Jarrolds. 1967
	The First of the Many.	Jarrolds. 1968
Musciano, W	*Eagles of the Black Cross.*	Oblensky. 1965
Pitt, B (Ed)	*Purnell's History of the Second World War.*	Purnell. 1966
	Purnell's History of the First World War.	Purnell. 1969
Obermaier, E	*Die Ritterkreuzträger der Luftwaffe. 1939–45.*	Dieter Hoffman. 1966
Postan, M, Hay, D and Scott, J D	*Design and Development of Weapons.*	HMSO. 1964
Price, A	*Instruments of Darkness.*	Kimber. 1967
	Battle over the Reich.	Allan. 1973
Richards, D and Saunders, H St G	*The Royal Air Force. 1939–45.* (3 vols)	HMSO. 1964
Robinson, D H	*The Zeppelin in Combat.*	Foulis. 1961
	Giants in the Sky.	Foulis. 1973
	The Dangerous Sky.	Foulis. 1973
Roskill, S	*War at Sea.* (4 vols)	HMSO. 1954
Rust, K C	*Fifth Air Force Story.*	Historical Aviation Album. 1973
	9th Air Force.	Aero. 1967
Schliepak, H	*The Birth of the Luftwaffe.*	Allan. 1971

Seversky, A   *Victory through Air Power.*   Hutchinson.

Shores, C with   *Pictorial History of the Mediterranean Air War.* (3   Allan. 1972–4
others   vols).

                           Fighters over the Desert.   ——   Spearman. 1969

                           Fighters over Tunisia,   Spearman. 1975

                           2nd Tactical Air Force.   Osprey. 1970

Slessor, J   *The Central Blue.*   Cassell. 1956

Taylor, J W R   *The Guinness Book of Air Facts and Feats*   Guinness Superlatives 1973
and others

Van Haute, A   *French Air Force.* Vol I.   Allan. 1974

Wagner, R (Ed)   *Soviet Air Force in World War II.*   Doubleday. 1973

Webster, C and   *Strategic Air Offensive against Germany in World*   HMSO. 1961
Frankland, N   *War II.* (3 vols).

Winterbotham, E   *The Ultra Secret.*   Weidenfeld and Nicolson.
                                                                                  1974

Index

A

Aachen, 148
Abyssinia–Italian War, 74, 75
Ace System, 28, 29, 196, 197, 219
Aden, 107
Afghanistan, 63
Ain Zara, 7
Aircraft, Makes of:
Australian
  Wirraway; 174
Austrian
  Etrich Taube; 6
British
  Armstrong Whitworth Siskin; 69
  Armstrong Whitworth Whitley; 88, 108, 121, 123
  Auster; 202, 207
  Avro 504; 15
  Avro Manchester; 101, 105
  Avro Lancaster; 126, 140, 148, 151, 202
  Avro Lincoln; 207
  Avro Vulcan; 200, 227
  BAC Lightning; 227
  BE 2; 7, 17, 28, 40, 41, 57
  BE 12; 57
  Blackburn Kangaroo; 59
  Blackburn Skua; 90
  Bristol F2A (Fighter); 39, 53, 57, 61–3
  Bristol MIC; 57
  Bristol Blenheim; 85, 87, 91, 93, 96, 104–6, 108, 129
  Bristol Beaufighter; 100, 174, 202
  Bristol Beaufort; 101, 143, 174

Bristol Bisley; 120
Bristol Bombay; 108
De Havilland 2; 25, 26, 33
De Havilland 4; 48, 49, 56, 58, 60, 64, 65, 235
De Havilland 5; 46
De Havilland 9; 49, 53, 54, 56, 57, 61, 63, 64
De Havilland 10; 63
De Havilland Mosquito; 105, 160, 167, 208
De Havilland Vampire; 202, 207
De Havilland Venom; 210
English Electric Canberra; 232, 235
Fairey Battle; 87, 92
Fairey Swordfish; 107, 116, 141, 143
Fairey Albacore; 116, 129
Fairey Fulmar; 116, 131
FE 2; 33, 41, 50, 51
Folland Gnat; 213
Gloster Gladiator; 91, 106–8
Gloster Meteor; 162, 163, 167, 168, 203
Handley Page o/100; 36, 48
Handley Page o/400; 37, 43, 49, 53, 54, 57
Handley Page V/1500; 63, 67
Handley Page Heyford; 84
Handley Page Hampden; 123, 124
Handley Page Halifax; 101, 105, 151
Handley Page Victor; 200
Hawker Hart; 70, 107, 235
Hawker Fury; 70, 107

Hawker Hurricane; 73, 85, 87, 91, 93–7, 101, 105–8, 111, 116, 129, 131, 194
Hawker Hunter; 210, 211, 213
Hawker Tempest; 162, 208
Hawker Typhoon; 160, 164
Hawker Siddeley Harrier; 234
Hawker Siddeley Nimrod; 235
Hawker Siddeley Buccaneer; 235
RE 8; 43, 50
Salmson A2; 62, 73
SE 5; 40, 41, 46, 53, 57
Short; 18, 19, 36
Short Stirling; 101, 105
Short Sunderland; 121, 199, 202
Sopwith Baby; 36
Sopwith 1½ Strutter; 36, 37, 40, 50
Sopwith Pup; 39, 40, 44, 45, 58
Sopwith Camel; 45, 46, 48, 50, 51, 53, 54, 56, 59, 61
Sopwith Triplane; 39, 44
Sopwith Cuckoo; 59
Supermarine Spitfire; 73, 85, 88, 94, 97, 100, 106, 118, 120, 126, 140, 144, 160, 170, 194, 202, 208
Supermarine Seafire; 193
Vickers FB; 23, 25
Vickers Vildebeest; 75, 129, 130
Vickers Wellesley; 107
Vickers Wellington; 85, 87, 88, 108, 169, 194
Vickers Valetta; 207
Vickers Valiant; 200
Westland Wapiti; 65
Westland Lysander; 87, 93

Westland Dragonfly; 202
Westland Scout; 201

French
Blériot; 6
Breguet IV; 36, 37
Breguet XIV; 49, 50, 52, 62, 64
Breguet XIX; 75
Breguet 691; 85
Breguet Alizet; 213
Caudron R4; 37
Caudron GIII; 50
Caudron G IV; 50
Dassault Mystère; 208, 211
Dassault Mirage; 210–13, 227
Dewoitine D27; 7
Dewoitine 520; 95, 112
Farman MF7; 70
Hanriot HD1; 50
Morane Saulnier; 16, 23
Morane 406; 85
Nieuport; 6
Nieuport 11; 25, 26, 33
Nieuport 12; 36, 37
Nieuport 17; 55
Nieuport 28; 50
Nieuport 29; 62
Nieuport Delage 52; 75
Ouragan; 208
Potez 25; 63–5, 73
Spad VII; 39, 40, 62
Spad XI; 50
Spad XIII; 46, 50, 62
Vautour; 210, 211
Voisin XIII; 20, 22, 26
Voisin V89; 12

German
Albatross D; 33, 37, 39, 41, 55
Aviatik B 1; 14, 23
Brandenburg D 1; 55
Dornier Do 17; 76, 96, 106
Dornier Do 24; 129
Dornier Do 28; 226
Dornier Do 217; 145, 146
Focke Wulf FW 190; 105, 140, 159, 194
Focke Wulf FW 200; 123, 146, 156
Fokker E; 23–6, 33, 37
Fokker DR 1; 46, 51
Fokker D VII; 46, 52
Fokker D VIII; 59, 62
Gotha G; 37, 41, 45, 48
Heinkel He 51; 75, 76
Heinkel He 59; 91

Heinkel He 111; 76, 85, 92, 93, 154, 155, 157
Heinkel He 177; 146, 156, 157, 167
Heinkel He 178; 84
Henschel Hs 126; 95
Henschel Hs 129; 156, 157
Henschel Hs 293; 146
Junkers Ju 52; 69, 75, 76, 87, 91, 92, 111, 144, 145, 154, 155, 202
Junkers Ju 86; 107, 154, 155
Junkers Ju 87; 87, 90, 108, 112, 120, 147, 154–6
Junkers Ju 88; 88, 90, 104, 140, 157, 194
Junkers Ju 290; 156
LVG C; 41
Messerschmitt Bf 109; 73, 76, 85, 87, 88, 90, 91, 96, 97, 101, 106, 108, 112, 120, 148, 155, 156, 194
Messerschmitt Bf 110; 86, 88, 90, 91, 104, 108
Messerschmitt Me 163; 153
Messerschmitt Me 262; 154, 159, 165, 168, 175
Messerschmitt Me 323; 145
Rumpler C IV; 49
Taube; 7

Holland
Fokker CV; 65
Fokker DXX; 88
Fokker F 27 (Friendship); 226

India
HF-24 Marut; 213

Italian
Ansaldo; 62
Cant Z1007; 106, 140
Caproni 32; 22
Caproni 111; 75
Caproni 133; 75, 106
Fiat CR20; 75, 76
Fiat CR32; 75, 76, 106
Fiat CR42; 85, 106, 108
Fiat G50; 106
Fiat G55; 208
Macchi C200; 106
Macchi C202; 120, 140
Meridionali Ro 1; 64, 65, 75
Meridionali Ro 37; 75
Savoia Marchetti S 79; 72, 76, 85, 108
Savoia Marchetti S 81; 75, 106

Savoia Marchetti S 82; 108, 145
Japanese
Aichi D3A (Val); 131, 136
Kawasaki Ki 10; 79
Kawasaki Ki 27; 80, 82, 128
Kawasaki Ki 43 (Oscar); 169, 202
Kawasaki Ki 84 (Frank); 168
Mitsubishi G3M; 78, 79, 85
Mitsubishi A5M (Claude); 79, 85
Mitsubishi A6M (Zero); 126, 127, 130, 131, 133, 136, 140, 176, 177, 179, 180, 182, 183, 193, 194
Mitsubishi G4M2 (Betty); 133, 140
Nakajima A1N; 74
Nakajima A2N; 70
Nakajima B5 N2 (Kate); 131
Nakajima B6N (Jill); 179
Yokosuka Y20 (Frances); 167
Yokosuka D4Y (Judy); 179

Polish
PZL P11; 86, 87

Russian
Antonov; 12
Ilyushin DB3; 89, 140
Ilyushin Il 2 (Schturmovik); 116, 117, 158, 159, 194
Ilyushin Il 10; 202
Ilyushin Il 28; 208, 226
Lavochkin La 3; 116
Lavochkin La 5; 157, 159
Lavochkin La 9; 205
Mikoyan MiG 3; 116
Mikoyan MiG 15; 203, 205, 207, 208, 210, 226
Mikoyan MiG 17; 208, 217, 226
Mikoyan MiG 19; 213
Mikoyan MiG 21; 210, 211, 213, 224, 227
Mikoyan MiG 25; 211, 212
Petlyakov Pe 2; 116, 159, 194
Petlyakov Pe 8; 167
Polikarpov I 15; 73, 76, 79, 80, 85
Polikarpov I 16; 73, 76, 79, 80
Sikorski, Le Grand; 22
Sikorski, Ilya Mourometz; 22
Sukoi Su 7; 211, 213
Sukoi SB 2; 72, 76, 79, 85, 88
Tupolev TB 1; 69
Tupolev TB 3; 72

Tupolev Tu 2; 205
Tupolev Tu 16; 212, 227
Yakovlev Yak 1; 116, 140
Yakovlev Yak 3; 168
Yakovlev Yak 9; 157, 159, 194, 202
Swedish
MF1 – 9B Minicon; 226
Saab J 29B; 226
USA
Bell P 39 (Airacobra); 116, 133, 140, 174
Huey; 219, 221
Boeing B 9; 72
Boeing B 17 (Flying Fortress); 105, 118, 120, 126, 128, 129, 133, 135–7, 140, 147–54, 159, 167, 173–5, 194
Boeing B 29 (Super Fortress); 171–3, 180, 186, 187, 189, 191, 200, 203, 205, 207
Boeing B 52 (Strato Fortress); 200, 221, 222, 225, 227
Boeing RB 47; 228
Boeing 218; 74
Boeing Chinook; 219
Brewster Buffalo; 130
Consolidated B 24 (Liberator); 123, 126, 132, 143, 147, 152–4, 169, 171, 176, 193, 194
Consolidated Catalina; 128, 129
Convair B 36; 200
Curtiss AB; 7
Curtiss H-8; 58
Curtiss Large America; 59
Curtiss Jenny; 65
Curtiss Hawk; 78, 87
Curtiss P 40; 106, 128–33, 174, 194
Curtiss C 46; 132, 169, 186
Curtiss Helldiver; 180
Douglas DC 3 (C47) (Dakota); 131, 132, 169, 194, 201, 202, 206–8, 219, 232
Douglas A 20 (Boston); 140, 160, 174, 184, 235
Douglas Dauntless; 133, 135–7, 177, 180, 202
Douglas Devastator; 135
Douglas A1 (Skyraider); 219
Douglas A-4 (Skyhawk); 211, 217
Grumman Martlet; 123
Grumman Avenger; 137, 163, 177, 179

Grumman F4F (Wildcat); 133, 135, 136
Grumman F6F (Hellcat); 177, 179, 180, 182, 184, 194
Grumman F9F (Panther); 203
Grumman A 6 (Intruder); 217, 223, 225
Grumman F14 (Tomcat); 232
Lockheed P 38 (Lightning); 120, 137, 145, 151, 160, 174, 176, 183
Lockheed Constellation; 230
Lockheed Hudson; 121, 123, 128
Lockheed F 80; 202, 203
Lockheed C 119; 206
Lockheed U 2; 228
Lockheed P 2 (Neptune); 228
Lockheed SR 71; 230
Martin B 26 (Marauder); 120, 133, 160
Martin P 4M (Mercator); 228
Martin 166W; 129
McDonnell F2H (Banshee); 203
McDonnell F4 (Phantom); 211, 216, 227, 235
North American B 25 (Mitchell); 131, 132, 134, 144, 160, 171, 174, 184, 193, 194
North American P 51 (Mustang); 151, 154, 160, 162, 168, 194, 203
North American F 82; 202
North American F 86 (Sabre); 203–5, 207, 213
North American F 100 (Super Sabre); 216
Northrop F-5E (Tiger); 212
Republic P 47 (Thunderbolt); 149–51, 160, 194, 207, 227
Republic F 84 (Thunderstreak); 203, 208, 210
Republic F 105 (Thunderchief); 216–18
Vought o2U; 65
Vought F4U (Corsair); 184, 194, 227
Wright Flyer; 4
Air defence systems, 20, 36, 37, 45, 52, 53, 77, 87, 96, 124, 125, 153, 180, 181, 189, 207, 217, 222–5, 227, 230, 231
Airships, 3, 34–6
Akagi, 135
Albania, 56, 106, 107, 110

Albert, M, 196
Albert Canal, 92
Aleutian Islands, 134
Algeria, 120, 207
Allam, M, 213
Allen, J, 4
Allmenrode, K, 44
Allon, M, 208
Ambon, 130
American Volunteer Group, 130–2
Ammunition, tracer, 17
Anshan, 172
Anti-aircraft guns, 3, 9, 20, 21, 43, 77, 93, 124, 163, 207, 211
Anti-aircraft missiles, 211, 212, 216–18, 222–5
Anti-tank aircraft, 155–9, 164
Antwerp, 13, 35, 163, 165
Arab League, 210
Arakan, 169
Arcadia Conferences, 141
Archer, 143
Ardennes Offensive, 1944; 165, 166
Area Bombing, 124–6, 147–54
Argus, 59, 107, 116
Armament, Aircraft: 4
    Machine-guns; 4, 5, 12, 23, 24, 43
    Cannon; 5, 73, 220
    Missiles; 17, 160, 207, 219, 220, 230, 232
Ark Royal, 91, 123
Armour Protection, 81, 82
Arnhem, 164, 165
Arras offensive, 1917; 38–41
Arrigi, J, 55
Artillery fire, Direction of, 18, 19, 34, 36, 174, 232
Assam, 132
Atlantic, Battle of, 121, 123, 124, 141–3
Aubers Ridge, Battle of, 20
Audacity, 121, 123
Augsburg, 126
Austro-Hungary Air Arm, 7, 55
Aviacione Legionaria, 76
AWACS, 230, 232

B

Baker Island, 177
Bali, 130
Balikpapan, 176
Balkans, 1941, 104, 107, 110, 111, 159

Ball, A, 40
Balloons, vii, 1–3, 7, 12, 45, 56
Balloon barrages, 45
Bangkok, 171
Banks, C, 48
Baracca, F, 29, 55
Barés, Cmdt, 14
Barker, W, 29, 54
Barmen-Wüppertal, 148
Beatty, D, 33
Beauchamp-Proctor, A, 29
Beaverbrook, Lord, 97
Belgian Air Force, 7, 50, 92, 93
Belgrade, 110
Bergen, 90
Bergendal, I du M de, 196
Berlin, 97, 116, 150, 152, 154, 199
Beurling, G, 196
Birksted, K, 196
Biafra, 226
Big Week, 151, 152
Biscay, Bay of, 121, 143, 146
Bishop, W, 29
Bismarck Sea, Battle of, 174
Biter, 141
Bloody April, 38–40
Bochum, 148
Bockholt, L, 48
Bödenplatte, Op, 166, 167
Boelke, O, 23, 24, 29
Boer War, 3
Bogue, 141
Bolivia, 73
Bomber Command (RAF), 99, 101,
    104, 123–6, 147–54, 164, 189
Bombs: 4, 7, 16, 36, 65, 70, 72, 99
    AZON; 171
    Fritz X; 145, 146
    Target Indicator; 147
    SD 1 and 2; 157
    Atom; 191, 200
    Para-frags; 174
    SMART; 221, 232
    Concrete Dibber; 211
Bomb-sights, 20, 43
Bonanzo, M, 77
Bône, 120
Bong, R, 197
Borneo, 129, 130
Bougainville, 176, 177
Brandenburg, E, 41
Bremen, 125, 148
Brest, 101, 105, 124
Britain, Battle of, 95–101
Brock, F, 17

Brocq, M, 21
Brown, A, 51
Brown, R, 203
Bruges, 36
Brunowski, G, 29, 55
Bulgaria, 110
Buna, 174
Burma, 130, 131, 169–71, 173
Burma Road, 130, 131

C

Caen, 164
Calcutta, 169, 172
Caldwell, C, 196
Cambodia, 128, 221, 224
Cambrai, Battle of, 46
Campbell, D, 52
Campbell, K, 101
Cantacuzene, C, 196
Canton, 132
Caporetto, Battle of, 55
Caroline Islands, 174
Castro, B de, 75
Cavendish, H, 1
Ceylon, 131
Chandler, C de F, 4, 5
Changsha, 169
Channel Ports, 94, 99
Charles, J, 1
Chenghsien, 172
Chengtu, 126, 172, 173
Chennault, C, 130–2, 169, 170
Chiang Kai-shek, 130
Chihkiang, 173
China incidents, 78, 79
China National Air Corporation,
    132
Chindits, 169
Chinese Air Forces, 73, 74, 78, 79,
    126, 169
Chinese (Nationalist) Air Force, 207
Chungking, 126
Circus, Ops, 100, 104
Citadelle, Op, 156, 157
Clark Field, 127, 184
Coastal Command (RAF), 104, 121,
    123–5
Codes and Cyphers, 133, 134, 176
Collishaw, R, 29, 44
Cologne, 104, 125
Command of the Air, The, 65
Communication systems, 3, 5, 6, 18,
    34, 82, 96, 228

Condor Legion, 76
Contact Patrols, 19, 20, 26, 34, 40
Coppen, W, 29
Coral Sea, Battle of, 133, 134
Corsica, 95, 106
Coutelle, Capt, 2
Coventry, 99
Crete, 111, 112
Crissy, M, 4
Cuba, 228
Cunningham, J, 100
Curtiss, G, 4
Cutler, H, 18
Cuxhaven, 15
Cyprus, 209

D

Daimler, C, 3
Dallas, R, 29, 44
Darwin, see Port Darwin
Davão, 129
Death ray, 82
Defoliants, 202, 221
Denikin, A, 61
Denmark, 89
Depth charges, 123
Deruluft, 68
Déscente en Angleterre, La, 2
Dien-bien-phu, 206, 207, 223
Dieppe, 118, 120
Dive bombing, 72, 90, 116
Dixmude, 202
Dog-fights, 40, 72, 13
Douhet, G, viii, 65, 67, 154, 193
Dover, 16
Dowding, H, 93
Dresden, 153, 154
Duisburg, 148
Duna River, 115
Dunkirk, 14, 20, 35, 44, 45, 94, 95
Dunning, E, 58
Dusseldorf, 15, 148

E

Eagle bombing radar, 189
Eagle, 118
Eaker, I, 126
Eben-Emael, 92
Ebener, K, 156
Egyptian Air Force, 208, 211
El Adem, 106

El Alamein, 120
Electronic Warfare, 99, 150, 216, 217, 225, 230
Ellyson, T, 5
El Salvadore, 227
Ely, E, 4
Emden, 150
Endau, 129
Engadine, 33, 36
Enterprise, 135-7
Eschwege, Lt von, 56
Essen, 125 148

F

Faroe Islands, 143
Fickel, J, 4
Fighter Command (RAF), 99, 104, 105, 167
Finish Air Force, 88, 89
Firth of Forth, 88
Flax, Op, 144
Fléchettes, 8
Fleet Air Arm, 90, 91, 173
Fleurus, Battle of, vii, 2
Fokker, A, 23
Formidable, 112
Formosa, 128, 172, 173, 182-4, 207
France, Battle of, 91-5
Frankfurt-am-Main, 150
Franklin, B, 1
Franklin, 182, 184
Frantz, J, 12
Freiburg, 14
French Air Arm, 7, 14, 26, 38, 40, 49, 51, 52, 54, 64, 67, 87, 92-5, 106, 112, 206-10
Freya, 104, 156
Friedrichshafen, 15
Fuel supplies, 132, 153, 189
Fullard, P, 29
Furious, 58, 59, 116

G

Galic, C, 197
Gallabat, 107
Galland, A, 99, 196
Gallipoli, 18
Garcia-Morato, J, 77
Garnerin, A, 3
Garros, R, 23
Gas, Poison, 22, 75

'Gee', 123, 125
Gentzen, H, 87
German Air Arms, 7, 14, 26, 33-5, 37, 41, 44, 48, 54, 67-9, 75-8, 86 et seq., 108 et seq., 144 et seq.
Gibraltar, 118, 120, 121, 123, 129
Gifford, H, 3
Gilbert Islands, 133, 177, 179
Gliders, 91, 92, 160, 164, 167
'*Glorious*', 90
'*Gneisenau*', 101, 124
Gnys, W, 86
Golan Heights, 211, 212
Göring, H, 54, 69, 93, 165
Göys, Cmdt de, 14, 21
Gran Chaco War, 73
Grave, 164
Gray, C, 196
Gray, S, 14
Graziani, Marshal, 107
Greece, 107, 110, 111
Greek Air Arm, 107
Grunne, R de H de, 77
Guadalcanal, 135-7, 173, 174, 176
Guam, 180, 182, 186, 221
Guernica, 76, 77
Guerrilla warfare, 48, 57, 147, 157, 200 et seq.
Guidoni, Capt, 4
Gumrak, 156
Guynemer, G, 29, 40, 46

H

Hackwill, G, 48
Hahn, M, 84
Haiphong, 132, 217, 221, 222, 225
Haller, General, 62
Hamburg, 148-50
Hankow, 78, 79, 172, 173
Hanoi, 170, 216, 218, 219, 221, 225
Happe, F, 24
Harris, A, 124, 150, 154
Hartmann, E, 196
Heglund, S, 196
Held, A, 87
Helicopters, 206, 207, 211, 214, 219-21, 224, 232, 234
Heligoland Bight, 15, 59
Henderson Field, 136, 137
Hermes, 131
Hertz, H, 82
Hiei, 137

Himmelbett, 104
Hindenburg, P von, 34
Hinton, B, 203
Hiroshima, 190-3
Hiryu, 135
Hitler, A, 97, 112, 124, 154
Hiyo, 180
Ho Chi Minh Trail, 214, 221, 224
Hoeppner, E von, 34
Hollandia, 174
Honan, 170
Honduras, 227
Hong Kong, 132
Hornet, 134, 137
Hosho, 73, 74, 78
Hump Route, 131, 169, 173, 186, 221
Hungarian Air Arm, 114
Hutnicki, 86

I

Iceland, 143
I-Go, Op, 176
Illustrious, 107, 108
Ilmen, Lake, 117
Immelmann, M, 23, 24, 29
Imphal, 170
Inchon, 203
Independence, 179, 182
Independent Air Force, 53, 54, 124
India, 64, 141
Indian Air Force, 212, 213
Indo-China, 126, 128, 170, 184, 201, 202, 206
Indomitable, 118, 129
Indonesia, 201, 207
Indo-Pakistan Wars, 208, 212, 213
Intruder ops, 100, 123, 124
Iraq, 64, 112, 211, 212
Iraqi Air Force, 211, 212
Isonzo, Battles of, 55
Israeli Air Force, 208 et seq., 232
Italian Air Force, 6, 55, 64, 67, 74-8, 95, 97, 106-10, 114, 144, 146
Iwo Jima, 184

J

Jablonna, 22
Jaime I, 75
Jamboli, 46
Japanese Army Air Force, 67, 73, 74, 79 et seq., 128 et seq., 169 et seq.

Japanese Navy Air Force, 67, 70, 73, 74, 78 et seq., 126 et seq., 176 et seq.
Java, 129, 130, 201
Jet propulsion, 84, 154
Johnson, H, 197
Jordanian Air Force, 211
Junkers, H, 68, 69
Jutland, Battle of, 33
Juutilainen, E, 196

K

Kabul, 63
Kaga, 73, 78, 79, 135
Kamikaze, 183, 184, 186, 230
Kammhüber, J, 104
Karlsrühe, 36
Kassel, 149, 150
Katanga, 226
Kazakov, A, 29
Kenya, 107, 108, 207
Kesselring, A, 69, 86, 117, 120
Kharkha river, 80
Khe Sang, 223, 224
Kiev, 61
Knickebein, 99
Kobe, 187
Koga, K, 79
Kohima, 170
Kokura, 191
Kolwezi, 226
Königsberg, 18, 90
Korean War, 202–6
Kos, 146
Kozhedub, I, 197
Krupps, 3, 148
Kunming, 126, 132, 169, 170
Kursk, 156, 157
Kut-el-Amara, 31, 32
Kuttelwascher, K, 196
Kwangsi, 170
Ky, Marshal, 214
Kyoto, 191
Kyushu, 172, 173, 186

L

Lacalle, A, 77
Lae, 174, 176
La France, 3
Lake Lesjaskog, 90, 91

Lampedusa Island, 145
Lancastria, 95
Laos, 206, 214, 219, 221, 224
Lawrence, T, 57
Lebaudy brothers, 3
Ledo, 173
Leipzig, 153
LeMay, C, 187
Le Prieur, Y, 17
Leros, 146
Lexington, 133, 134
Leyte Island, 182–4
Libya, 64, 112
Liège, 8, 13
Linke-Crawford, F, 55
Lipetsk, 68
Little, R, 44
Liu, Chi Sun, 196
Lock, E, 99
Loehr, Gen, 86
Loewenhardt, E, 29
London, 15–17, 41, 45, 48, 53, 82, 97, 100, 162
Lorenz Beam, 82
Losses of aircraft (aggregate), 55, 193, 212, 213, 220, 224
Lowe, T, 3
Lucchini, F, 196
Ludendorff, Gen, 37
Lufthansa, 69
Luukkanen, E. 88
Luxeuil, 36, 37, 41
Luxor, 208
Luzon, 129, 184

M

Maastricht, 92
Macedonian front, 56
MacLaren, D, 29
MacNamara, R, 221
Madrid, 76
Mainz, 53
Malaya, 128, 129, 201, 202, 207
Malayan People's Liberation Army, 202
Malta, 106–8, 111, 118, 120, 121
Manado airfield, 129
Manchester, 16
Manchuria, 73, 78, 80, 172, 205
Mandalay, 169
Manica, 18
Mannock, E, 29
Marat, 116, 119

Marconi, G, 5
Marcus Island, 177
Mariana Islands, 173, 180, 182, 186
Marshall Islands, 133, 179
Master Bomber, 149
Matapan, Battle of, 112
Mathy, H, 16
Mau Mau uprising, 207
McConnell, J, 206
McCudden, J, 29
McKellar, A, 99
Meerbeck, 153
Mesopotamia, 31, 32, 57, 63
Messines, Battle of, 44
Meusnier, J-B, 3
Mexico, 7
Midway, Battle of, 134, 135, 141
Milch, E, 69
Mindoro Island, 184
Mines, Aerial laying of, 36, 91, 104, 106, 124, 153, 179, 187, 189, 225
Mitchell, W, viii, 54
Mitla Pass, 208
Möhne, dam, 148
Mölders, W, 77, 99, 115, 196
Montgolfier, brothers, 1
Morocco, 63, 64, 75
Morosovskaya, 154, 155
Mortain, 164
Moscow, 61, 115, 116
Moulmein, 169
Murmansk, 60
Musashi, 182
Musashino, 187
Mussolini, B, 74
Myitkina, 170

N

Nablus, 57
Nagasaki, 172, 191, 193
Nagoya, 187
Nagumo, Adml, 127
Nakajima factory, 186, 187
Namsos, 90
Nanking, 78, 79
Napalm, 137
Napoleon, 2
Narvik, 3, 90
Navigation, 20, 43, 82, 99, 101, 123, 124, 147
Nesterov, P, 12

Netherlands Army Air Force, 93, 129, 130
Netherlands Army Naval Air Force, 129, 130
Neuve Chapelle, Battle of, 18, 19
New Britain, 133, 177
New Guinea, 141, 173, 174, 176
New Hebrides, 136
New Ireland, 177
Nicaragua, 65
Nigeria, 226
Nijmegen, 164, 165
Nimitz, C, 186
Nishazawa, H, 196
Nixon, R, 225
Nomonham incident, 80–2
Normandy, Battle of, 153, 159–64, 179
North Korean Air Force, 202, 203
North Vietnamese Air Force, 214, 216
Norway, Battle of, 90, 91, 95, 105
Norwegian Air Force, 90
Notoro, 73
Nowotny, W, 196
Nuclear bombs, 191, 227
Nürnburg, 151

O

Oahu, 127
Oberndorf, 36, 37
Oboe, 147
Ohain, H von, 84
O'Hare, E, 133
Oil refineries, 124
Okinawa, 182, 184, 186, 193
Omura, 172
Osaka, 187
Oslo, 90
Ostend, 16, 35, 45
Ostrov, 115

P

Pakistan Air Force, 212, 213
Palau, 179
Palembang, 130, 172, 173
Palestine, 57
Pantelleria, 145
Papua, 133, 176
Parachutes, 3

Parachute troops, 72, 91, 93, 108, 130, 160, 164, 167, 211, 232
Paraguay, 73
Paris, 12, 95
Parmalee, P, 4
Pathfinders, 99
Pattle, M, 110, 111, 197
Pearl Harbor, 127, 134
Peenemünde, 149, 150, 162
Peuty, Cmdt du, 26, 28, 31, 40
Philippine Islands, 128–30, 179, 182–4, 193
Philippine Sea, Battle of, 179, 180, 185
Photography from the air, 7, 19, 26, 56, 58, 105, 228, 230, 233
Piazza, Capt, 6
Pitomnik, 154, 156
Ploesti, 107, 153
Poland, Battle of, 1919; 61, 62
Poland, Battle of, 1939; 86, 87
Policing by air, 63–5
Polish Air Force, 61, 62, 86, 87, 147
Poplavko, Lt, 23
Port Darwin, 130, 132
Port Moresby, 133, 173, 174, 176
Port Said, 210
Power plants, recip engines, 68, 69, 73
Preece, W, 5
Prince of Wales, 129
Princeton, 177
Propaganda effects, 7, 32, 207
Production of aircraft, 56, 193, 194

R

Rabaul, 132, 136, 137, 173, 174, 177, 179
Radar, 82, 84, 96, 101, 102, 121, 124, 130, 143, 147, 148, 150, 160, 169, 216, 217, 228, 230
Rangoon, 130, 131, 169
Rapallo, Treaty of, 68
Red River, 221
Red Sea, 107
Regensburg, 149
Remagen Bridge, 167
Remotely piloted vehicles, 233
Repulse, 129
Rezny, R. 196
Rhubarb, Ops, 100, 104
Rhys Davis, A, 46

Richthofen, L von, 28, 40
Richthofen, M von, 28, 29, 38, 40, 51
Rickenbacker, E, 29
Robinson, W, 17
Rocket engines, 84, 153
Rocket Missiles, 143
  V1; 160, 162–4
  V2; 163–5, 167
Rolling Thunder, Op, 214, 216–19
Roma, 145
Rommel, E, 110, 117
Rosen, Count von, 226
Rosenthal, Baron von, 12
Rotterdam, 91, 93, 101
Royal Air Force, viii, 51, 52, 60, 63–5, 67, 87, 88, 90 et seq., 200–2, 209, 210, 235
Royal Australian Air Force, 128–30, 203
Royal Canadian Air Force, 205
Royal Flying Corps, 7, 26, 33, 44, 49
Royal Naval Air Service, 14–16, 36, 37, 44, 45, 49, 57–9
Rozier, F de, 1
Rudel, H-U, 116, 119
Ruhr, 101, 148
Rumania, 87, 107, 110
Russia, Battle of, 112–17
Russian Air Force, 7, 22, 60–2, 67–9, 79 et seq., 88, 89, 112–17, 157–9, 200, 230
Russo-Finish War, 88, 89
Ryujo, 78, 136

S

Saigon, 129, 214
St Lo, 183
St Nazaire, 95
Saipan, 179, 182, 186, 187
Salas, A, 76
Salerno, 145
Salmond, J, 64
Salonika, 56
Salt, 228
Samar, Battle of, 182
Samos, 146
Santa Cruz, Battle of, 137
Santa Elena, 33
Santee, 182
Santo Domingo, 65
Santos-Dumont, A, 3
Saratoga, 177
Sarawak, 129

Sardinia, 106, 145
Sarvanto, J, 89
Satellites, Orbiting, 228, 230
Saulnier, R, 23
Scarf, A, 129
Scharnhorst, 101, 124
Scheer, R, 33
Schlief, Hpt, 86
Schneider, F, 23
Schneider Trophy, 73
Schweinfurt, 149, 150
Searchlights, 45, 124
Sedan, 93
Seoul, 203
Shanghai, 73, 79
Shimada, Capt, 80
Shinohara, H, 80–2
Shook, A, 45
Shoho, 133
Shokaku, 134, 180
Short, R, 74
Sicily, 106, 108, 110, 112, 118, 120,
    144, 145, 157
Sidi Barrani, 107
Siegert, W, 14
Sikorski, I, 22
Sinai, 208, 211
Singapore, 128, 129, 173
Six Day War, 210
Skalski, I, 87, 196
Skip bombing, 174
Slava, 33
Smart, B, 58
Smolensk, 115
Smuts, J, 52
Solomon Islands, Battles of, 133, 136,
    137
Somme, Battle of, 33, 34
Soryu, 135
South African Air Force, 107, 147,
    203
South Korean Air Force, 203
South Rhodesian Air Force, 107
South Vietnamese Air Force, 214
Spanish Air Arms, 64, 75–7
Spanish Civil War, 75–8
Sports Flying Association (German),
    68
Spruance, R, 180, 184
Stalingrad, 145, 154–6
Stimson, H, 191
Stoyanov, S, 196
Strategic Air Command (US), 199,
    203
Stuttgart, 150

Submarines, Anti, 5, 35, 36, 57–9,
    121, 123, 141–4, 151, 160,
    234, 235
Sudan, 3, 64, 107, 108
Sueter, M, 6, 36
Suez Canal, 106, 117, 208–12, 230
Sulaimaniya, 64
Sumatra, 129, 130
Supply by air, 31, 32, 64, 75, 131,
    132, 144, 145, 154–6, 169–74,
    186, 199, 200, 206, 207, 219,
    223, 224, 232
Surigao Strait, 182
Sweeney, Lt. Col, 191
Syria, 112, 208, 210–12
Syrian Air Force, 208, 211
Szentgyorgyi, D, 196

T

Tactics, 20, 23, 24, 38, 42, 53, 72, 78,
    81, 121, 135, 138, 150, 151,
    179, 205
Taiho, 180
Takoradi, 106, 112
Taranto, 107
Tazinskaya, 154, 155
Tebaga Gap, 144
Tet Offensive, 224
Thailand, 128, 206, 218, 219
Thanh Hoa, 221
Thomsen. H. 34
Tibbets, P, 191
Tinian. 182, 191
Tinker, F, 77
Tito, 147
Tobruk, 106, 110
Tokyo, 134, 177, 182, 184, 186, 187,
    193
Tonkin, 206, 218
Torpedoes, 4, 18, 45, 101, 135, 143,
    145
Tournachon, G, 7
Tragino, 108
Trenchard, H, viii, 26, 28, 53, 65,
    124, 154, 193
Tripoli, 106, 108, 121
Triumph, 202
Trondheim, 90, 91
Truk, 174, 176, 177, 179
Tsingtao, 12
Tulagi Island, 133
Tunisia, 95, 106, 120, 121, 144, 145
Turgud Reis, 18

Turkish Air Arm, 7
Tyneside, 97

U

U boats, see submarines
Uchatius, F, 2
Udet, E, 29, 165, 196
Ukraine, 60, 62
United Nations, 226
United States Air Force, 200 et seq.
United States Air Transport Com-
    mand, 132
United States Army Air Force, 4, 38,
    50, 51, 54, 67, 72, 118, 121,
    123, 126 et seq., 147 et seq.,
    159 et seq.
United States Marine Corps, 65, 70,
    127, 133–7, 184, 186, 223, 234
United States Navy Air Arm, 67, 70,
    72, 123, 127, 133 et seq., 159,
    177 et seq., 216 et seq.

V

Venice, 2, 3
Vera Cruz, 7
Verdun, 26, 34, 38
Versailles Treaty, 67, 162
Vichy France, 120
Victoria Cross, 101, 129
Victorious, 116
Vietcong, 214 et seq.
Vietminh, 202, 206
Vietnam War, 202, 206, 214–25
Vikrante, 213
Vindex, 33, 36
Visconti, A, 196
Vlotman, C, 196
Voss, J von, 2, 12
Voss, W, 46
VTOL aircraft, 234

W

Wake Island, 133
Walcheren Island, 165
Walter, H, 84
Warneford, R, 16
Warsaw, 13, 62, 86, 87, 147
Wasp, 118
Wau, 174
Western Desert War, 106, 110, 117

Westkapelle, 165
Wever, W, 69
Wewak, 174, 176
White Russian Air Arm, 60, 61
Whittle, F, 84
Wick, H, 99
Wilhelmshaven, 59, 147
Window, 148, 150, 160
Wintgens, K, 23
Wolfert, K, 3
Wolff, K, 46
Wright brothers, 4
Würzburg, 104

X

X-Gerät, 99

Y

Yalu River, 205
Yamamoto, I, 176
Yarmouth, 15
Yawata, 172
Yom Kippur War, 211, 212
Yorktown, 133–5, 184

Ypres, Battle of, 46
Yugoslavia, 110, 147
Yugoslavian Air Force, 110, 114
Yunnanni, 169

Z

Zeebrugge, 35, 36, 45
Zeppelin, F, 3
Zeppelins, 3, 4, 8, 9, 13–18, 26, 33, 34, 36, 46, 48, 58, 59
Zuikaku, 134

M T W TH F S

M T W TH F S

M T W TH F S

M T W TH F S

M T W TH F S

M T W TH F S

M T W TH F S

M T W TH F S

M T W TH F S

M T W TH F S

M T W TH F S

M T W TH F S S

26 S